国家汉办/孔子学院总部
Hanban/Confucius Institute Headquarters

Li Bai

Collection of Critical Biographies of Chinese Thinkers

(Concise Edition, Chinese-English)

Editors-in-chief: Zhou Xian, Cheng Aimin

Author: Zhou Xunchu   Tong Qiang
Translator: Curtis D.Smith
Expert: Zhang Jing

Nanjing University Press

《中国思想家评传》简明读本 – 中英文版 –

主 编 周 宪 程爱民

李 白

著 者／周勋初　　　童 强
　　　　Zhou Xunchu　Tong Qiang
译 者／Curtis D. Smith
审 读／张 静 Zhang Jing

南京大学出版社

Editor: Zhao Li
Cover designed by Zhao Qin

First published 2010
by Nanjing University Press
No. 22, Hankou Road, Nanjing City, 210093
www.NjupCo.com

©2010 Nanjing University Press

Chinese Library Cataloguing in Publication Data
The CIP data for this title is on file with the Chinese Library.

ISBN10: 7-305-06609-2(pbk)
ISBN13: 978-7-305-06609-2(pbk)

Books available in the collection

Confucius
《孔子》
978-7-305-06611-5

Laozi
《老子》
978-7-305-06607-8

Emperor Qin Shihuang
《秦始皇》
978-7-305-06608-5

Li Bai
《李白》
978-7-305-06609-2

Cao Xueqin
《曹雪芹》
978-7-305-06610-8

Du Fu
《杜甫》
978-7-305-06826-3

Zhuangzi
《庄子》
978-7-305-07177-5

Sima Qian
《司马迁》
978-7-305-07294-9

Mencius
《孟子》
978-7-305-07583-4

Mozi
《墨子》
978-7-305-07970-2

总序

General Preface

China is one of the cradles of world civilization, enjoying over five thousand years of history. It has produced many outstanding figures in the history of ancient thought, and left a rich philosophical heritage for both the Chinese people and the entire humanity. The fruit of these thinkers was to establish unique schools that over the long course of history have been continuously interpreted and developed. Today much of these thoughts are as relevant as ever and of extreme vitality for both China and the rest of the world. For instance, the ideal of "humaneness" and the concept of "harmony" taught by Confucius, the founder of Confucianism, have been venerated without ceasing by contemporary China as well as other Asian nations.

Ancient Chinese dynasties came and went, with each new dynasty producing its own scintillating system of thought. These rare and beautiful flowers of philosophy are grounded in the hundred schools vying for attention in pre-Qin times and the broad yet deep classical scholarship of Han and Tang times and in the simple yet profound occult learning of the Wei and Jin dynasties together with the entirely rational learning of Song and Ming Neo-Confucianism. The fertile soil of religious belief was Buddhism's escape from the emptiness of the sensual world and Daoism' s spiritual cultivation in the search for identification with the immortals. The founders of these systems of thought included teachers, scholars, poets, politicians, scientists and monks— they made great contributions to such disparate cultural fields in ancient China as philosophy, politics, military science, economics, law, handicrafts, science and technology, literature, art, and religion. The ancient Chinese venerated them for their wisdom and for following moral paths, and called them sages, worthies, saints, wise men, and great masters, etc. Their words and writings, and sometimes their life experiences, constitute the rich matter of ancient Chinese thought distilled by later generations. The accomplishments of Chinese thought are rich and varied, and permeate such spiritual traditions as the harmony between humans and nature, the unification of thought and action, and the need for calmness during vigorous action, synthesizing the old and innovating something new.

Nanjing University Press has persisted over the last twenty years in publishing the 200-book series, *Collection of Critical Biographies of Chinese Thinkers*, under the general editorship of Professor Kuang Yaming, late honorary president of Nanjing University. This collection is the largest-scale project of research on Chinese thinking and culture undertaken since the beginning of the twentieth century. It selected more than 270 outstanding figures from Chinese history, composed their biographies and criticized their

中国是世界文明的发源地之一，有五千多年的文明史。在中国古代思想史上，涌现出了许许多多杰出的思想家，为中华民族乃至整个人类留下了丰富的思想遗产。这些思想成果独树一帜，在漫长的历史中又不断地被阐释、被发展，很多思想对于今天的中国乃至世界而言，仍然历久弥新，极具生命力。比如，儒家学派创始人孔子"仁"的理念、"和"的思想，不仅在当代中国，在其他亚洲国家也一直备受推崇。

古代中国朝代更迭，每一个朝代都有灿烂夺目的思想文化。百家争鸣的先秦诸子、博大宏深的汉唐经学、简易幽远的魏晋玄学、尽心知性的宋明理学是思想学术的奇葩；佛教的色空禅悦、道教的神仙修养是宗教信仰的沃土；其他如经世济民的政治、经济理想，巧夺天工的科技、工艺之道，风雅传神、丹青不老的文学艺术……都蕴涵着丰富的思想。这些思想的创造者中有教师、学者、诗人、政治家、科学家、僧人……他们在中国古代的哲学、政治、军事、经济、法律、工艺、科技、文学、艺术、宗教等各个文明领域内贡献巨大。古代中国人尊敬那些充满智慧、追求道德的人，称呼他们为圣人、贤人、哲人、智者、大师等，他们的言论、著作或被后人总结出来的经验构成了中国古代思想的重要内容，在丰富多彩中贯穿着天人合一、知行合一、刚健中和等精神传统，表现出综合创新的特色。

南京大学出版社坚持20余年，出版了由南京大学已故名誉校长匡亚明教授主编的《中国思想家评传丛书》，这套丛书共200部，是中国20世纪以来最为宏大的中国传统思想文化研究工程，选出了中国历史上270余位杰出人物，为他们写传记，

intellectual accomplishments; all in all, it is a rigorous and refined academic work. On this foundation, we introduce this series of concise readers, which provides much material in a simple format. It includes the cream of the crop of great figures relatively familiar to foreign readers. We have done our best to use plain but vivid language to narrate their human stories of interest; this will convey the wisdom of their thought and display the cultural magnificence of the Chinese people. In the course of spiritually communing with these representative thinkers from ancient China, readers will certainly be able to apprehend the undying essence of thoughts of the Chinese people.

Finally, we are deeply grateful for the support from Hanban/ Confucius Institute Headquarters, and the experts from home and abroad for their joint efforts in writing and translating this series.

Editors
November, 2009

评论他们的思想成就，是严肃精深的学术著作。在此基础上推出的这套简明读本，则厚积薄发，精选出国外读者相对较为熟悉的伟大人物，力求用简洁生动的语言，通过讲述有趣的人物故事，传达他们的思想智慧，展示中华民族绚烂多姿的文化。读者在和这些中国古代有代表性的思想家的心灵对话中，一定能领略中华民族思想文化生生不息的精髓。

最后，我们衷心感谢国家汉办/孔子学院总部对本项目提供了巨大的支持，感谢所有参与此套丛书撰写和翻译工作的中外专家学者为此套丛书所做的辛勤而卓有成效的工作。

编者
2009年11月

目录
Contents

2 Contents ⚘

引言: 一百四十年, 国容何赫然

Introduction: One Hundred Forty Years / How Amazing the Empire Is

When speaking of classical Chinese poetry, one cannot pass over Tang poetry; when speaking of Tang poetry, one cannot pass over Li Bai.

Li Bai is a great poet of the Tang Dynasty (618—907). He was born in 701, during the reign of Wu Zetian, and died in 762, during the reign of Tang Emperor Daizong. He lived most of his life during the "High Tang" period, which was the strong Kaiyuan and Tianbao administrations of the reign of Emperor Xuanzong. Li Bai was an extraordinarily talented poet. His poems are full of emotion and fantastic imagination, using clear and fluent language to cover a broad range of topics. His descriptions are rich and dynamic, not merely recording his rich life and fascinating internal realm, but also expressing the spirit of the "High Tang," and the social and political changes he met. Li Bai is often associated with another great poet of the Tang Dynasty— Du Fu; they are known as "Li Du." These two poetic geniuses are often referred to as the two brightest stars in the brilliant heaven of Tang poetry.

There were many factors which contributed to Li Bai becoming a great poet, but it was mainly the social environment in which he lived, and especially the unique element of the High Tang society, which created this great poet. In the early years of the Tang Dynasty, the emperors were liberal and progressive, and the political atmosphere of the empire was unstrict. This contributed to the flourishing literary culture that cultivated great poets such as Li Bai.

In 618, Li Yuan unified China and established the Tang Dynasty, ending four hundred years of warfare and division. Nine years later, his son Li Shimin, known as Tang Taizong, assumed the throne. With this, Chinese history turned a new leaf.

Not only was Tang Taizong an outstanding military strategist, but also a liberal politician. He knew how to learn from history, and understood the Chinese proverb that "water supports the boat, but can also overturn the boat." The minds and hearts of the people are invaluable in maintaining long-lasting government and peace. With this understanding, many policies of the Tang government encouraged social development and benefited the prosperity of the people. Economic prosperity and military strength made the Tang into a great empire.

With social stability and economic prosperity, and especially convenient transportation, exchange and interaction between the Han People and surrounding ethnicities became increasingly frequent. As the Tang ruling

　　说起中国古典诗歌，就不能不说到唐诗；说起唐诗，就不能不说到李白。

　　李白是唐代伟大的诗人，生于武则天的长安元年（公元701）；卒于唐代宗的宝应元年（762）。他的大半生经历的是"盛唐时期"，即唐朝最为强盛的开元、天宝（唐玄宗的年号）年间。李白具有极高的诗歌创作天赋。他的诗歌，激情饱满，境界开阔，想象奇异，语言清新流畅，形象丰富生动，不仅记录了他丰富多彩的生活经历和微妙复杂的内心世界，而且也体现出当时的"盛唐气象"和他所遭遇的社会变化。李白与唐代另一位伟大诗人杜甫齐名，世称"李杜"。这两位大诗人，被人们称之为灿烂的唐诗星空中一对耀眼的双子星。

　　李白之所以能够成为一位伟大的诗人，有多方面的原因，但其中社会环境，特别是盛唐时代的社会特征造就了这位大诗人。唐帝国建立之初，皇帝颇有四海一家的胸怀，王朝的政治氛围相对宽松，这对促进唐代文学的繁荣发展、培育李白这样的大诗人确实起到了很好的促进作用。

　　公元618年，李渊统一中国，建立唐朝，结束了自汉末以来长达四百年之久的分裂局面。九年之后，其子李世民即位，后世称为唐太宗。自此，中国历史翻开了新的一页。

　　唐太宗不仅是一位出色的军事家，也是非常开明的政治家。他懂得吸取历史的经验与教训，深知中国传统所说的"水能载舟，亦能覆舟"的道理，懂得民心向背对于王朝长治久安的重大影响。基于这一出发点，唐朝当时推行的许多政策都比较有利于社会生产的发展，有利于百姓安居乐业。经济的繁荣、军事实力的加强，使唐帝国成为一个强大的国家。

　　社会相对稳定，经济繁荣，特别是交通便利之后，汉民族与周边民族以及海外的交流日益频繁起来。唐代皇室具有中国

family had ethnic minority heritage, Taizong encouraged the peaceful interaction between the Han People of the heartland and the ethnic minorities of Central Asia, which formed the harmonious relation known as "the family of Hun and Han." He respected the customs and religions of the minority groups, and permitted them to establish their own religious institutions within Tang borders. The foreign policies of the Tang were also relatively liberal, encouraging the assimilation of different ethnicities and interaction between the Chinese and foreign cultures. Throughout the Tang Dynasty, interaction of trade, culture, and arts between the various ethnic groups and the Han nationality was quite common. The various ethnic groups of the western regions, and even Asia and Europe, traded over both land and sea routes. At the time, the trade routes of Hunnish traders covered the whole empire, and temples and monasteries of Hunnish monks could be found in major cities such as Chang'an and Luoyang. Such trade not only brought Central Asian goods such as gold and silver to the Tang people, but more importantly, it introduced cultural treasures. Chinese literary culture absorbed foreign and exotic artistic qualities, giving it a fresh and interesting style. This was the fertile ground in which Tang literature, and especially poetry, flourished.

As society became prosperous during the "High Tang" period, along with the improvements in land and water transportation, it became convenient for poets to travel and gain experience. Most High Tang poets enjoyed traveling. It could increase their knowledge and expand their horizons. As for poetic composition, travel facilitated merging literary styles of different regions.

Tang poets were generally open to different artistic styles and cultural practices. Southern Dynasties literature was delicate yet weak; Northern Dynasties literary styles were strong and forceful, yet not subtle enough. Tang poets were able to avoid the shortcomings of styles in the Southern and Northern periods and synthesize the delicate Southern style with the strong Northern style. The "Four Masters of the Early Tang," Wang Bo, Yang Jiong, Lu Zhaolin, and Luo Binwang, were already able to combine the Northern toughness and Southern delicacy fairly well. After them, an important poet, Chen Zi'ang, continued experimenting in this direction, resulting in the new Tang style. In the High Tang period, the characteristics of the Northern and Southern style were combined even more effectively, resulting in a style unique to Tang poetry. The Southern and Northern intellectual and poetic styles were combined to provide an extremely favorable climate for further development of cultural arts, especially

少数民族的血统，在民族政策上，唐太宗提倡西域各民族与中原汉族和睦共处，即所谓"胡汉一家"。他尊重少数民族的乡土习俗和宗教信仰，允许他们建立各自的寺院。唐朝的对外政策也比较开明，相关的政策促进了各民族之间的融合以及中外文化的交流。整个唐代，各民族之间以及中外的贸易、文化、艺术上的交流十分频繁。西域各民族以及亚洲、欧洲国家的商人有的通过陆路，有的经过海上，进行贸易。在当时，胡商的足迹遍布海内，胡僧的寺院也云集长安、洛阳等地。这种交流不仅给唐人带来了西域以及中亚各民族的金银器物等有形的东西，更重要的是，带来了许多无形的文化财富。华夏文艺创作与充满异域风光与兴味的艺术风格相互融会，呈现出多彩多姿的风貌。这是唐代文学艺术，特别是诗歌得以蓬勃发展的沃土。

盛唐时期的民众生活比较富裕，加上当时水路和陆路交通都相对便利，诗人墨客外出旅行颇为方便。这为盛唐诗人的物质生活和游历活动提供了基本的条件。盛唐诗人大多喜好漫游。对于诗人而言，这可以增长见识，开阔视野；对于诗歌创作而言，游历活动大大促进了不同地域之间文风的融合。

唐诗人性情开朗，对于各种艺术风格、文化现象，大多没有什么偏见，南朝诗文，风格优美，但不免纤弱；北朝文风刚劲有力，但不够含蓄，唐诗人则能避免南北文学的短处，而将南朝清丽和北朝刚健结合起来，融二者于一炉。"初唐四杰"王勃、杨炯、卢照邻、骆宾王的诗歌作品，已经能够把刚毅的骨气与华美的词句较好地结合起来。随后的一位重要诗人陈子昂，继续沿着这一方向探索，开创出唐诗的新风尚。盛唐之时，南北文学各自的特点更是在诗人手中充分融合，诗人们努力创作，展现出真正属于唐诗自身的独特风貌。南方与北方学风、文风的结合给文化艺术的发展，特别是诗歌创作，提供了极好的精

poetic writings.

Chinese tradition has always valued poety; people love to recite poems, study poems, and compose poems. When selecting officials for the imperial government, the abilities of the candidates to compose poems were tested. If a candidate wrote poems well, his chances of being selected for official service were higher. Besides their aesthetic qualities, poems were also very practical. Composition was required for many social occasions. When departing on a long journey, friends would throw a going-away banquet, at which poems would be composed and exchanged. The mutual sorrow of parting would be expressed in graceful poetry. In ancient China, the ability to compose poems was a mark of high scholarly ability. Most government officials in ancient China wrote poetry. With such a poetic tradition, several emperors of the Early Tang also emphasized poetry and respected poets. Emperors often assembled men of letters at banquets to recite poems and paint paintings, appreciate dance and song, and even held poetry contests to see who could compose the best verse in the shortest time. The best poet, of course, was recognized by the emperor and court officials. At the time, composition was generally free of restrictions, in that the court would not interfere with the topics of composition. This was quite beneficial to the composition of poetry.

The spiritual realm of the Tang people was extremely unique. It was a refreshing, bright realm, full of the spirit of optimism. The economic vitality, social stability, and imperial strength of the Early Tang were the foundation for the broad enthusiasm and fervor of most intellectuals. As far as the Tang were concerned, though, the material factors of their times were only partially responsible for their spirit of optimism and progress. There were times after the Tang that also exhibited similar qualities, but the spirit of the Tang was unrecoverable. The society of this period was like a youth during a growth spurt. The Early and High Tang periods experienced war and disaster, and the people also encountered all sorts of difficulties and challenges, sadness and sorrows, but what is truly surprising is that despite all of this, the Tang were always confident and full of hope. Sorrows were temporary, and sighs were light. Deep in the Tang spiritual realm, there were fewer worries, sorrows, and disappointments. There was always a spirit of vitality, vigour, and progress. To use a phrase of some scholars, "this was a healthy era." ❶

神氛围与发展方向。

中国传统一向重视诗歌，人们喜爱读诗、学诗、写诗。有时选拔文官也会考察候选者诗歌的写作能力，诗歌写得好，那么，被朝廷录用为官员的可能性更大一些。诗歌除了美感价值，还很"实用"，许多社交场合都需要写诗。一人远行，朋友都会设宴送别，席间赋诗相赠，彼此之间依依惜别之情都是通过优美的诗句来表达。能够写诗在中国古代是受到良好教育的标志，古代大部分的官员都会写诗。在这样一个诗歌传统中，唐初的几位帝王自然也都比较重视诗歌，尊重诗人。帝王经常召集文士游宴，吟诗作画，欣赏歌舞，还举行诗歌创作比赛，看谁在最短的时间里写出最好的诗篇。最佳的诗人自然受到皇帝以及朝臣们的推崇。当时的诗人写作比较自由，一般情况下，朝廷不会干涉诗歌的内容。这种状况十分有利于诗歌的创作活动。

唐人的精神世界非常独特，那是一种清新、明朗、充满乐观精神的世界。唐初经济繁荣、社会稳定、国力强盛，这是广大士人具有激情昂扬的精神状态的基础。当然，对于唐人乐观向上的精神面貌而言，这些物质因素只提供了某种可能性，唐以后的某些时期也曾出现过类似的局面，但唐人的那种精神气息却是一去不复返了。这一时期的民族好似正在成长中的青年。初、盛唐时期尽管也有战争、灾难，士人百姓也都遭遇种种困难、挫折，也有忧郁、悲伤，但令人惊叹的是，唐人始终都是那样的自信，充满希望。尽管悲伤，却是短暂；虽然叹息，总是轻盈。在唐人的精神世界的深处确实较少担心、哀伤和失望，通体散发出一种蓬勃、昂扬、向上的气息。有学者说得好，这是"一个健康的时代"。❶

---

❶ 冯至《杜甫传》。

❶ Feng Zhi's *Du Fu Zhuan* (*Biography of Du Fu*).

Not only was this the period during which the Tang Dynasty was ascending toward its zenith, it was also the era during which the culture was advancing toward maturity. Not only the doors of China, but also the hearts of the people, were wide open. It was with this open spirit that the people of Tang encountered the cultures of exotic lands and foreign peoples. Not only did they not feel threatened, they took the initiative to actively extract beneficial aspects from these new cultures. During such exchanges, music is often the first to be disseminated. When the Tang people, accustomed to the subtle and slow sounds of sophisticated court music and the delicate "Lotus Picking Melody," first heard the Central Asian Swirling Dance and Galloping Dance, they were instantly attracted by the swift rhythms and strong lively dances. The refreshing new music enraptured the Tang people. As an example of the influence the foreign music had, the Early Tang court established "Ten Schools of Music," of which four schools came from minority ethnic groups within the empire, and four from foreign lands. It was evident that music from the minorities and foreign countries had occupied the major position. Most of these schools were accompanied by unique dance. The choreography, costumes, musical instruments, and rhythms were all very different from those used in local Chinese dance and music. From the emperor and high officials in the central court all the way to the commoners, everyone enjoyed these new songs, dance, and music. The Tang people were interested in all aspects of exotic cultures, whether it be music, dance, painting, or sculpture. They were able to not only accept, but to absorb, the new content and form. The techniques of foreign painting also entered into China, influencing traditional Chinese painters. Each time Tang poets composed poems describing paintings, they would describe their new experiences appreciating the exotic styles.

Tang society was stable, the military was strong, and the people were rich. The culture of the people was mature, and their hearts were open and full of progressive optimism. The scholarship and culture were developed, and especially the composition of poetry had a solid foundation in society and rich intellectual resources from which to draw. On top of the foundation of the combined Southern and Northern intellectual and literary traditions, the Tang people absorbed and assimilated the new cultural content and styles of the Central Asian and other foreign cultures, creating a new dynamic and beautiful form of expression with which they expressed their own culture and realized a new culture. This new culture reached its zenith in the High Tang. The spirit of this new culture is what is referred to as the "High Tang climate."

Li Bai lived during the High Tang, experiencing the influences of this

　　此时，不仅是唐帝国走向鼎盛的时期，也是民族的心智走向成熟的时代。当时的中国不仅门户敞开，而且民族的心扉也是敞开着的。正是这种开放的心灵，唐人面对纷至沓来的异域外族文化，不仅不感到什么威胁，反而主动地从中获取于己有利的各种滋养。在这种交流中，音乐常常是最先传播的内容。当听惯了凝重迟缓的雅乐和轻柔婉转的"采莲曲"的唐人初次接触西域的胡旋舞、胡腾舞时，一下子便被吸引住了，那快速急促的节奏、活泼有力的舞姿、令人耳目一新的音乐样式着实让唐人着迷。唐初宫廷中设有"十部乐"，其中四部来自境内的少数民族，四部来自国外，可见当时外族异域的音乐占了很大的比例。这些音乐大多配合有独特的歌舞，舞蹈的编排、装扮、舞姿以及乐队组成、旋律都与中国原有的乐舞样式大相径庭。上至君主官员，下至平民百姓，都很喜爱这些样式新颖的歌舞音乐。唐人对各种外来文化都很有兴趣，无论是音乐、舞蹈，还是绘画、雕塑，都能够十分关注，并且广泛吸收其中的新内容与新形式。国外的绘画也传入中国，在技法等方面影响到本土的画家。唐代诗人每有咏画之作，借此表达他们对各种新画风的新鲜感受。

　　唐代社会安定，国力强盛，人民生活富裕；民族心智成熟，心胸开阔，充满积极向上的精神；学术文化发达，特别是诗歌创作具有良好的社会基础和文学积累。唐人在充分融合南北学风、文风的基础上，又积极吸收西域各民族以及海外文化的新内容、新形式，从而创造了一种既具有生动优美的表达形式，又能够反映自身民族精神面貌和现实生活的新文化。这种文化在盛唐时期达到了高峰，其内在的精神，大体就是前人所谓的"盛唐气象"。

　　李白生活在盛唐时期，亲身感受到盛唐文化的影响。他出

High Tang culture. He was born in Central Asia, and then moved to Sichuan. He spent most of his life journeying to all parts of China, encountering different religions, cultures, customs, and practices, including tales and myths, folk songs, music, and dance. His poetic compositions express his amalgamation of this multivariate culture. Li Bai had an open heart and mind, bold and uninhibited character, rich imagination, and literary talent. Most of his poetry, composed during this period, is the most direct and dynamic expression of the "High Tang climate."

生在西域，后到四川，一生中大部分时间都在游历各地，接触到各种宗教文化、民族风情、地方习俗，包括大量传说神话、民歌民谣、音乐舞蹈，他的诗歌创作体现出对这些多元文化、异质元素的有机融合。李白胸襟开阔，性格豪放，想象丰富，富有文学天才，他的大部分诗歌都写作于这个时代，是"盛唐气象"最直接、最生动的写照。

明代画家笔卜的四川地貌

Geography of Sichuan in the painting of a Ming painter

一　孕育: 蜀国多仙山

Chapter　Ⅰ　Childhood: The Shu Kingdom Has Many
　　　　　　　Immortal Mountains

According to Li Bai himself, he was the descendent of the Western Han general Li Guang, and the ninth generation descendent of the founder of the Western Liang kingdom, Li Hao, and so a relative of the Tang ruling family. One branch of the Li clan ended up in western China and became the famous "Longxi Li" aristocratic clan, so historians refer to Li Bai as a descendent of the Longxi clan. In the late years of the Sui Dynasty, China was in a state of chaos, and Li Bai's ancestors moved west to take refuge in Suiye, where they settled. Suiye is near modern Ak-Beshim, Kirgizstan. It was an important oasis along the silk route. At the time, it was on the frontier of the Tang Empire.

Li Bai was born in 701 A.D. in Suiye. The Tang people saw Li Bai as a genius, and such a genius could not have had a common birth. According to legend, before Li Bai was born, his mother dreamt that the star Changgeng fell into her belly. The star Changgeng is the planet Venus, which rises at dusk in the west. Before dawn, it is in the east, and so is called the Morning Star. This star is very bright, and the ancient Chinese placed great importance on it. The star Changgeng is also known as the *Taibaijinxing* (Great White Metal Star), and so his father named him Li Bai, alias Taibai. At the time, people could not believe that a genius such as Li Bai was of the human realm, and so said he must be the embodiment of the spirit of the planet Venus. Only this could explain how extraordinary he was. When he was young, Li Bai dreamt that the tip of the brush with which he was writing blossomed into flowers. People believed this must be an important omen. Later, his poetry did become extraordinary, known throughout the empire and beyond. Since then, the saying "to dream that one's brush blossoms" is used to imply that a person's literary skills are extraordinary.

The Empress Wu Zetian died in 705 A.D. Her son assumed the throne, becoming Emperor Zhongzong. In this year, Li Bai's father encountered difficulties, and so quickly moved his family out of Suiye and into mainland. Li Bai was five years old.

Usually, those entering China from Central Asia would follow "the silk route," traveling southeast to Chang'an or Luoyang. At the time, many Central Asians lived in Chang'an, and were involved in all sorts of business, trade being the most common. Other big cities also had populations of Central Asians, including Yangzhou, Guangzhou, and even such small town as Liyang (in modern Jiangsu Province). In his poem "Song of the Fierce Tiger," Li Bai said: "Liyang tavern in the spring of April / Willow catkins floating about, killing with sorrow / A Hun youth with green eyes playing the jade flute / The Wu song 'White Sack,' dust flying from the beams." In a tavern in Liyang,

按照李白自己的说法，他是西汉名将李广的后代，是五胡十六国时西凉创业君主李暠（hào）的九世孙，因此与唐皇室是同宗。李氏中的一支后来流落到中国西部，成为唐代著名郡望中的"陇西李氏"，所以，史书中称李白是陇西成纪人。隋朝末年，天下大乱，李白的祖先西迁到碎叶避难，并在那里定居。碎叶在今天的吉尔吉斯共和国境内，靠近托克马克城，是古代丝绸之路上的重要城市，当时属于唐王朝的疆域。

长安元年（701），李白在碎叶出生。在唐人的心目中，李白是一位天才。这样的天才，出生自然不同寻常。据说，李白出生时，他的母亲梦到长庚星落入怀中。长庚星即金星，傍晚出现在西边，称为长庚星；天亮前出现在东方，又称为启明星。这颗星非常明亮，古人特别看重。长庚星又称太白金星，因此，他的父亲给他取名白，字太白。当时人认为李白这样的天才不可能生于人间，一定是"太白之精下降"，就是说，是太白金星的灵气、精气凝聚而成，才使他如此才能出众。李白少年时，曾梦见所用毛笔的笔头上开放出鲜花。人们以为这是个重要的征象，日后李白的诗歌创作果然精妙奇绝，名闻天下。后来，汉语中常用成语"梦笔生花"来形容一个人文才出众。

神龙元年（705），女皇帝武则天去世，她的儿子中宗继承王位。此时，李白的父亲因为在西域遭遇麻烦，便急切地带着家人离开碎叶，来到内地。此时李白五岁。

一般来说，从西域过来的人都会沿着"丝绸之路"东下，来到长安、洛阳等地。当时留居在长安的胡人数量很多，他们从事各种职业，但主要是经商。其他的大城市也会有胡人居住，扬州、广州等地固不必说，就像溧阳（今属江苏省）这样县级的小地方，也有胡人的身影。李白《猛虎行》中说："溧阳酒楼三月春，杨花茫茫愁杀人。胡雏绿眼吹玉笛，吴歌《白纻》

the poet met a green-eyed Central Asian youth playing the flute.

Li Bai's family were ethnic Han, and so when they returned to China, they could have settled in a large city such as Chang'an or Luoyang, but they chose to settle in Sichuan. This was not a common route for Central Asians to follow. Li Bai's father was certainly concerned about attracting attention, and so did not dare enter large cities. Rather, he settled in the sparsely populated and remote village of Qinglian, in Changlong County, Mianzhou. Changlong is modern Jiangyou City, Sichuan Province. At the time, Changlong was but a small and remote county of several thousand households surrounded by mountains. Considering that Qinglian Village was seven kilometers from the Changlong County, and thirty kilometers from Mianzhou, it seemed even more remote. Qinglian Village was on the banks of the Fujiang River, nearby Dakuang Mountain. The scenery was beautiful and serene, and quite suitable for a stranger to go to avoid trouble. This was indeed a good place for Li Bai's family to settle.

People called Li Bai's father "Li Ke (Guest Li)." Scholars believe this was not his true name. Because his father moved from distant Central Asia to Sichuan and settled as a guest in this place, yet no one knew his true name, they referred to him as "Li Ke," or the stranger named Li. Li Ke returned with members of his extended family, and Li Bai was the twelfth born among his brothers and cousins, and so was sometimes called "Li the twelfth."

When he was five years old, Li Bai followed his family to Sichuan, and lived there twenty years. These were the formative years of his life, during which he grew up and received an education. These years are important to everyone because they can influence the rest of one's life, but for Li Bai, they were even more important; not only important, but extraordinary.

Li Bai's experiences during his youth were affected by three facets. One was the culture of Central Asia. Central Asia has wide open spaces and large deserts. Most people there live following the water and grass. They tend to be fierce and good at fighting, enjoy singing and good at dancing. Both in daily life and cultural customs, they are quite different from Chinese. Li Bai's ancestors lived in Central Asia for a long time, and had close ties to the people there. Their life, customs, and ideas must have been influenced by the local culture. Traditional Chinese always speak of the sun and the moon, saying the sun rises in the east, and the moon in the west. Therefore, the moon represents the West. Li Bai had a little sister named "Yueyuan (Round Moon)," implying a longing for her place of birth. Li Bai's compositions also often mention the

飞梁尘。"在溧阳的酒楼上,诗人就遇到碧眼的西域少年吹笛子。

李白一家本为汉人,他们从西域返回,行程万里,本可以在长安、洛阳这样的大城市定居,但他们却来到蜀地。这并不是西域人常走的路线。李白的父亲一定是怕招惹是非,不敢到名都大邑去,才在人口较少、相对偏僻的绵州昌隆县后称青莲乡的村落中定居。昌隆即今天的四川省江油市。昌隆县在当时不过是一个只有几千户人家的小县,周围群山环绕,比较偏远。青莲乡距昌隆县城7公里,距绵州城30公里,显得更加僻静了。它靠近涪江,附近有大匡山,景色秀丽,倒是外乡人躲避麻烦的好去处。李白一家定居在这里,确实非常适宜。

李白的父亲,人称"李客",研究者认为,这恐怕不是他的本名。因为李家万里跋涉,从西域来到川蜀,客居此地,当地人不晓得李白的父亲的名字,直接称他为"李客",即姓李的外乡人的意思。李客是同家族中人一起回来的,李白在堂房兄弟中排行第十二,别人有时称他"李十二"。

李白五岁随家来到蜀地,在那里生活了二十年。这正是一个人从童年接受教育,成长为青年的时期。对任何人而言,这一时期的经历都非常重要,因为它常常影响人的一生,但对李白而言,就更加重要了。不仅重要,而且奇特。

李白早年的经历受到三方面的影响。一是西域文化。西域地方广大,有很多沙漠,当地人大多逐水草而居,性格勇猛善战,能歌善舞,无论是生活习惯,还是文化习俗,都与中原地区的人有较大的差别。李白的祖先长期居住在西域,与胡人的关系密切,其生活、习俗、观念等必然要受到当地文化的影响。中国古代总是"日"与"月"相对而言,日出东方,月生西边。因此,月代表着西方。李白有个妹妹,名字就叫"月圆",蕴含着对出生之地西域的怀恋。李白的诗作中也常提到"月",

moon, such as "Frontier Pass Moon," in which he says:

> The bright moon appears over Tianshan;
> Distantly, among the sea of clouds.
> The long wind, over several tens of thousands of miles;
> Blows through Yumen Pass.

Li Bai describes the moon in the Central Asian landscape, expressing his deep feelings for Central Asia. Li Bai spent his life wandering, not minding much his family and children. His personality was uninhibited. This was in some part due to the influence of the Central Asian culture.

The second facet was the influence of traditional Chinese culture.

Although the Li family lived a long time in Central Asia, they were not Central Asians. Their ancestors originally lived in Longxi, and so the family retained much of their Chinese culture and traits. Li Bai recalled later that when he was young, his father would often have him recite the "Rhapsody on Sir Vacuous" written by Sima Xiangru of the Han Dynasty. Reciting poems and rhapsodies is a characteristic of Chinese education. From this, one can see that Li Ke had an understanding of traditional Chinese culture.

The Li family's life in Central Asia was cause for an unusual phenomenon: The Chinese culture which they retained was no longer the Chinese culture of the time. There were some substantial differences. Why? The Li family originally lived in Longxi, but moved to Suiye at the end of the Sui Dynasty, bringing with them the customs and practices of Chinese culture from the Han and Wei periods. In the remote circumstances of Central Asia, these family customs did not change much. The Sui Dynasty had ended over one hundred years before the birth of Li Bai, though, and the customs of China had continued to evolve. The customs of the Li family therefore appeared rather "traditional" to others of the time. In ancient times, children began their education around the ages of seven or eight, but Li Bai was exceptionally bright, and began reading at five. He himself said that "at five, I could recite the *six jia*." What is the "*six jia*"? In the Daoist canon, there is an odd book titled "Six Jia," but Li Bai's education would certainly not begin with reading such books. "*Six jia*" here refers to a kind of children's educational material. In the Han and Wei periods, children would enter school at the age of eight and begin learning the "*six jia*," or the calculation of the *jiazi* counting system. The traditional way of keeping track of the order of years, months, and days was to use the "heavenly stems" and "earthly branches." *Jia, yi, bing, ding, wu, ji, geng, xin, ren,* and *gui* are the ten stems, or ten heavenly stems. *Zi, chou, yin,*

如《关山月》中说:

> 明月出天山,苍茫云海间。
>
> 长风几万里,吹度玉门关。

说的是西域景色中所见的月亮,传达着李白对西域的深厚感情。李白一生漂泊,不甚顾念家庭孩子,性格豪放,多少与他受到西域习俗文化的浸染有关。

二是中原传统文化的影响。

李家虽然长期生活在西域,但他们并不是西域人,李氏的先祖本来就生活在陇西,因此家族在很大程度上仍然保留着汉族文化、中原文化的特点。李白后来回忆,小的时候,父亲经常让他背诵《子虚赋》。背诵诗赋是中原文化教育的方式。从这里还可以看出,李客对中国传统文化是有所了解的。

李家西域生活的经历还造成一个不寻常的现象,这就是李家固守的中原文化与当时现实的中原文化,实际上有所区别。为什么?李家本来生活在陇西,隋末,家族迁至碎叶,带走的是汉魏时期的中原文化习俗。这种家族的文化习俗在西域相对隔绝的情况下,不太容易发生很大的变化。但隋末到李白的时代,已经过去了一百多年,中原地区的文化习俗沿着自己的方向悄然发生改变。所以李家的文化传统对于当时人来说显得尤为"传统"。古人大约在七八岁时开始读书,李白自幼聪颖,五岁时就开始读书识字,他自称"五岁诵六甲"。"六甲"是什么?道教典籍中有一种奇怪的书叫"六甲",李白启蒙教育自然不会从读这类书开始。这里的"六甲"是针对儿童的一种教育内容。汉魏时期的儿童八岁入小学,开始学习"六甲",掌握六十甲子的名称以及推演方法等。古时标记年、月、日的次序采用特殊的"干支"方法。甲、乙、丙、丁、戊(wù)、己、庚、辛、壬、癸十个名称为十干,也

mao, chen, si, wu, wei, shen, you, xu, and *hai* are the twelve branches, or the twelve earthly branches. The heavenly stems are aligned with the twelve earthly stems in order: *jia-zi, yi-chou, bing-yin,* and so on, until reaching *ren-xu* and *gui-hai,* resulting in sixty combinations. Each year is assigned one name, until it repeats after sixty years, thus the common saying of "sixty, a graying *jiazi,*" when referring to a person reaching sixty years of age. The ordering of days and months also follow this system. Children of the Han and Wei Dynasties began their education with learning these characters and the associated mathematics. By the Tang Dynasty, though, children rarely learned the "*six jia.*" Upon returning to Sichuan from Central Asia, Li Bai's father still taught his son with this "*six jia*" system of reading and mathematics, and not the system commonly used by the Tang Dynasty people. One can see that the conservative traditional culture of the Li family was not the same as the contemporary customs of the Chinese.

After growing older, Li Bai began reading on his own, saying of himself that "at ten, I had read the books of the hundred schools." The "hundred schools" here refers to works of various different schools of thought. This reading interest of his was quite different from that of his contemporaries. Ancient China had a special method of choosing candidates for official service called the *keju* examinations. The Sui Dynasty initiated the *keju* system. Candidates were assigned official positions according to their grades in official palace examinations. After receiving an official position, they could receive a court salary, called "*Fenglu*" at that time, along with other benefits. This is why many scholars were very enthusing about participating in these examinations. In the early years of the Tang Dynasty, the court published *Proper Explanations of the Five Classics* as the standard for examinations. In order to successfully pass the examinations, students would begin studying the Confucian classics from a very young age, yet Li Bai put his main energies on studying the "hundred schools." The "hundred schools" naturally included the Confucian classics, but ever since the Han Dynasty, the Confucian classics were the dominant orthodoxy, unlike the "hundred schools." As Li Bai emphasized that he had read all "hundred schools," we can be sure that his interests were not limited to the Confucian classics.

He did not only study the "hundred schools," but also enjoyed reading "unconventional books." In his second poem of "Two Poems Given to Zhang Xianghao," Li Bai said that "At fifteen, I read unconventional books / I wrote rhapsodies competing with Xiangru." This is to say, at fifteen, he enjoyed reading "unconventional books" and composing pieces that exceeded the

称天干。子、丑、寅、卯、辰、巳（sì）、午、未、申、酉、戌（xū）、亥十二个名称为十二支，也称地支。天干顺着次序与地支组合，即有甲子、乙丑、丙寅……壬戌、癸亥等六十个名称，一个年份用一个名称，六十年重复一次，俗称"六十花甲子"。日期的编排等等也用这种方法。汉魏时期的儿童学习之初，就是接受这种童蒙的识字计数教育。可是，到了唐代，儿童的启蒙已经很少再学"六甲"了。李白的父亲从西域回到蜀地，教儿子识字计数，仍然采用"六甲"，其教育方式与唐人通常的做法并不一致。可见，李家恪守的传统文化与当时的中原文化不尽相同。

长大一些，李白开始自由阅读，自称"十岁观百家"。这里的"百家"指的是不同流派的著作。他这样的阅读兴趣与当时的读书人完全不同。中国古代文官选拔有特殊的制度，称为科举。隋朝开始实施科举制度，候选人通过朝廷专门的考试，即可按照成绩的等第不同授予官职。获得官职后，可以得到朝廷发给的薪水，当时称为"俸禄"，还可以享受其他的特权，因此当时的士子都很热衷于参加这样的考试。唐初，朝廷颁布《五经正义》作为考试的准则，学生为了能够顺利通过考试，在很小的时候即开始熟读儒家经书。但李白却把主要精力放在阅读"百家"上。"百家"当中自然包括"儒家"，但汉代以来，儒家受到独尊，显然不同于"百家"。李白强调遍观"百家"，至少可以说明他的兴趣不限于儒家。

他不仅钻研"百家"，还喜欢阅读"奇书"。李白《赠张相镐（hào）二首》其二中称自己"十五观奇书，作赋凌相如"。意思是说，他在十五岁时就爱读各种"奇书"，写作水平超过

quality of those of the great Han scholar Sima Xiangru. The "unconventional books" here obviously do not refer to the Confucian classics. The Confucian classics were mandatory material for students to study. The content discusses mostly government and education, ritual and etiquette, and certainly cannot be referred to as "unconventional." Li Bai was obviously concerned with subjects beyond those in the Confucian classics. He was interested in rare and unusual books, with new and remarkable ideas. In Sichuan of the time, there were certainly plenty of "unconventional books" from the "hundred schools." For example, the famous poet Chen Zi'ang came from Sichuan. His fifth generation grandfather Chen Fangqing once received *Mozi*'s *Five Elements Secret Script* and *White Tiger Seven Transformations*. These are secret scripts, not to be found in other records. Li Bai's friend Zhao Rui, also from Sichuan, once wrote *Important Methods of the Long and Short*, also called *Classic of the Long and Short*. According to the contents of the books, they certainly belong to the category of "unconventional books of the hundred schools." The books discuss many books that later generations have not seen. The fact that contemporary scholars focused on the *keju*, and read exclusively Confucian classics, while Li Bai read the "hundred schools" and loved unusual books, was at least in part due to his special family background. The Li family was different from central Chinese families because they had been in Central Asia for a long time and were influenced by the Central Asian culture, but also because, unlike Central Asians, they had the characteristics of Chinese culture. In fact, they had Chinese characteristics of the ancient Han and Wei Dynasties, thus differentiating them from the contemporary Chinese families.

The third facet was the geographical influences of Sichuan.

Sichuan is a basin. The Chengdu plain, with its fertile soil and well developed agriculture, is known as a land of plenty. To the east are the sheer three gorges of the Yangtze River, to the west is the Tibetan plateau, to the south is the Yungui plateau, and to the north are the Qin mountain range and Mount Ba. Transportation is extremely inconvenient. Due to its confinement, it is also known as the "land of four impediments." Although the location is confined, the culture is definitely not lacking. During the reign on Wendi of the Han Dynasty, the local area emphasized education and produced many men of letters and scholars, the best known of which were Sima Xiangru and Yang Xiong. Sima Xiangru was a Western Han man of letters. He received the attention of the emperor with his rhapsodies. He was also skilled at governing. He led the policy of arbitration and conciliation with the southwestern minority tribes, and was quite successful. Yang Xiong was also from Sichuan. In his earlier years, he

了汉代的大文学家司马相如。这里的"奇书"显然不是指儒家典籍。儒家著作是当时学者必读的经典,内容大多关乎政治教化、伦理日用,谈不上"奇"。李白关注的显然是儒家经典之外的各种珍奇、奇异的书籍,不仅难得,而且立论卓异,观念新奇。而当时的蜀中确实多有"百家"的"奇书"。如诗人陈子昂,家乡在蜀地,他的五世祖陈方庆曾得"墨子五行秘书、白虎七变(法)",这是不见于其他记载的秘籍;李白的朋友赵蕤(ruí)也是四川人,曾著《长短要术》,又称《长短经》,根据书中的内容来看,确实属于耐人寻味的"百家奇书"。书中谈到的不少典籍,后人绝少见过。当时学子热衷于科举,苦读儒家经典,而李白却遍观百家,爱读奇书,造成这种差别至少有一部分原因是李白家庭的特殊文化背景。李家不同于中原士人家庭,因为他们长期生活在西域,有西域文化的影响;又不同于西域人,他们有中原文化的特征,而且是比较古老的汉魏时代的中原文化的特征,这又使得他们不同于当时的中原士人家庭。

三是蜀地风土的影响。

川蜀实际上是一个盆地——四川盆地,其中成都平原,土地肥沃,农业发达,称为天府之国。盆地四周,东有长江三峡之险,西有青藏高原之阻,向南是云贵高原,向北是秦岭巴山,交通极为不便,颇为封闭,所以又称为"四塞之国"。地方虽然不免闭塞,可是当地的文化并不落后。汉文帝时期,当地大力兴办文化教育,涌现出不少文学家和学者,最著名的莫过于司马相如和扬雄。司马相如是西汉文学家,以擅长写赋而得到汉武帝的赏识。他又有政治才能,曾奉命前往西南少数民族地区进行安抚工作,颇有业绩。扬雄也是四川人,早年赋作仿效

emulated Sima Xiangru in composing rhapsodies, for which he gained praise. In fact, he received an official appointment due to a rhapsody he composed. Later, he declared rhapsodies to be "carving insects and etching script, not what a real man does." Being a real man, he looked down upon such petty matters and took up philosophic studies, and became one of the Han Dynasty's greatest scholars. The local predecessors and the cultural environment had an influence on Li Bai. Li Bai appreciated Sima Xiangru and Yang Xiong very much. In his "Rhapsody on the Great Hunt," Li Bai compared himself favorably to Sima Xiangru, claiming that his works could surpass Sima's. He always had the ambition to surpass Yang Xiong and Sima Xiangru.

The religious environment of Sichuan was very rich, and unlike other regions. During the Wei, Jin, and Northern and Southern Dynasties periods, a minority ethnic leader led a large group of refugees into Sichuan, where he received the support of the Daoist Fan Changsheng. With this, he founded a small kingdom with Daoism as state religion. As for this, Daoism has had a broad and deep influence on Sichuan. Many sorts of Daoist myths and tales abound throughout the mountains and rivers of the area. The Tang imperial family had the clan name of Li, and therefore recognized Laozi (Li Er) as their ancestor and supported Daoism. Therefore, Daoist tales of immortality spread throughout the empire. Having grown up in Sichuan, Li Bai was deeply influenced by Daoism since childhood.

There are many minority ethnic groups in Sichuan, and the religious cultures of the minority groups display all sorts of exotic colors. The Qiang ethnic group lives in Sichuan, and their religious practices had a special influence on Li Bai. Scholars believe that the religious beliefs of the Qiang are closely related to the origins of Daoism.

The origins of the Qiang are very ancient. The oracle bone inscriptions of the Shang Dynasty recorded the Qiang. When the Zhou led the eight hundred nobles to conquer the Shang king Zhou, the Qiang participated. Because the Qiang do not have a written script, later generations know little about their religious beliefs. The Qiang still use cremation, and scholars suggest that this is an ancient practice of this ethnic group, passed on through the generations, up until today.

According to ethnologists and religious scholars, Chinese beliefs in immortals originated in the eastern coastal regions of Yan and Qi. The mirages visible along the coastal regions make it easy to believe that there may be immortals living on the seas. The ideas of immortality could evolve from this. Other scholars believe, though, that Qi was a fiefdom of Grand Duke Jiang

司马相如，享有声誉，以献赋得官。后来他以为辞赋是"雕虫篆刻，壮夫不为"，自以为大丈夫不屑于做这样的事情，于是转向哲学研究，成为汉代著名的学者。当地的先贤和蜀地的文化氛围对李白极有影响。李白非常欣赏司马相如和扬雄，他写作《大猎赋》，自认为可以和司马相如的作品相媲（pì）美，在他的内心中一直有超越扬、马成就的雄心与抱负。

四川的宗教气氛十分浓郁，很不同于其他地区。魏晋南北朝时，一个少数民族的首领率领众多流民进入四川，得到道教徒范长生的支持，在此建立了一个小朝廷，并以道教作为当地的国教。因此，道教之于四川，具有广泛而深入的影响，境内诸多名山大川流传着各种神仙故事。唐代的皇帝姓李，认老子李耳为始祖，推崇道教，因此，道教仙风更是遍布朝野。李白生长在蜀中，自幼时起即深受其影响。

四川少数民族很多，少数民族的宗教文化更是呈现出各种奇异的色彩。四川有羌族，羌族的宗教习俗对李白颇有影响。有学者认为，羌族的原始宗教与道教的兴盛密切相关。

羌族的起源十分古老，殷商的甲骨文中即有关于羌的记载。周王率八百诸侯伐纣（zhòu），其中就有羌族参加。羌族没有系统的文字记载，因此有关他们的宗教信仰，后人知道的很少。羌族至今仍然实行火葬，学者推测，这是这个民族十分古老的习俗，世代相传，延续至今。

按照民族学者与宗教学者的研究，中国的神仙思想产生于东部沿海的燕国、齐国之地。沿海地区出现的海市蜃（shèn）楼的景象，很容易使人形成海上存在着仙山神人的想法，从而进一步产生神仙学说。但有学者提出不同看法，以为齐国是太

Shang, and Grand Duke Jiang was the leader of the Qiang ethnic group. Therefore, the belief in immortality still originated with the Qiang. The Qiang people use cremation, and as the flames rise and a person's body transforms into smoke and billows upward, people believe that the spirit is being released from the body and ascending to heaven. The belief that the soul is eternal gradually developed into the belief in immortality.

The Qiang people have always been active in the west of China, from the western Yellow River Basin, to the Guanzhong region, through Qinghai and Sichuan, all the way into the region that is modern Yunnan. Wherever the Qiang influence reaches, the belief in immortals is popular, and this just happens to be the birthplace of Daoism. In the late Han Dynasty, Zhang Lu organized people with the Five Pecks Daoist movement and established a theocratic state. The ancestral founder of the Heavenly Masters school of Daoism, Zhang Daoling, studied Daoism on Mount Heming, along the eastern bank of the Min River in western Sichuan, in modern Renshou County. One can infer that the popularity of Daoism in the western region of Sichuan is related to the primitive religious beliefs of the Qiang.

Li Bai grew up in western Sichuan, where there are many famous mountains, the most famous of which is Mount Emei. This is an area where the Qiang live, Daoism is prevalent, and many tales of spirits and the fantastic flow. Fantastical mountains and waters, billowing clouds and mists, and all kinds of miraculous myths and religious stories stimulated Li Bai's surprising imagination. Before leaving Sichuan, Li Bai visited Mount Emei. In his poem "Climbing Mount Emei," he wrote:

> Sichuan has many immortal mountains;
> Emei's profundity is difficult to match.
> Traveling about, I try to climb and view;
> The ultimate oddities, how can they be known?
> The green darkness unfurls against the sky;
> Multivarious colors, as if from a painting.
> Lightly, I swallow the purple mist;
> I have truly achieved the techniques of the brocade sack.
> In the clouds, I play the jade flute;
> On the rock, I strum the jeweled zither.
> All my life, I have had some accomplishments;
> Laughter from here ends.
> The misty tone appears on my face;
> The accumulated dust suddenly vanishes.

公姜尚的封地，而姜太公即为羌族首领，因此齐燕之地的神仙思想根源还在于羌人。羌人实施火葬，烈火升腾，人的肉体化为云烟冉冉上升，人们也就认为灵魂开始脱离躯壳而上升天国。灵魂不灭的观念逐渐形成了神仙思想。

羌族的主要活动地区一直集中在中国的西部，自河西走廊起，到关中地区，经过青海、四川一带，一直南延到今天的云南等地。羌族影响所及的地区，神仙信仰十分流行，道教也正是兴起于这些地区。汉末张鲁凭借五斗米道组织民众，建立政教合一的政权；天师道的祖师张道陵则学道于西蜀的鹤鸣山，就在今天的岷江东岸仁寿县境内。可以推知，四川西部地区盛行的道教，与羌族的原始信仰有关。

李白生长在西蜀，蜀地多名山，名山之中又以峨眉山为最。此地既是羌族聚居之地，也是道教盛行的区域，流传着许多关于神异的传说。蜀中奇异的山水、缥缈的云气，以及各种奇妙的神话、宗教故事大大激发了李白令人惊叹的想象力。李白出川之前，曾到峨眉山游赏。他在《登峨眉山》诗中说：

> 蜀国多仙山，峨眉邈难匹。
> 周流试登览，绝怪安可悉？
> 青冥倚天开，彩错疑画出。
> 泠然紫霞赏，果得锦囊术。
> 云间吟琼箫，石上弄宝瑟。
> 平生有微尚，欢笑自此毕。
> 烟容如在颜，尘累忽相失。

> If I should meet Master Goat Rider;
> We would hold hands and ascend to the white sun.

In the poem, he says that the most renowned of all immortal mountains in Sichuan is Mount Emei. Climbing it and exploring it, one encounters too many "ultimate oddities," fabulous scenes, and miraculous stories. At the end, the poet says how much he wishes to meet Master Goat Rider and follow him to the land of the immortals. Master Goat Rider is the ancient immortal Ge You. Fables say Ge You was an artist who enjoyed carving wooden goats. He usually took the goats he carved and sold them in the market to earn a living. It was amazing that if he blew on the wooden goats, then, they would come to life. People knew he had immortal powers, and wished to learn from him. One day, the people saw him riding a goat up Mount Emei. Many people chased after him. The tales say those people became immortals with him, never again to return to the mortal realm. Master Goat Rider was an ethnic Qiang, so this story ought to be a Qiang myth. From the many Qiang shrines below Mount Emei, it is obvious that the local people still believe strongly in the Qiang immortals. It is worthy of notice that Li Bai's family's residence was always near Qiang territory. The Qiang culture and Daoist environment had great influences on Li Bai as he grew up.

In conclusion, the cultural environment and geographical surroundings which nurtured this great poet were very special. On the one hand, because the Li clan experienced life in Central Asia, they were influenced by Central Asian culture; but on the other hand, because they had moved to Central Asia in the last years of the Sui Dynasty, the clan also brought the special Han period culture with them. Because the clan lived in Central Asia, this Han culture did not evolve or change over time. The result was that the customs and ideas of the Li clan were different from those of other aristocratic families of the times. When a family with such diverse cultural influences moved into Sichuan, their open-minded attitudes easily accepted the influences of the local ethnic peoples, religions, and beautiful mountains and rivers. All these factors miraculously came together to provide unusually rare circumstances for the poet to grow up in.

倘逢骑羊子，携手凌白日。

诗中说蜀中的仙山最著名的就是峨眉山，登临游览，山中各种"绝怪"，那些奇异的景色、神奇的故事实在太多。诗人最后说，他多么想遇见骑羊子，好随他一同到仙国去。骑羊子是古代的仙人葛由。传说葛由喜欢雕刻木羊，还是一位艺术家，他平时雕刻木羊就拿到集市上去卖，以此为生。但神奇的是，他对着木羊吹一口气，木羊立刻就变成了活羊。人们知道他有仙道，都想跟他去学仙。一天，人们见他骑着一头羊上了峨眉山，许多人都追随他而去，据说他们都成了神仙，再也没有回到人间。骑羊子是羌族人，这个故事也应该是羌族的神话。峨眉山下有羌人的祠堂数十处，足见当地祭祀羌族神仙的香火十分旺盛。值得注意的是，李白家族的定居点始终靠近羌族的活动区域。羌人的文化、道教的风气对李白青少年时期的成长形成了很大的影响。

总之，孕育李白这样一位伟大诗人的文化氛围、地理环境非常奇特。李氏家族一方面由于西域的生活经历，受到了西域文化的影响，又由于他们是在隋末从中原搬迁到西域的，因此，家族本身又带着汉魏时期中原文化的特点，这一特点由于家族生活在西域的环境中，并没有发生很大的变化。这使得李氏家族在文化习俗、思想观念方面不同于当时一般的士族家庭。这样一个具有多元文化交互影响的家庭迁至川蜀之后，具有开放的心态，更容易接受当地民族、宗教文化以及秀美的山川地理环境的熏染。各种奇妙的因素神奇地汇集在一起，为诗人的成长提供了异常难得的机会。

李白书法
Calligraphy of Li Bai

二 成长: 十五观奇书

Chapter Ⅱ　Youth: At Fifteen, I Read Unconventional Books

Li Bai's youth was spent primarily on studying, encountering new things, and experiencing for himself never before experienced feelings. There are several points we should emphasize about this period.

First is his discovery of his interest in and talent for literature. Li Bai said: "At fifteen, I read unconventional books / I wrote rhapsodies competing with Xiangru." This means his compositions were already mature at fifteen, but he discovered his love and talent for literature even earlier.

In the Tang Dynasty, a love of poetry was a career with a bright future, because society at the time valued literature, and the court desired people with poetic talent. For this reason, Li Bai's interests received encouragement and support of his family, as is evident from his father's having him memorize and recite the "Rhapsody on Sir Vacuous." At the time, though, learning to compose poetry was not easy.

In ancient China, literary composition was much esteemed and valued. Besides requiring that the content be good, precise, and logical, the structure, syntax, parallelism, and historical allusions had to follow many prescribed specifications. Compositions which followed these specifications would be more appreciated. Of course, superior compositions not only followed these specifications, but also had creative innovations in their content and form, expressing a quality and ambiance which transcended the language. This is not the simple descriptive essay we learn in today's education. It is a *belles-lettres* which requires long-term training and practice to accomplish.

The ancients had a simple and practical method of learning composition. First, they would recite from memory. From the day that he began studying, Li Bai memorized and recited large numbers of outstanding compositions. Second was imitation, imitating previous masterpieces in one's own compositions. When Chinese students practice calligraphy, they must first imitate model calligraphy ❶ of earlier masters. When learning painting, students must first imitate model paintings ❷ . When learning to write literature, one must also imitate model works of earlier masters. Li Bai learned to write poems, rhapsodies, and ballads from earlier works, and his compositions showed the

青少年时代的李白主要就是学习，接受各种新鲜事物，体验从未经历过的感受。这一段经历有几个方面值得我们注意。

首先是文学的爱好和文学天赋的发现。李白自称："十五观奇书，作赋凌相如。"意思是说，他十五岁时的作品已经相当成熟了。这样说来，李白爱好文学并被发现具有文学天赋的时间更早。

在唐代，爱好诗赋绝对是一项有前途的事业，因为当时的社会普遍重视文学，朝廷也需要有诗赋才能的士人，所以李白的兴趣肯定得到了家人的鼓励与支持，这从李白的父亲让他背诵《子虚赋》就可以看出来。不过，那个时候，学习诗文写作绝非易事。

在中国古代，文章具有极高的地位和价值，被人们看得很重。各种文体除了表达的内容要好，要准确，要合乎道理，还要在篇章结构、遣词造句、对仗排偶、典故象征等方面遵循许多约定俗成的规范。符合规范的文章更能为人们所欣赏，当然，更高层次的文章是要能够在遵循成规的同时，又能在内容与形式方面有所创新突破，表现出超越言词表达之外的神韵、气象。这就不是我们今天只要受过教育，就可以写成的基本能够传情达意的文章，而是需要长期的学习与训练才能写作的美文。

古人学习写作有简单而实用的方法，第一是背诵记忆。自读书之日起，李白熟读、背诵了前人大量的优秀作品。第二就是临摹，面对优秀范本进行模仿。中国学生练习书法时，先要有一番临帖❶的功夫；学画时，先要经过临摹画谱❷的训练；习文时，也要模仿前人的典范之作。李白的诗、赋、乐府等众

---

❶ 帖，前人的书法范本。
❷ 画谱，前人绘画范本。

❶ model calligraphy: the model of calligraphy of former generation.
❷ model paintings: the model of paintings of former generation.

marks of imitation. This was a common method of the ancients, and was especially emphasized by scholars of the Han, Wei, and Six Dynasties periods. During his foundational training in poem and prose composition, Li Bai expended great energy imitating masterpieces of the ancients, and even "imitated the *Wenxuan* (*Selections of Refined Literature*) three times."

Wenxuan is the earliest anthology of Chinese literature extant today. It was compiled by a team of literati organized by Xiao Tong, eldest son of Emperor Wu (502—549) of the Southern Liang Dynasty. Xiao Tong was posthumously enfeoffed as the Prince of Brilliance, and so the anthology is also known as *Zhaoming Wenxuan* (*Prince of Brilliance's Selections of Refined Literature*). The anthology collected over seven hundred works of poetry, prose, and rhapsodies from before the Qin Dynasty to the Liang Dynasty. With representative pieces from all genres, it is a collection of outstanding masterpieces from earlier ages. The Tang valued this anthology very much. When Li Bai "imitated the *Wenxuan* three times," he chose a composition from the *Wenxuan* and practiced imitating it in his own composition. For example, Li Bai imitated Jiang Yan's "Rhapsody on Regret" and "Rhapsody on Parting." *Wenxuan* has over seven hundred pieces, and Li Bai imitated it three times. That means he imitated over two thousand pieces. One can see how hard he worked on composition. Li Bai held himself to very high standards. He burned the compositions with which he was not satisfied, leaving only the two rhapsodies, "Rhapsody on Regret" and "Rhapsody on Parting." In the modern collection of Li Bai's works, only the "Rhapsody on Regret" remains. "Rhapsody on Parting" has been lost.

It is not a very easy task for a young child or youth to constantly recite and imitate literature he cannot fully understand. Legend says that when Li Bai was young, he did not want to continue with his studies. He threw down his books and went out to play. As he passed over a stream, he saw an old woman intently grinding a steel pole. Li Bai was curious, and so asked the old woman why she was grinding the pole. She responded by saying she wanted to grind it into an embroidery needle. How long would it take to grind a thick steel pole down to an embroidery needle? Li Bai was greatly moved, and so continued his studies vigorously. This stream still flows through Changlong (modern Jiangyou City). The locals call it "Needle-Grinding Stream." The Chinese historical allusions "to grind a pole to a needle" and "the steel pole becomes a needle" refer to this story. In ancient China, even a person of such exceptional talent as Li Bai must work very hard to learn to compose prose and poetry. Through his studies and training, Li Bai learned much. He gained a rich

多作品，都曾广泛地向前人学习，留有摹拟的痕迹。这是前人普遍遵行的法则，特别是在汉魏六朝时期，这一做法尤其受到士人的重视。李白在苦练诗文写作的基本功时，用了很大气力摹写前人的优秀作品，曾经"三拟《文选》"。

《文选》是中国现存的最早一部诗文总集，由南朝梁武帝（502—549）的长子萧统组织文人共同编选。萧统去世后被称为昭明太子，因此，书又称"昭明文选"。书中选录了从先秦到梁代的诗、文、辞赋等作品七百多篇，各种文体的主要代表作大体具备，是前代优秀作品的大汇集。唐人非常看重这部选集。李白前后"三拟《文选》"，就是对照着《文选》中每一篇作品，自己练习写作一篇。如选集中有江淹的《恨赋》和《别赋》，李白就模拟《恨赋》和《别赋》各一篇。《文选》作品七百多篇，他模仿了三遍，合计也有二千多篇，可见为了写作他所付出的努力。李白对自己的要求很高，模拟的作品不满意，就烧掉，最后只留下《恨赋》和《别赋》。今天的《李白集》中仅存《恨赋》一篇，《别赋》散失了。

要让一个儿童、青少年不断地背诵、摹写那些他自己还不能完全理解的文字，并不是一件容易而愉快的事情。传说李白小时，不想再读书了。他扔掉书籍，外出玩耍，经过一条溪水时，看到溪边一位老奶奶正在全神贯注地磨一根铁杵（chǔ）。李白非常好奇，便问她磨铁棒做什么。老奶奶说："要把它磨成绣花针。"要把一根粗铁棒磨成细细的绣花针，那要磨到什么时候！李白受到了极大的触动，从此发愤读书。昌隆，即今天的江油市的这条溪水现在还在，人们称之为"磨针溪"。汉语成语"磨杵成针"、"铁杵成针"指的都是这个故事。中国古代的诗文写作，即使像李白这样天资卓越的人，也要下过苦功夫。通过读书和写作训练，李白学到了很多东西，掌握了丰富

knowledge of literature and history and built a solid foundation for poetic composition.

Li Bai was extremely curious. The Daoism and tales of immortals that he encountered in his early years became extremely attractive to him.

In his youth, he was fascinated in learning Daoism and techniques of immortality. In "Written on the Mountain Abode of Hermit Yuan Danqiu of Song Mountain," he wrote:

> Home was originally on Purple Cloud Mountain;
> The Daoist customs have not yet waned.
> I have deep ambitions of Danqiu;
> Empty wishes, return to solitude.

Purple Cloud Mountain is a famous center of Daoist activity. In his early years, Li Bai was active in Daoist temples in the mountains.

Around the age of seventeen or eighteen, Li Bai visited the recluse Dong Yanzi, and lived in seclusion with him on Mount Min, practicing Daoist cultivation techniques. Li Bai said that he lived several years in the mountain without ever entering a town. They also raised many exotic birds. When they called the birds, the birds would fly onto their hands and tamely eat from their palms.

Why did the poet tell this story? Li Bai wanted to demonstrate how advanced he had cultivated his Daoist techniques. Daoists generally believe that the universe is a unity. Humans and the birds and beasts are all similar in that they are all parts of nature. Humans and the birds and beasts are close, belonging to nature, and abide by the Way of Heaven. Describing Confucius entering the wilds, the "Shanmu" (Mountain Woods) chapter of *Zhuangzi* says that "when he entered, the beasts did not intermingle; when he entered, the birds did not intersperse." This is to say that, when he met with the birds and beasts, they did not panic and become chaotic. To be able to intermingle with the birds and beasts is a sign of a perfected person. *Liexian Zhuan* (*Biographies of Immortals*) has a record of an immortal named Old Chicken Man Zhu who raised chickens at the foot of the mountains for over one hundred years. The chickens roamed freely during the day, and slept in trees at night (Chickens in ancient China could easily fly into the tree). He had over one thousand chickens, and each one had its own name. If he called their names, they would instantly come to him. *Nanqi Shu* (*The History of the Southern Qi*) has a record of a Daoist named Cai who raised decades of rats in the mountains. When the Daoist adept called them, they would come to him. When he excused them, they would disperse. He was known as the "exiled

的文史知识，诗歌写作方面也打下了坚实的基础。

李白具有强烈的好奇心，早年接触到的神仙道术，对他形成了极大的吸引力。

他在青少年时期，就热衷于学道求仙。《题嵩山逸人元丹丘山居》诗曰：

家本紫云山，道风未沦落。

沉怀丹丘志，冲赏归寂寞。

紫云山是著名的道教活动地区，李白早年即出入山上的道观。

十七八岁时，李白拜访隐士东岩子，并和他在岷山一同隐居，修炼道术。李白说，自己住在山上，一连几年都不到城市中来。他们还在山上养了许多奇异的禽鸟，一呼叫它们，就飞到手掌中吃食，一点也没有惊吓、防备的样子。

诗人为什么说这个故事呢？李白想说明自己修道很深了。因为，道家一贯认为，万物一体；人与禽兽类同，均为大自然中的成员；人与禽兽相亲，合乎自然，顺乎天道。《庄子·山木篇》表达这一观点，书中假托孔子，说他到旷野之中，"入兽不乱群，入鸟不乱行"，即与鸟兽相遇，不会引起它们的恐慌、混乱。能与鸟兽为群，这是有道之人的表现。《列仙传》记载，有一个仙人叫祝鸡翁，他在山下养鸡，养了一百多年。他养的鸡，白天随处放养，晚上栖息在树上（中国古代家中饲养的鸡都能轻而易举地飞到树上），有一千多只。竟然每只鸡都有自己的名字，一叫到它们的名字，就立刻能跑到跟前。《南齐书》上说，有一位姓蔡的高士在山中养了数十只老鼠。高士叫它们来，就都跑过来；让它们走，就都跑开去。被人们看做

immortal." The "Yanyu" (Spoken Words) chapter of *Shishuoxinyu* (*New Account of Tales of the World*) records a lecture that the Buddhist Emperor Jianwen of the Liang Dynasty said to followers in the Garden Hualin that one did not need to travel far to understand that "the universe and I are one." This truth can be comprehended within the forests, where one can experience the tameness of the birds, beasts, and fish. When Li Bai told of how he fed many tame birds, he was implying that he had already reached a certain level of Daoist cultivation. Indeed, as soon as word of Li Bai feeding birds spread, the local officials investigated, personally visiting their abode, and recommended the two to accept official positions. Both turned down the offer.

As a youth, Li Bai studied Daoist techniques. Later, he became a certified Daoist priest. He was in all ways a Daoist. Most Daoists liked to work alchemical concoctions and ingest elixirs, as they believed that ingesting plants such as calamus, or sweet flag, can give one a "complexion like a plum blossom" and for one to "eternally be a perfected person," approaching a state of peaceful longevity, free of hardship and illness. Li Bai consistently ingested calamus. In his poem "The One Picking Calamus on Mount Song," he wrote: "I came to pick calamus / Ingesting it can prolong one's life." Another interesting plant that Li Bai ingested was *zhushi* (vermillion fruit). In the poem "Viewing the Dawn on Tiantai," he said: "Climbing the vine to pick the vermillion fruit / I ingest the medicine to cultivate metal bones." Besides herbal medicines, there was an even more miraculous alchemical medicine called "golden elixir." Daoists had great faith in the golden elixir, and even emperors ingested it. Many Tang emperors ingested the golden elixir, eventually dying from poisoning. The Emperor Taizong of the Early Tang and Emperors Muzong and Wuzong of the Middle Tang all met with this end. Living in these times, Li Bai also experimented with working the elixir and ingesting it.

He was very interested in learning the techniques of alchemy. In the poem "Climbing Mount Jingting and Gazing South, I Reflected upon Ancient Times and Wrote This for Assistant Magistrate Dou," he said: "I wish to follow Ziming / Working the flames and firing the golden elixir." In "At Sunset, I Remembered Being in the Mountains," he said: "I wish to leave to wander in the famous mountains / To learn the Dao and fly off with the elixir of immortality."

It appears as though Li Bai had actually worked alchemical elixirs. In his poem "Composed upon Parting with All the Officials at Caonan and Going to Jiangnan," he said: "Seal the sword in the glazed case / Work the elixir in the

"谪仙"（被贬到人间的仙人）。《世说新语·言语》中记载，简文帝在华林园中，对随从说：能够领会"万物与我为一"的道理并不需要走远，在园林之中，也能感觉到鸟兽禽鱼，自来亲人。所以，李白讲述自己饲养许多驯服的禽鸟，是想说明自己修道已经达到一定水平了。果然，李白饲养禽鸟的故事一经传出，地方官闻讯，亲自来到他们的住处，推荐两人出来做官。他俩婉言谢绝了。

李白年轻时就学习道术，后米正式成为道士，名副其实地是道教中人。道教中人大多喜好炼丹服食，他们相信，长期服食一些植物，如菖蒲，即可"面如桃花"、"永是真人"，步入无灾无病、幸福安康的长生境界。李白坚持服食菖蒲。《嵩山采菖蒲者》诗曰："我来采菖蒲，服食可延年。"另一种奇异的植物——朱实，他也吃。《天台晓望》诗曰："攀条采朱实，服药炼金骨。"除了草药，当时还有一种更加神奇的药物"金丹"。道教徒十分相信金丹，皇帝也吃。唐代君主每每服食金丹，最后中毒而死，唐初的唐太宗，中唐时期的穆宗、武宗都是如此结局。李白处在当时这样的环境中，尝试炼丹吃药，也是风气所致。

他学习炼丹的热情很高。《登敬亭山南望怀古赠窦主簿》曰："愿随子明去，炼火烧金丹。"《落日忆山中》曰："愿游名山去，学道飞丹砂。"

看起来，李白真的是炼过丹的。他在《留别曹南群官至江南》诗中说："闭剑琉璃匣，炼丹紫翠房。"《留别广陵诸公》

purple and emerald room." In "Composed upon Parting the Gentlemen of Guangling," he said: "Working the elixir expends much fire / Picking herbs exhausts the mountains and rivers." In his preface to "The Gathered Scholars of Jinling Send Off Quan the Eleventh (Quan Zhaoyi)," he states it even more plainly: "I wish to emulate Guang Cheng ... and receive the precious method ... I plucked the beautiful girl in Jianghua, and gathered the river wheel in Qingxi. Together with Quan Zhaoyi, I attended to the duties of the crucible flames for a long time." This is to say, Li Bai long admired the immortal Guangchengzi, and practiced secret Daoist alchemical techniques. The "beautiful girl" refers to quick silver, or elixir mercury, and "river wheel" is lead, also called the proper qi* of the North. Li Bai collected these basic ingredients for the elixir of longevity in various locations, and worked the alchemical elixir with Quan Zhaoyi for a long time.

In fact, Li Bai cultivated Daoist techniques of alchemy as a way to express his search for a utopia. Daoist cultivation techniques were only a pathway, whereas his true goal was to obtain immortality, or the lifestyle of an immortal. Therefore, he was not too concerned with the theory behind Daoism, and took no heed of the restrictions of Daoism.

He was fascinated by immortality, and longed to live as an immortal, and also loved the word "immortal." If others called him an immortal, he was very happy. A famous poet at the time, He Zhizhang, called Li Bai an "exiled immortal," meaning that Li Bai was originally an immortal, belonging in the heavens, but was exiled to live among humans as a form of punishment. Li Bai was very pleased, saying this title was quite accurate, as he enjoyed such activities of the immortals as cultivating Daoist alchemical techniques and ingesting medications, drinking wine and composing poems, and wandering about in the clouded peaks of famous mountains. He was completely unconcerned with the vulgar activities and concerns of the human realm.

Besides Daoist techniques of immortality, Li Bai was quite fascinated by chivalry.

"Chivalry (xia)" was a very influential idea in ancient China, but it is difficult to define the term. According to historical records, the actions of chivalrous men can be divided into two categories. One kind appeared during the social chaos and unrest of political power shifts. Chivalrous figures would gather heroes and raise armies, either following a new leader, or settling an area oneself. The ultimate goal was to fulfill one's abilities to restore order. The other kind of chivalrous hero had a more distant relationship with the politics. In times of social stability, men of chivalry developed reputations of

诗又说："炼丹费火石，采药穷山川。"《金陵诸贤送权十一（权昭夷）序》说得更具体："吾希风广成……素受宝诀……尝采姹女于江华，收河车于清溪，与天水权昭夷服勤炉火之业久焉。"意思是说，李白倾慕古代的仙人广成子，学习过道家修行炼丹的秘密方法。这里的"姹女"即水银，亦称丹汞；"河车"是铅，一说北方正气。李白在不同的地方采集这些炼丹的基本材料，与权昭夷共同炼丹，持续了很长时间。

实际上，李白修道炼丹，不过是他追求理想之境的表现而已。修道炼丹只是路径，仙境，或者说仿佛仙人一般的生活方式本身才是他向往之所在。所以他对道教的理论不很关心，对道教的戒律也无心遵守。

他热衷于"仙境"，渴望着像仙人一样生活，也喜爱"仙"字。别人称他"仙"，他就很开心。当时著名的诗人贺知章称李白为"谪仙人"，即是说，李白本是仙人，居于天上，只是受到贬谪处罚，才屈尊降临人间。李白很得意，说这个称号完全符合实际。因为他在人间，修道服食，饮酒赋诗，云游名山，都是仙人之所为，而世间俗人所关心、所做的事情，他都不屑去做。

除了神仙道术，李白还十分热衷于侠士的举动。

"侠"在中国古代很有影响，但这个字的意思很难界定。据史传中侠士之所为，大体可以归结为两类。第一类是在王朝更替、社会动荡之际，侠士招揽豪杰，起兵征战，或割据一方，或追随新主，总之，试图为建立一个新的秩序，发挥自己的作用。第二类侠士与政治的关系较为疏远。在社会稳定时期，任侠之士修行砥名，一诺千金，仗义好施，救人于危难之中，由

---

* *Qi*, also written as *ch'i*, is the vital energy that, in the microcosm, flows throughout the body, and in the macrocosm, throughout the universe.

integrity and righteousness, doing good acts and helping those in need. In doing so, they developed strong reputations and held great influence in their local communities. During the chaotic times of Wang Mang, the usurper of the Han throne, Dai Zun feigned illness and retired to his homeland. His biography says his "family was rich, and he enjoyed giving. He was chivalrous, and kept three to four hundred guests." ❶ He was very influential in his homeland. Both sorts of chivalry were similar in that they required bravery and strength. They were daring, upheld principles, and gave to the needy. They were heroic.

During the Warring States Period, chivalrous knights-errant and political strategists were two separate kinds of people, but by the Han Dynasty, the empire was unified, and the environment in which one could wander from state to state maneuvering for influence no longer existed. Stratagem became something that interested individuals could discuss, but they could rarely act upon their ideas. These interested individuals were often strong and heroic men of chivalry, full of political enthusiasm.

In Sichuan, there were many such men of chivalry. These men of chivalry were also very interested in stratagem. The Sichuan poet Chen Zi'ang was a man of great valor, and enjoyed acts of chivalry. By the age of seventeen, he had not committed himself to his studies. He enjoyed stratagem, and traveled about the regions of Chu and Yan, displaying the unique characteristics of Sichuan scholars, who enjoyed both stratagem and acts of valorous chivalry. The famous Sichuan scholar Zhao Rui was also "chivalrous and charismatic, skilled at stratagem." He had a direct influence on Li Bai's interest in chivalry.

In 719, at the age of eighteen, Li Bai set out for Zizhou (modern Santai County, Sichuan Province). This area does not have any famous mountains or historical sites; it was Zhao Rui that attracted him to this location. In their interactions, the two established a deep friendship. Later, in his poem "Expressing My Feelings While Lying Sick in Huainan, Sent to Soldier Zhao Rui in Sichuan," Li Bai said: "My old friend cannot be seen / My deep dreams, with whom can I share?" This is to say, after having parted with Zhao Rui, of whom should he dream? Their friendship is evident.

Zhao Rui was an avid reader, he enjoyed stratagem, and he liked to perform chivalrous acts for the sake of righteousness. He lived the life of a recluse in the mountains, focusing on his studies. He wrote *Classic of the Long and Short*, a book on government that was popular in the Sichuan area. Zhao Rui believed that one must first determine the condition of the state, whether it was a time of order or chaos, before one can properly govern. Only then can one

此获得极大的声名，在地方上形成一定的势力。王莽时，戴遵称病归乡里。他"家富，好给施，尚侠气，食客常三四人"❶，在当地颇有影响力。这两类侠士实际上都有共同点，勇猛刚强，行为果敢，仗义好施，充满豪气。

战国时代，游侠与纵横家本是两种不同类型的人，但到汉代之后，国家统一，像战国时代那样可以往来于各诸侯国之间、纵横捭（bǎi）阖（hé）的社会环境消失了，纵横术由此转变为热衷者可以谈论但很难实行的东西。热衷者常常就是那些富有政治热情、豪爽刚健的好侠之士。

蜀中多侠士，这些侠士又特别喜好纵横术。四川诗人陈子昂豪气过人，尤好侠义之举，到了十七八岁之时，也没有用功读书，但是喜好纵横术，往来楚、燕各地，体现了蜀地文士既好纵横术又崇尚游侠之风的特点。蜀中名士赵蕤（ruí），也是"任侠有气，善为纵横学"。他对于李白的好侠有着直接的影响。

开元七年（719），十八岁的李白出游梓州（今四川省三台县），这里没有多少名山胜迹，吸引他的正是当地的奇士赵蕤。两人在交往中建立了很深的情谊。李白日后曾在《淮南卧病书怀，寄蜀中赵征君蕤》诗中说："故人不可见，幽梦谁与适？"意思是说，与赵蕤分别了，那么，做梦该梦见谁呢？可见两人交情十分深厚。

赵蕤读书很多，喜纵横之术，好行侠仗义，隐居山中，专心学术。他写了一部书，专门讨论国家的政治，在蜀中地区广为流传，名叫《长短经》。赵蕤认为，国家治理首先必须确切地了解国家的状况，是处在治世，还是乱世，然后采取相应的

---

❶《后汉书》，卷83《戴良传》。

❶ *Hou Han Shu* (*Book of the Latter Han*), volume 83.

determine the appropriate measures to employ, such as the measures of a king, of a hegemon, or of a despot. His opinions were influenced by Warring States Period schools of Legalism and Stratagem. Zhao Rui admired such figures of the past as Fu Yue, Taigong, Su Qin, Zhang Yi, Lu Zhonglian, Han Emperor Gaozu, Han Emperor Guangwu, Zhang Liang, Han Xin, Zhuge Liang, and Xie An. He especially admired Zhuge Liang, who was originally a recluse. Without leaving his hut, he already understood much of current affairs. Later, he served Liu Bei and left behind a timeless reputation. Zhao Rui saw Zhuge Liang as a model to be emulated.

Li Bai was deeply influenced by Zhao Rui. Zhao Rui's ideas on stratagem left a strong impression on Li Bai's thought. In his poems, Li Bai praised all of the people Zhao Rui admired. Lu Zhonglian, Zhang Liang, and Xie An appeared especially frequently in Li Bai's poems. During the Warring States Period, Su Qin and Zhang Yi came from lowly backgrounds, but relying only on their talent, they became influential advisors to their rulers. Li Bai often compared himself to Su Qin and Zhang Yi, longing to use his skills in stratagem to gain a position in the political realm.

Zhao Rui liked chivalry, and so did Li Bai. Li Bai's chivalry is evident in the poems he composed, and in records written by his contemporaries. People of his time said that when Li Bai was younger, he thought of himself as a gentleman of chivalry. He never concerned himself with where his daily necessities would come from. His reputation reached as far as the capital. Wei Hao wrote in his "Preface to *Li Bai's Collected Works*" that "when young, he was chivalrous, felling several people with his blade."

Li Bai was very proud of his youthful acts of chivalry. In his poem "Recalling the Past, Presented to Lu Tiao, Magistrate of Jiangyang," Li Bai described himself in his youth as being debonair, dressed extravagantly, with his sword by his side, wandering about the entertainment districts of large cities. At a cock fight, Li Bai once became entangled in a dispute with the local gentries. They detained Li Bai, who was released only through the help of his friends. Such experiences cannot be easily met by other men of literature. The Tang men of chivalry were unrestrained and extravagant, enjoying leisure and entertainment. They led lives very different from the common person, indulging in wine and women, and sometimes even battle and killing.

On the one hand, these men of chivalry were able to help their states in times of trouble, and on the other, they were able to serve justice to the people.

措施，或施行"王道"，或施行"霸道"，或施行"强道"。这些观点受到了先秦法家、纵横家观点的影响。赵蕤极为赞赏古代傅说（yuè）、太公、苏秦、张仪、鲁仲连、汉高祖、汉光武帝、张良、韩信、诸葛亮及谢安等人。赵蕤特别喜爱诸葛亮。诸葛亮原是一个隐士，未出茅庐，已知天下三分，后跟随刘备，建功立业，名垂青史。对赵蕤来说，诸葛亮的经历无疑是他可以直接仿效的模式。

李白受赵蕤的影响极深，赵蕤的纵横家思想在李白的脑海中留下深深的印迹。赵蕤欣赏的这些人物，李白诗中差不多都赞叹过，鲁仲连、张良、谢安更是李白诗中经常出现的传奇人物。战国时期的苏秦、张仪出身卑微，然而凭借自己的才能，说服君主，在当时的政坛上叱（chì）咤（zhà）风云。李白每每自比苏秦、张仪，渴望以纵横家的方式在政坛中一显身手。

赵蕤好侠，李白也好侠。李白的任侠之风，在他的诗篇里以及当时人的记载中都曾提到。当时人都说，李白少年时代就把自己当做侠士，从不考虑自己的生活来源等琐碎的事情，京城都知道他的名声。魏颢《李翰林集序》说他"少任侠，手刃数人"。

对自己年轻时期的豪侠作风，李白很是得意。他《叙旧赠江阳宰陆调》诗中说：当初风流年少，穿着华美的服饰，佩带着长剑，往来于大都市中的游乐之地。在一场斗鸡中，李白与豪门子弟发生冲突。他们把李白抓了起来，多亏了友人才把他解救出来。李白的这种经历，恐怕其他文人很少遇到过。唐代的侠士豪奢逸乐、纵酒狎妓，甚至斗殴杀人，与常人的生活有很大不同。

从大的方面说，侠客能够为国解难；从小的方面说，能够打抱不平。不论怎样，这些都需要侠士有些武功，击剑打斗是

All else aside, skills in battle and swordplay were fundamental to these men. Li Bai said of himself that "at fifteen, I enjoyed swordplay," meaning that he had learned to fight with the sword when he was young. Li Bai's good friend Cui Zongzhi praised him, saying that when Li Bai "got up and danced, waving his long sword / Everyone there raised their eyebrows." ❶ One can see that Li Bai was quite skilled at the sword. No matter where he went, he always brought his sword. He enjoyed practicing swordplay. In his poem "Presented to Zhang Xianghao," he said:

> Caressing my sword, I whistle into the night;
> My lofty aspirations travel a thousand miles by day.

In "Presented to Censor Cui," he also said:

> My long sword, a cup of wine;
> The simple heart of a man.

The sword became a representation of his ambitions, and a symbol of his chivalry. Besides his sword, Li Bai sometimes kept a dagger concealed in his sleeve. Again, in "Presented to Li the Twelfth," Cui Zongzhi said:

> In your sleeve, you have a dagger blade;
> In your bosom, Maoling's* writings.
> Your two pupils shine with brilliance upon others;
> Rhapsodies surpass Xiangru.

One must not use today's standards of morality when judging Chinese gentlemen of chivalry. They had their own set of principles, known as "*yi*" (righteousness). *Yi* is justice, doing that which is right. When deciding what must be done, the "*xiayi*," chivalrous righteousness, approach to making decisions is uniquely impulsive, and not based on common sense and logic. Accomplishing a goal based on such decisions fulfills the ambitions and desires of the chivalrous gentleman. When seeing a woman being harassed, he must draw his sword and come to the rescue; when seeing a person starving, he must offer his last bowl of rice; when a friend is in need, he can suffer stabs to his ribs; when witnessing a father being killed, he must fight fearlessly to the death; and if someone insults him, he must fight to the end, even if his opponent is far stronger than he. These are all examples of the principles of chivalry. Men of chivalry value forthrightness and valor above all. Once valor is invoked, emotions flare, and there is no turning back. Indecision and cowardice are never a factor. When they must do something, they must unconditionally overcome all obstacles and difficulties. When they must act,

一个侠士的基本功。李白自称"十五好剑术",就是说他少年时代就学习过剑法。李白的朋友崔宗之称赞他"起舞拂长剑,四座皆扬眉"❶,可见,他的剑术还比较高明。无论到哪里,李白都喜爱佩戴长剑,喜爱抚弄长剑。他在《赠张相镐》诗中说:

抚剑夜吟啸,雄心日千里。

《赠崔侍御》诗中又说:

长剑一杯酒,男儿方寸心。

剑成了他雄心壮志的象征,也是他作为侠士的标记。除了长剑,李白有时还袖藏匕首。崔宗之《赠李十二》诗曰:

袖有匕首剑,怀中茂陵书。

双眸光照人,词赋凌相如。

对于侠士,很难用现在的道德标准、处事原则去衡量他们。他们有自己独特的原则,这就是"义"。义就是正义,做应该做的事情。"侠义"的独特之处在于,侠士经常是从自己的本性出发,确认那些必须做的事情,而不是从世人的常识、理智出发去衡量;而完成这些应该做的事情,能够极大地满足侠士的情志与意愿。看见别人欺侮女性,一定要拔刀解救;看见饥饿的人,一定要拿出自己最后的一碗饭来共享;知己有难,可以两肋插刀;看见杀父之仇,一定要以死相拼,毫不怯懦;有谁侮辱自己,即使对手的力量远远超过自己,也得较量到底。诸如此类,都体现出侠士做人的原则。侠士最重豪爽与血气,一旦血气上涌,激情勃发,则永无回头之时,更不用说犹豫、摇摆、懦弱的表现了。当他们必须去做什么的时候,任何阻碍与困难都必须无条件克服;当他们必须行动的时候,理智、法

---

❶ 崔宗之《赠李十二》。

❶ Cui Zongzhi, "Presented to Li the Twelfth."

* Maoling refers to the Han Dynasty scholar Sima Xiangru.

logic, law, and even death will not deter them. Gentlemen of chivalry use their own lives to protect and elevate the status and value of "righteousness." In the eyes of the chivalrous, "righteousness" transcends logic, law, and life. It is for just this reason that chivalry was suppressed in later societies.

Li Bai valued chivalry, and so he did not consider the results of his chivalrous actions. When necessary, one must draw one's sword and kill. In his "Song of the Chivalrous Traveler," he wrote: "Take ten steps, kill one man / One thousand miles, never slow down." In "Song of a White Horse," he wrote: "Kill men as if cutting grass / Making alliances to travel off together." These are all *yuefu* ballads. The verses borrow ancient phrases and topics. For Li Bai to "take ten steps, kill one man" and "kill men as if cutting grass" was not very likely. In his poem "Presented to My Cousin Hao, District Defender of Xiangyang," Li Bai said:

> Eliminate Qin, and receive no reward;
> Attack Jin, is it for the merit?
> Commit one's life to the white blade;
> And kill men in the world.
> The court promotes high righteousness;
> Society honors heroic deeds. ❶

To eliminate Qin and attack Jin are actions to aid the state. To face blades and flames, and to throw oneself into battle, these are actions of "high righteousness" that the court rewards and the "heroic deeds" that society values.

Wei Hao wrote in his "Preface to *Li Bai's Collected Works*" that "when young, he was chivalrous, felling several people with his blade." To say this in the preface is not the same as Li Bai saying so in a poem. There ought to be some basis for his statement. In his "Song of Meeting the Traveler among the Youths," Li Bai wrote: "Finish a cup of wine in laughter / Kill a man in the middle of the city market." There may be some shadow of truth, but we cannot know for sure. In fact, whether or not Li Bai killed a man is not important. What is important is his glorifying attitude toward actions such as "killing a man in the red dust." Even when appraising "rightful" battles of the court, poets such as Du Fu do not approve of killing. When describing bravery, Wang Wei mostly made statements such as: "Drawing my sword, I have already cut the arm of the Hun / Returning to my saddle, we drink by the targets." ❷ Wang

律甚至生命都不足以阻挡他们的脚步。侠士们正是用自己的生命捍卫并提高了"义"的地位与价值。"义"在真正侠士的心目中确实超越于理智、法律甚至生命之上。正因此，侠义在后来的社会中逐渐受到抑制。

李白重侠，那就必须不顾侠举的一切后果。必要时，必须动刀杀人。他在《侠客行》中说："十步杀一人，千里不留行。"《白马行》中说："杀人如剪草，剧孟同游遨。"这些都是乐府诗，词多承袭古语或古诗主题，诸如"十步杀一人"、"杀人如剪草"，在李白身上似乎不太可能。李白在《赠从兄襄阳少府皓》诗中说：

> 却秦不受赏，击晋宁为功？
> 托身白刃里，杀人红尘中。
> 当朝揖高义，举世钦英风。❶

却秦、击晋，显然是为国解难的行为，因此，面对刀山火海，持刀拼刺，冲锋陷阵，这是朝廷奖赏的"高义"，举世推重的"英风"。

不过，魏颢《李翰林集序》中说他"少任侠，手刃数人"。在序文当中说这话，不同于李诗中的描写，当是有所根据。李白《结客少年场行》曰："笑尽一杯酒，杀人都市中。"或许有些事实的影子，但实情均不能知道了。事实上，关键并不在于李白是否真的杀过人，而在于他在诗歌中对"杀人红尘中"之类行为竭力颂扬的态度。像杜甫之类的诗人即使在评价朝廷的"正义"战争中，也不主张多杀人。王维描写英勇，也多半是说"拔剑已断天骄臂，归鞍共饮月支头"❷，用的是典故；

---

❶《李白集》宋刊本等有后四句，多数版本无。
❷ 王维《燕支行》。

❶ The last four lines are found in the Song Dynasty edition of *Li Bai Ji* (*The Collected Works of Li Bai*), but most editions do not include them.
❷ Wang Wei, "Song of Yanzhi."

Wei uses allusion. "One life turns away, three thousand miles to fight in battle / One sword once fought ten thousand troops." ❶ Wang Wei avoids overtly describing killing. He uses detailed description to create an image of bravery. This is unlike Li Bai, who describes in a direct and exaggerated manner "killing men like cutting grass."

Li Bai's youth was spent mostly on his studies. He did not wander past the local counties. He did not get to know many people, but those with whom he did become acquainted were extraordinary. Later, he wandered further, visiting nearby Mount Ziyun, Mount Daitian, and Mount Dakuang to study Daoist methods of immortality. The rich Daoist customs of Sichuan, along with the unusual regional ethnic minority cultures, had a strong influence on Li Bai's unique thought and poetic style, along with his later behavior.

"一身转战三千里，一剑曾当百万师"❶，避免直接描写杀人，都是通过其他方面的细节描写来塑造勇敢者的形象，而不像李白这样直接并夸张地说出"杀人如剪草"。

李白早年在西蜀的生活主要是读书学习，足迹不出附近州县，结交的人不多，但多特异之士。时而云游在外，前往邻近的紫云山、戴天山、大匡山等地，学仙求道。蜀地浓郁的道教的气氛以及周边奇异的少数民族文化，对于李白奇特的思想、独特的诗歌风格以及日后的立身行事，都产生了巨大的影响。

---

❶ 王维《老将行》。

❶ Wang Wei, "Song of the Old General."

李白行吟图

Painting of Li Bai, walking and reciting poems

三　远游：大鹏一日同风起

Chapter Ⅲ　Journeys: The Great Roc Bird, in One Day, Flies with the Wind

In the autumn of 724, at the age of twenty-four, Li Bai left Sichuan and began his life of roaming in hopes of expanding his opportunities of building upon his skills and realizing his ambitions.

Where did he want to go? What did he want to do?

In his "Letter to Anzhou Administrator Pei," Li Bai wrote:

> The life of a scholar is like a mulberry bow and reed arrow; it can be shot in all four directions. I therefore take my sword and leave my homeland, parting from my family and traveling afar. I will go south beyond Mount Cangwu, and east across the deep sea.

After a boy was born in ancient China, the parents would make a bow of mulberry wood and six arrows made of reed stalks. They would then ask someone to represent the newborn and shoot the arrows in all directions, indicating the idea that a true man sets his ambitions in all directions of the world. Li Bai therefore took up his sword and took leave of his family to go out into the world and seek his fortune; however, Li Bai said only that he was going to go beyond Mount Cangwu (modern Jiuyi Mountain in Hunan Province), east to the eastern coast of China. The question is: Where was he going? What was he going to do?

Tang society was very different from society today. After graduating today, students have a wide choice of careers, but in the Tang Dynasty, after students finished their studies, they had very few options. The best career was to become a government official. The Tang government had many different kinds of examinations, such as the Presented Scholar Examinations, the Clarification of the Classics Examinations, and the Special Examinations. Intelligent commoners could study and participate in the examinations. If they passed the examinations, they could be employed by the court as officials and advance into the upper levels of society.

The Tang Dynasty examination system had some peculiarities, though. One was that the number of successful examinees in the Presented Scholar Examinations was small relative to later dynasties, making it more difficult to pass the examinations. The second was that the Tang Dynasty examination system did not rely solely on the examination. Before the Sui and Tang Dynasties, selection of officials relied on recommendations of potential candidates from established officials and aristocracies. From the Tang Dynasty, selection was based mainly on official examinations, but the Tang Dynasty examination system had the signs of a transitional system, relying both on examination results and recommendations from high officials and aristocrats.

　　开元十二年（724）秋，二十四岁的李白，为了寻找施展才能的机会，实现远大的抱负，离开了四川，开始了漫游的生活。

　　他要到哪里去？他要做什么？

　　李白《上安州裴长史书》中说：

　　　士生则桑弧蓬矢，射乎四方，故知大丈夫必有四方之志。乃仗剑去国，辞亲远游。南穷苍梧，东涉溟海。

　　中国古代男子出生后，就用桑木做成弓，用蓬草茎做成六支箭，请人代表他射向天地四方，表明男子汉大丈夫有志于天地四方的意思。所以李白要告别亲人，带着剑离开自己的故乡，到外面的世界去闯荡一番。但李白只是说，自己向南到了苍梧山，即今湖南九嶷山，向东到了中国东部沿海。可问题还是：他要到哪里去？他要做什么？

　　唐代与现代社会有很大差别。在现代，学生毕业之后，可以从事许多职业，而在唐朝，读书人完成学业后，出路比较狭窄。最好的出路就是做官。唐代有各种不同性质的考试，如进士、明经与制科等，百姓子弟聪明好学，则可以读书求学，参加朝廷举行的科举。考试通过，即可被朝廷录用授官，进入仕途，步入上层。

　　但唐代科举选拔进士有几个特点：一是，相对于后代而言，唐代中进士的人数很少，这无形中增加了应试的难度。二是，唐代科举不完全依赖考试。隋唐以前选拔人才主要依靠官员、贵族的推荐，唐代以后则主要通过官方的考试，而唐代的科举呈现出一种过渡状态，既看考试的成绩，也要考虑名公巨卿的推荐。

Despite such opportunities, Li Bai did not even bother to try. He never once participated in the official examinations. This path held not attraction for him.

From the very beginning, Li Bai saw himself as being extraordinary. He had always thought of himself as an immortal, and not a common person. He had always thought of himself as having extraordinary literary and political talents. Even when facing the setbacks of reality, when the common person would feel defeated, Li Bai never lost confidence in his own abilities. Even during his lowest point, he never forgot that he was the poet immortal, the drunken immortal, the exiled immortal; nor did he forget that he was a peer of Xie An and Zhuge Liang. At no point did he ever loose his sense of self-importance. *Zhuangzi* tells of a great bird called *peng*:

> As for the back of the *peng*, I do not know how many miles it is;
> With full force it flies, its wings are as the clouds hanging in the
sky.

Li Bai often compared himself to the *peng*:

> The great *peng* rises into flight in one day;
> Stroking and flapping, it rises ninety thousand miles. ❶

In Chinese literary history, very few poets have ever compared themselves to the *peng*. Even when he did not have money to pay for wine, he declared that if he "strewed one thousand pieces of gold, it would come back." He enjoyed boasting, and often exaggerated, causing most people to be suspicious of what he said. Li Bai was aware of this: "When common people see me, they take me as unusual / When they hear me exaggerate, they all sneer." ❷ No matter how much ridicule he received, though, Li Bai still believed in his exaggerations, and believed that he was a true genius.

This is the quality of a genius.

He was truly too naive. His poetic naivety enabled him to deny all the criticism of the practical world. Practicality had no persuasive force on him. It was within this obstinate denial of the practical world that Li Bai's ideal realm, the immortal realm, managed to take form.

Not only did Li Bai advocate the longevity of immortality, he also emphasized the extraordinary wisdom and abilities of immortals. As for the transcendence of immortals, Li Bai's immortals transcended the common person, and the common lifestyle. This kind of immortal is different from the

即使这样的机会，李白也不屑于尝试。他一生从未参加过科举，这条道路对他没有吸引力。

李白始终自命不凡，他始终想象着自己是仙人，是与众不同的人物，他始终相信自己具有非凡的文学才能和政治才干。即使面对现实的挫败，常人往往心灰意冷，可是李白却从未失去自我肯定的力量；即使在最为落魄的时候，他也没有忘记自己是诗仙、酒仙、谪仙人，也没有忘记自己是与谢安、诸葛亮一样的人物，更没有失去对自己卓越才能的高度自负。《庄子》书中有一种巨大的鸟称之为鹏：

> 鹏之背，不知其几千里也；
>
> 怒而飞，其翼若垂天之云。

李白常常自比大鹏：

> 大鹏一日同风起，扶摇直上九万里。❶

中国诗坛上，自比大鹏的诗人并不多。就在他连酒钱也付不起的日子里，他也宣称"千金散尽还复来"。他喜好大言，说话夸张，这让一般人简直不敢相信他的话。李白自己也知道这一点："时人见我恒殊调，闻余大言皆冷笑。"❷可是，再多的讥讽，李白仍然相信自己的大话，相信自己是一位真正的奇才。

这是天才的品质。

他实在太天真了。他的天真，诗人般的天真，竟然能够拒绝现实对他的各种评断；现实在他的面前，竟然哑然失声，失去了所有的说服力。正是在这种拒斥之中，李白的理想之境——仙境才得以一种执著而完整的形态呈现。

李白既宣扬仙人的长寿、长生，也强调仙人超凡的智慧与能力。就超越性而言，李白的仙人是超越常人、超越世俗生活

---

❶ 李白《上李邕》。
❷ 李白《上李邕》。

❶ Li Bai, "Submitted to Li Yong."
❷ Li Bai, "Submitted to Li Yong."

modern elite. The modern elite receive high positions and the recognition of society through their successful careers. Li Bai's ideal immortals had no direct relation to the success of the mortal world. He was transcendent god, disdainful of matters of the mortal world. Even if he achieved great accomplishments in the mortal world, he would laugh it off and retire into seclusion.

Of course, it would be inaccurate to say that Li Bai's immortals were completely removed from the mortal world. After all, Li Bai lived in this world, and understood his society and life. He said: "Vast, the South and the North / The way is straight, but affairs difficult to harmonize." ("Spring Reflections") One cannot say he was oblivious of the affairs of the world. He was concerned about this world, and followed with interest the struggles and conflicts of his time. Especially after the rebellion of An Lushan, he desired to participate in the central government and rescue the people, but Li Bai imagined using his own unique way of improving the state of society and resolving the conflicts of his time. He imagined himself as an extraordinary genius suddenly descending from the heavens, and with a wave of his hand, the world would be filled with brilliance, fortune, and happiness.

We cannot say that this idea of Li Bai's was completely without basis, because such characters have appeared in Chinese history. Fu Yue originally lived in the wilds of Fuyan, but when he one day became the advisor to the King of Yin, he instantly assisted the ruler in establishing the Shang Dynasty. The Grand Duke of Jiang used to butcher oxen and fish in the Pan River. One day, he became the advisor to King Wen of Zhou and quickly achieved great accomplishments. Su Qin and Zhang Yi came from common backgrounds, but as soon as they became grand ministers, they accomplished great deeds. Zhuge Liang and Xie An were originally recluses, but once they came out of the mountains, the world was quickly pacified. Li Bai anticipated just such a political career for himself, believing that he could resolve the problems of his day with a few words over a few banquets. It is difficult to know how many times Li Bai went over this scene in his mind, or how many times he spoke of it, but those around him probably never took him seriously. In response to the suspicion of those around him, Li Bai said: "Great talents are unpredictable, fools are volatile / In the years before, they seemed quite like the average person." ❶ He meant that those who achieved great accomplishments seemed at first no different from the common person. The

形态的人。这种仙人不同于现代精英。现代精英大多是通过事业的成功而赢得较高地位和普遍认可的杰出人物，而李白心目中的仙人，从某种意义上说，与世俗领域中的成就没有太多直接的联系。他本来就是超越尘世的神人，不屑于世俗事务；即使在世俗领域中获得巨大成就，他也会淡然一笑，退身江湖。

当然，要说李白的仙人完全不食人间烟火，又是不准确的。李白毕竟生活在这个世界上，他了解当时的社会与人生，他说："茫茫南与北，道直事难谐。"（《春感》）不能说他不谙世事。他关心这个世界，关注现实中的矛盾、冲突。特别是安史之乱爆发后，他更是渴望能够参与国家政治，拯救苍生。不过，改善当时的社会状况，解决当前的现实矛盾，李白想象的却是以他自己的独特方式：他就是举国上下都盼望出现的超凡的奇才，突然降临人间，大手一挥，世界一下子就充满了光明、幸福和温暖。

不能说李白的这种想法丝毫没有根据，因为中国历史上确实曾出现过类似的人物。傅说（yuè），起先筑于傅岩之野，一旦成为殷王的辅佐，立刻帮助君主实现王朝的兴旺。姜太公屠牛朝歌，钓于磻（pán）溪，一朝为周文王的辅臣，迅速成就大功业。苏秦、张仪出身下层，一朝位至卿相，叱咤风云。诸葛亮、谢安起初皆隐居不仕，一旦出山，谈笑之间天下安定。李白为自己设计的就是这样一种参与政治的路径，他经常自比谢安，并相信自己就是筵席之上谈笑风生而使四海安定的奇士。这一理想，在李白的心中不知道回味过多少遍，也不知道讲述过多少次，可是，周围大概没有一个人会当真。面对周围人怀疑的目光，李白说："大贤虎变愚不测，当年颇似寻常人。" ❶ 他说，那些成就不朽功业的人，起初与平常人没有两

---

❶ 李白《梁甫吟》。

❶ Li Bai, "Chant on Liang Fu."

average person had no way of differentiating them, and could not foretell their capablities. This is why, when he heard the ridicule of others, Li Bai did not mind, and continued to firmly believe that he was the one to bring stability and peace to the empire.

He was not interested in participating in the examination system. He did not wish to follow the path of the average scholar participating in government, sitting for the examination, becoming an official, and rising through the ranks. He imagined jumping directly from being a civilian to becoming a minister, then immediately implementing his grand ambitions. This is why, although most scholars actively participated in the examination system, he never did. He turned down most normal recommendations from officials. The records say he "did not pursue a lowly position, thinking himself capable of overseeing the realm." ❶ This is quite true. An early work of his, "Letter Written for Mount Shou in Response to Officer Meng's ' On moving' ," is even more able to express this point. In the letter, Li Bai came down from Mount Emei and resided in seclusion on Mount Shou. He was truly an immortal like there had never been before:

> Child's face returning to spring, true vital energy ever more profuse. He will wish to rely on his sword to the horizon, and hang his bow on the *Fusang* tree.*
>
> Float on the four seas, and cross the eight wilds; depart the wide expanses of the universe, mount the vast boundlessness of the clouds and heavens.

Is this not an immortal? Yes, this is Li Bai's imaginary image of himself. He would not, however, feel satisfied simply roaming beyond the clouds of heaven. Li Bai raised his head toward the heavens and gave a long sigh, saying to his friend that he could not just leave like this: "If successful, one should attend to the world; if unsuccessful, one should attend to one's self. How could you feast on your purple mists and cool yourself under the green pines; ride on your cranes, and drive your dragons; one day fly off and become a resident of [the immortal islands of] Fangzhang and Penglai?" If one is poor and unsuccessful, one can be a good person. If one is successful and very influential in society, one can help and improve society. If one were to succeed in cultivating the Dao and fly off to become an immortal, one will not be able to contribute to society. This is not acceptable. This is why Li Bai continued with:

> Thus, he rolls up his cinnabar (Daoist) scriptures and boxes his jade zither; elucidates the doctrines of Guan [Zhong] and Yan [Ying],

样，一般人根本识别不出来，根本无法预料。正因此，听到他人的讥讽，李白毫不介意，依然坚信自己是安邦定国的人物。

科举之路他不感兴趣。他并不想沿着一般读书人应试、入仕、晋升的道路，参与政治，而是想象着从布衣一下子跃至公卿，并立刻在政坛上发挥巨大的作用。所以，唐代一般士子积极参加科举，他从没有参加过；官员一般的推荐，他都谢绝了。传记中称他"不求小官，以当世之务自负"❶，确实如此。他早期写作的《代寿山答孟少府移文书》更能充分显示出这一点。文中说，李白从峨眉山来，隐居于湖北寿山。他真是自古以来，从未有过的仙人啊！请看：

> 童颜益春，真气愈茂，将欲倚剑天外，挂弓扶桑。浮四海，横八荒，出宇宙之寥廓，登云天之渺茫。

这不是仙人吗？是的，这就是李白想象中的自我形象。不过，就这样逍遥于云天之外，他又不能感到完全的满足。李白仰天长叹，对友人说：我不能就这样走了。"达则兼济天下，穷则独善一身。安能餐君紫霞，荫君青松，乘君鸾鹤，驾君虬龙，一朝飞腾，为方丈蓬莱之人耳"！人若穷困而不能做什么时，可以做一个好人；人若通达而富有社会影响力，则可以帮助社会，改善社会。自己一旦修炼成功，飞腾成仙，对社会没有益处，这也不可行。因此：

> 乃相与卷其丹书，匣其瑶瑟，申管、晏之谈，谋帝

❶ 刘全白《李君碣记》。

❶ Liu Quanbai, "Eulogy for Sir Li."

* The *Fusang* tree is a mythical tree at the end of the earth.

exercises the strategy of emperors, and executes their wisdom, hoping to assist the ruler, defining the world and clarifying the boundaries. Once the duties of serving the ruler are completed, and the glory of the family achieved, then he can join Tao Zhu and Duke Liu, floating upon the five lakes, playing among the vast lands. This should not be too difficult to accomplish.

He wants to put away his scriptures and zither and begin discussing the doctrines of Guan Zhong and Yan Ying, researching the theories of government, to be of assistance to the ruler's government and realize the prosperity of the government and the people. After having accomplished this, he will then retire into the mountains and practice the techniques of immortality.

This is what Li Bai most desired in life.

However, Li Bai had a very real problem: How can he jump directly from being a commoner to being a minister? How can he let the emperor know that he is such an extraordinary man of superiority?

During the Tang Dynasty, the solution to these problems was to roam about and to become a recluse.

The ancient Chinese had some very odd ideas about government. The ancients believed that authority should not be given to those who were anxious to achieve success in government. On the contrary, those who were detached from fame and fortune, those who were dedicated to personal cultivation, could be entrusted with the heavy responsibilities of state. This is why some rulers of ancient China valued those recluses distant from the central court. In 718, Lu Hong, a recluse on Mount Song, was summoned to court and appointed as minister. During the reign of Emperor Zhongzong, Lu Cangyong, a recluse who traveled between Mounts Shaoshi and Zhongnan, was very well known. Even if he accepted high positions of power and was slandered, those scholars who withdrew from society and isolated themselves in the mountains and country always had better reputations.

Of course, living in seclusion in just one location limits one's experiences and social interaction. This is not beneficial to broadening one's perspectives and gaining notoriety. For this reason, besides living in seclusion, scholars often traveled about. This is obvious when looking at the biographies of poets of that era. In his "Petition upon Submitting the Rhapsody on the Three Great Rites," Du Fu said: "I have been roaming in Your Highness's lush grasses and tall forests since I came of age." Du Fu expressed doubtless approval and appreciation of his youthful travels. In "Sent to Henan Governor Wei," he said:

王之术，奋其智能，愿为辅弼。使寰区大定，海县清一。
事君之道成，荣亲之义毕。然后与陶朱、留侯，浮五湖，
戏沧洲，不足为难矣。

他要把丹书、瑶琴收拾起来，开始讨论管仲、晏婴的学说，研究治理国家的办法，为君主的政治提供帮助，实现国泰民安，繁荣昌盛。功成之后，他再隐遁江湖，悠然仙去。

这就是李白一生中最想做的事情。

不过，李白眼下有一个最现实的问题，这就是：如何从布衣一跃而至公卿？如何让君主知道你是一位奇士高人？

在唐代，可行的办法中有漫游与隐居。

围绕着政治，中国古代有一些颇为独特的观念。古人认为，那些汲汲于功名的人，不能将权力交给他；相反，那些淡泊名利、潜心修身的人，可以担当治国的大任。所以中国古代君主有时更看重那些远离朝廷的隐士。开元六年（718）隐于嵩山的处士卢鸿被召至京，拜为谏议大夫。唐中宗时，卢藏用往来于少室、终南二山，隐居不仕，颇有声誉。尽管他后来专事权贵，受到非议，但可以看出，那些隐于江湖山林之中的士人，往往可以获得较好的名声。

当然，固定地隐居在一个地方，阅历不广，交往有限，不利于扩大视野，传播名声，因此，除了隐逸，士人经常还云游四方，只要看看当时诗人的生平就不难发现这点。杜甫在他的《进三大礼赋表》中自称"浪迹于陛下丰草长林，实自弱冠之年矣"，对于自己早年的游历无疑是肯定和自赏的口气。他在《奉寄河南韦尹丈人》中说："有客传河尹，逢人问孔融：青囊

"A guest forwarded from Governor of Henan / Meeting up, asks about Kongrong / Is the diviner still in reclusion / Is the scholar still west and east? ..." The meaning is, Wei Ji, the governor of Henan, sent someone to ask Du Fu whether he was still in seclusion studying Daoism, or was he traveling about. One can see that the traveling and seclusion were valued during this time. Meng Haoran traveled extensively during his life, reaching Hunan, Zhejiang, Jiangsu, Sichuan, Yunnan, and central China. Other poets, such as Wang Wei, Li Qi, Gao Shi, and Cen Shen were all the same—they read voraciously and traveled voraciously. While traveling, poets could broaden their perspectives and cultivate their dispositions, thereby composing even more beautiful poems and making more friends. By interacting with friends, drinking wine and appreciating flowers, and writing poems to each other, they could develop and expand their reputations. Li Bai was no exception. Most of his life was spent traveling. After leaving Sichuan, he traveled frequently to the southeast, southwest, and northeast of China.

Li Bai said goodbye to his family and left Sichuan, following the Yangtze River through the Three Gorges, past Hubei, toward Jiangsu and Zhejiang.

After passing the Three Gorges, he arrived at Xiangyang, Hubei, where he spent some time. Once the Yangtze River reaches Hubei, the landscape becomes wide and open, matching Li Bai's free and open disposition. He composed many masterpieces, such as "Upon Departing, Passing Through Jingmen" :

> Passing through Jingmen,
> Coming to the region of Chu to roam.
> The mountains end, leading into flat wilds;
> The river flows, entering into the great expanses.
> Under the moon, the soaring heavenly mirror;
> Clouds are born, becoming towers in the sea.
> I still miss the waters of my home;
> Which carried my boat ten thousand miles.

Mount Jingmen is in northwest of Yidu County, Hubei Province. The first two lines are grandiose, expressing Li Bai's bold and open disposition. Critics have called this "Li Bai's grandiose language." The last two lines, in which he longs for his homeland, are hesitant, expressing the complex emotions of leaving home for a long journey.

Following the Yangtze River, as he passed Jingzhou (modern Jiangling, Hubei Province), he composed "Song of Jingzhou." The song says:

> By the walls of Baidi, I travel the waves;

仍隐逸，章甫尚西东？……"意思是说，河南尹韦济托人问候杜甫，问他现在是在隐逸学道，还是在东西漫游。可见，漫游隐逸在当时很受推崇。孟浩然一生游历甚广，足迹遍及湘楚、吴越、川蜀、中原等地。其他诗人王维、李颀（qí）、高适、岑参等人莫不如此，读万卷书，行万里路。诗人在漫游的过程中，可以开阔眼界，陶冶情性，写出更多优美的诗篇，还可以结识许多朋友。朋友相处，赏花饮酒，酬赠诗篇，自己的诗名也随之传播开去。李白也不例外，一生中的大部分时光都是在漫游中度过。出蜀之后，多次游历梁宋、湘楚、吴越、齐鲁等地。

李白告别亲人，离开川蜀，沿着长江东下，出三峡，经湖北，再往江苏、浙江一带。

他出了三峡，到达湖北襄阳，并在那里逗留了一段时期。长江进入楚地即湖北以后，地形变得开阔，这与李白开放阔大的心胸正相吻合。他写下了很多杰出的诗篇，如《渡荆门送别》曰：

渡远荆门外，来从楚国游。

山随平野尽，江入大荒流。

月下飞天镜，云生结海楼。

仍怜故乡水，万里送行舟。

荆门山在湖北宜都县西北。"山随"二句，气象壮阔，突现出李白豪迈开放的胸襟。诗家一向称之为"太白壮语"。结尾二句留恋故乡，悠然不尽，表现出了离家远游时的复杂心情。

李白沿江东下，路过荆州（今湖北江陵）时，写下了《荆州歌》。歌曰：

白帝城边足风波，瞿塘五月谁敢过？

Qutang in summer, who dares pass?
Jingzhou wheat is ripe, cocoons become moths;
Silk threads of longing, leads are tangled.
The black bird calls in flight, "What-to-do?"

This song is very interesting. "Song of Jingzhou" was originally a *yuefu* folk ballad. After Li Bai arrived in Jingzhou, he composed this poem imitating the style of the folk ballad. The entire poem is five lines, with seven characters in each line. This is different from the average scholar's poem. The wheat ripens in Jingzhou at the same time the silkworms spin cocoons. One step in sericulture is called "*saosi*," in which the cocoons are soaked in hot water, after which the silk threads are drawn. One has to find the lead of the silk thread before the thread can be drawn. The problem is that there are many cocoons, and the leads can become tangled. In his poem, Li Bai uses the word *si* (silk), which is a homophone of the character *si* (to long after, or to miss). The tangled leads of the silk threads allude to the tangled thoughts of a young girl's longing. This was a common technique in Southern Dynasties *yuefu* ballad poetry, yet Li Bai uses it in a very unaffected and natural way. It is quite moving. Critics throughout history have given great praise to this poem, claiming it to be the only Tang poem equal to the *yuefu* of the Han and Wei periods.

Just like other Tang poets, Li Bai liked folk songs very much. Some of his compositions were based on contemporary and earlier folk songs. His accomplishments in this area stand out among those of Tang poets. On his way out from Sichuan, Li Bai passed through the Three Gorges, which is the location of the ancient district of Ba. This area is rich in folk songs. Li Bai was deeply impressed, and so imitated the folk song style when composing "Song of the Ba Maiden" :

The Ba River rushes as if it were an arrow;
The Ba boat leaves as if it were flying.
Traveling three thousand *li* during ten months,
When shall the young man return?

The current of the Ba River is swift, and boats travel quickly. One can travel three thousand *li*, or one thousand miles during ten months. The traveler (the young man) left home for ten months, but has not yet returned. The poet borrows a common device of the folk ballads, writing in the voice of a young maiden longing for her loved one. It is quite moving.

In approximately fall of 724, Li Bai decided to leave Jingmen and continue east. In "Departing Jingmen in Fall," he wrote:

　　荆州麦熟茧成蛾，缲丝忆君头绪多，

　　拨谷（即布谷鸟）飞鸣奈妾何？

这首诗非常有意思。《荆州歌》本来是乐府，有民歌的特色。李白到了荆州之后，就模仿民歌的风格写作这首诗。全篇五句，每句七言，即每句七个字，这与一般的文人诗不同。荆州麦子熟黄正是桑蚕结茧之时，女子养蚕纺丝，其中一道工序是"缲丝"，即将蚕茧浸在热水中抽丝。找到茧丝的头绪，就可以顺利抽出来。可是蚕茧很多，头绪很乱。李白的诗中以"丝"谐音"思念"的"思"，缲丝、头绪比喻女子思念时心绪杂乱。这是南朝乐府中常见的抒情手法，不过，李白写来纯朴自然，极为生动。前人以为唐人诗只有这一首可以归入到汉魏乐府诗中，评价很高。

　　像其他唐诗人一样，李白非常喜爱民歌，他的一些作品都是在学习当地民歌和前代乐府的基础上写成的。在唐诗人当中，他这方面的成就十分突出。李白出川途经三峡，三峡一带古为巴郡，民歌丰富多彩，诗人深有感受，仿照民歌样式与风格，作《巴女词》：

　　巴水急如箭，巴船去若飞。

　　十月三千里，郎行几岁归？

巴水流急，船行快速，十月可行三千里，可是远行者（郎）离家十月，至今未归。诗人继承了民间歌谣中的常用手法，用女子的口吻抒发思念之情，十分动人。

　　大约在开元十二年（724）的秋天，李白决定离开荆门东下。《秋下荆门》诗云：

The frost descends upon Jingmen, the river trees are bare;
The linen sails are in fine condition, hung in the autumn wind.
This trip is not for roasted bass;
I just love famous mountains, and so depart for the Shan River.

As frost forms, the autumn winds fill the sails. That which attracts him to the Wu (Jiangsu) and Yue (Zhejiang) regions is not the famous tastes of watercress soup and roasted bass, but the famous mountains and rivers of the Shan River area.

Before he traveled far, though, he met his friend Wu Zhinan from Sichuan, and the two decided to roam about Hubei together. Li Bai was very loyal to his friends. He himself said that while traveling throughout Yangzhou, in less than one year, he "gave out over three hundred thousand in silver" helping down and out gentlemen. To value righteousness and disdain money is a basic characteristic of the chivalrous gentleman. Li Bai was a self-proclaimed gallant and chivalrous man, and befriended the brave and gallant, so he devalued money and material belongings. He said: "In life, friends are dear / What need is there for gold and coin?" [1] "When gold leaves the hand, pleasure is exhausted / Yesterday I depleted my treasury, and today am poor." [2] Upon reaching Lake Dongting, though, Wu Zhinan died. Li Bai wore mourning and cried. He was as sad as if he had lost a close relative. When strangers heard the news, they were all very sad for him. Li Bai buried his friend temporarily by the shores of Lake Dongting, brushed away his tears, and continued toward Jinling (modern Nanjing, Jiangsu Province).

A few years later, Li Bai returned to the shores of Lake Dongting and prepared to give his friend a proper burial. The remains were still there, so with tears, Li Bai personally washed the remains and removed the remaining flesh from the bones. He put the bones in a bag and carried them on his back to the east of Echeng (modern Wuchang, Hubei Province), where he chose a plot and performed a proper burial.

Such friendship is rare, and Li Bai's burial method was also quite unusual. There are almost no records of this sort of burial after the Tang Dynasty. Researchers did not understand it until a recent discovery. [3] According to experts, this kind of burial is called defleshing. Ethnologists call it secondary excarnation. The origins of this practice are very old. It is most common in the ethnic minority regions of southwest China. Li Bai's family lived in the south of Changlong County of Mianzhou, Sichuan, which is considered to be a region of the southern ethnic tribes. The Nanzhao Kingdom of the Erhai region

霜落荆门江树空，布帆无恙挂秋风。

此行不为鲈鱼脍（kuài），自爱名山入剡（shàn）中。

秋霜降落，秋风吹动帆船。吸引他到吴越的并不是人们熟知的味道鲜美的莼（chún）羹（gēng）、鲈鱼脍，而是剡中那些名山大川。

还没有行多远，就遇到了蜀中的朋友吴指南，于是，二人相约同在湖北一带游赏。李白对朋友很讲义气。他自称，在扬州等地游历，不到一年，"散金三十余万"，都救济了当时许多的落魄公子。重义轻财，这是侠士的基本作风，李白自称豪侠，结交豪雄，对金钱财物看得很轻。他说："人生贵相知，何必金与钱"❶；"黄金逐手快意尽，昨日破产今朝贫"❷。到了洞庭湖，吴指南却不幸病逝。李白穿上丧服，泪如泉涌，悲痛欲绝，仿佛失去了亲人。路人听说，无不为之伤心。李白暂且将朋友葬在洞庭湖滨，挥泪前往金陵（今江苏南京）。

几年以后，李白回到洞庭湖滨，准备给友人正式下葬。遗骸筋肉尚在，李白含泪，亲自清洗，持刀将骨骸上的筋肉剔除。用袋子装裹遗骨，自己背着，一直步行走到鄂城（今湖北武昌）的东面，找了一块好地方，为友人举行正式的葬礼。

情义如山，李白此举难能可贵，而他葬友的做法，更是奇特。对于这种葬法，唐以后的文献几乎没有任何相关的记载，研究者也都不甚了了，直到最近才有学者揭开此中的秘密。❸按照专家的说法，这种葬法，称为剔骨葬，民俗学上称为二次捡骨葬。起源非常古老，主要流行于中国南方少数民族地区。李白家居四川绵州的昌隆县，南边即是所谓的南蛮地区。云南

❶ 李白《赠友人》。
❷ 李白《醉后赠从甥高镇》。
❸ 参见周勋初《李白评传》。

❶ Li Bai, "Presented to a Friend."
❷ Li Bai, "Presented to My Nephew Gao Zhen After Getting Drunk."
❸ See Zhou Xunchu, *Li Bai pingzhuan* (*Critical Biography of Li Bai*).

of Yunnan Province was populated mostly by the Black *Man* (predecessors of the Yi) and the White *Man* (predecessors of the Bai). Their funerary practices were different. The Black *Man* used cremation, whereas the White used burial, and also secondary excarnation. Li Bai's home in Sichuan bordered the kingdom of Nanzhao, and he was obviously quite familiar with the local funerary customs. This is a very typical example of Li Bai's complex cultural heritage. This is one difference between Li Bai and other poets.

After leaving Lake Dongting, Li Bai continued to Jiangxi, where he naturally visited the beautiful Mount Lu. He climbed Mount Lu, where he left behind many famous compositions on the beauty of the scenery. For example, the seven-character quatrain "Viewing the Waterfall at Mount Lu" :

> The sun shines upon Incense Brazier, emitting a purple haze;
> In the distance, I see the waterfall, dangling from the river before it.
> Flying current straight down three thousand yards;
> I suspect it to be the Milky Way, falling from the nine heavens.

In the sunshine, Incense Brazier Peak of Mount Lu seems to be giving off a purple haze. In the distance, the waterfall pours down from high above, flowing straight down. Waterfalls are often described as appearing to be a white sheet hanging before a mountain, yet Li Bai says: "I suspect it to be the Milky Way, falling from the nine heavens," as if it were the Milky Way falling out of the sky. His remarkable imagination and grandiose style are difficult to match.

Li Bai quickly arrived at Jinling (modern Nanjing). Jinling was an ancient capital of the Six Dynasties period, an important city in the southeast of the Tang Empire. With Mount Zhong to its back and the Yangtze River at its front, Jinling was often referred to as "crouching tiger, winding dragon." Li Bai traveled to all the famous sites, paying tribute to the earlier empires. Jinling was a vibrant city, with colorful flowers, rich wines, and beautiful women. Li Bai felt very comfortable in this environment, and wrote many poems describing the beautiful women:

> With one smile from the beauty, one thousand in gold;
> Flowing gauze and dancing silk, the refined music arises.
> Sing not of the white snow in Yin;
> The Wu "Midnight Song" moves the gentleman's heart.
> The Wu knife cuts colored silk to sew dancing robes;
> Bright rouge and beautiful clothes please the spring eye.

洱海地区的南诏国主要由乌蛮（彝族先民）与白蛮（白族先民）组成。他们的葬礼方式有所不同，乌蛮实行火葬，白蛮则实行土葬，还实行二次捡骨葬。李白四川的老家靠近南诏国，显然熟悉当地土著的葬礼仪式。这个事例十分典型，不难看出，李白的文化背景相当复杂，所受文化影响的来源非常多元。这是李白不同于其他诗人的地方。

离开洞庭湖，李白继续前行。路经江西时，自然不会错过风景秀丽的庐山。于是登庐山玩赏，留下了不少歌咏庐山的名篇，如七言绝句《望庐山瀑布》云：

> 日照香炉生紫烟，遥看瀑布挂前川。
>
> 飞流直下三千尺，疑是银河落九天。

阳光照射，庐山的香炉峰呈现出紫色的光彩，远远望去，庐山瀑布高悬，喷涌而出，飞流直下。人多形容瀑布仿佛山前挂着的白练，而李白却说，"疑是银河落九天"。仿佛银河自九天之上落下。想象奇特，气势宏大，他人难以相比。

李白很快来到金陵（今南京）。金陵是六朝古都，唐帝国东南的重镇。背负钟山，面临长江，素有"虎踞龙蟠"之称。李白游览各处名胜，凭吊前朝遗迹。金陵是繁华的都市，花红酒绿，美女如云。这种场合，李白总是十分惬（qiè）意自如，他有不少诗篇描写动人的美女：

> 美人一笑千黄金，垂罗舞縠（hú）扬哀音。
>
> 郢中白雪且莫吟，子夜吴歌动君心。
>
> 吴刀剪彩缝舞衣，明妆丽服夺春晖。

> Raise a brow and turn a sleeve as flying snow;
> The timeless beauty stands alone, so rare in this world. ❶

Li Bai always praised the lovable actions, beautiful appearance, exceptional artistic skills, and elegant temperament of a young maiden:

> Grape wine, golden cups;
> The Wu singing girl of fifteen, on the back of a delicate horse.
> Dark mascara, painted brows, red brocade boots;
> She recites the words wrong, but sings so sweetly. ❷

What a realistic description.

Li Bai once had a singing girl concubine called "Jinlingzi." In the fourth poem of his series "Four Poems on Presenting My Songstress Concubine Jinlingzi to Lu Liu," he said: "The young concubine Jinling sings in a Chu accent." It is evident that she sang well. Li Bai's interaction with such women can also be seen in a different light, though. Li Bai had always admired the Eastern Jin scholar and official Xie An. When Xie An lived in retirement on Eastern Mountain, he often took songstresses on outings. Li Bai also often took songstresses on outings. This was, in some part, in emulation of Xie An.

> The breeze blows the willow blossoms, the whole restaurant is fragrant;
> The Wu maiden presses the wine, calling guests to taste.
> The Jinling gentlemen come to see each other off;
> Ready to leave, yet not leaving, they delay each cup.
> Please ask the gentleman of the eastern flowing river;
> The regret of parting and this, which is longer?

This poem, "Parting at a Jinling Tavern," is true to the emotions. Li Bai was parting from his friends of Jinling to continue to the Wu and Yue regions. At the farewell banquet, the one parting and those seeing him off all drink their fills. In the end, the poet asks, the hesitant pains of parting and the Yangtze River, which flows longer, and which flows shorter? Li Bai valued friendship deeply, and many of his farewell poems are very well written. Take "Presented to Wang Lun" for example:

> Li Bai boards the boat, all ready to leave;
> But suddenly hears, from the shore, the sound of song.
> The water of Peach Blossom Pool is deep one thousand yards;
> Yet does not reach the depths of Wang Lun's friendship upon parting.

When the poet Wang Changling was exiled to Longbiao (modern Qianyang,

扬眉转袖若雪飞，倾城独立世所稀。 ❶

女性可爱的举止、动人的美貌、高超的才艺、高洁的品性，李白总是发出赞美：

蒲萄酒，金叵罗，吴姬十五细马驮。

青黛画眉红锦靴，道字不正娇唱歌。 ❷

刻画传情逼真。

李白曾有一位歌妓叫"金陵子"，其《出妓金陵子呈卢六四首》之四说："小妓金陵歌楚声。"可见她唱歌很好。不过，李白与这样的女性交往，有时还有其他的含义。李白一向倾慕东晋名臣谢安，谢安隐居东山时，常携妓游赏；李白也时时携妓出游，多少是仿效谢安的意思。

风吹柳花满店香，吴姬压酒唤客尝。

金陵子弟来相送，欲行不行各尽觞。

请君试问东流水，别意与这谁短长？

这首《金陵酒肆留别》写得情真意切。李白要告别金陵的朋友，前往吴越。告别的酒席上，欲行与送行的人都尽情痛饮。诗人最后说，我们依依惜别之情与长江流水，到底哪个长，哪个短呢？李白十分珍惜朋友情谊，他有许多告别诗、送别诗写得都十分精彩。如《赠汪伦》：

李白乘舟将欲行，忽闻岸上踏歌声。

桃花潭水深千尺，不及汪伦送我情。

诗人王昌龄被贬谪到龙标（今湖南黔阳），靠近夜郎，李白

---

❶ 李白《白纻辞三首》其二、其三。
❷ 李白《对酒》。

❶ Li Bai, "Song of the White Linen," second and third of three.
❷ Li Bai, "To the Wine."

Hunan Province), near Yelang, Li Bai wrote "Sent afar upon Hearing that Wang Changling Had Been Sent to Longbiao." The last two lines say: "I send my saddened heart and the full moon / Along with the breeze, all the way to west of Yelang." This is truly deep friendship.

The beautiful landscape of the Wu and Yue regions, along with the highly developed culture, resulted in plentiful traces of the many scholars of the Six Dynasties period. During his travels in the countryside, Li Bai composed many poems praising the landscape.

The girls of the Wu and Yue regions are very cute, and the folksongs they sing are very beautiful. Li Bai composed many pieces in imitation of these folksongs, such as the second and third of "Five Lyrics of the Yue Maiden" :

> Wu girls are mostly fair and radiant;
> They enjoy playing rock the boat.
> Casting glances at the spring heart;
> They pick a flower to flirt with the traveler.
> In the Ye Stream, the maiden picking lotuses,
> Sees the guest, and sings a verse back.
> Her smile goes into the water lilies;
> Feigned modesty, her head does not come up.

Ye Stream is the Ruoyefu Stream in Zhejiang. The poem presents the playful and lovable nature of the girls of the Wu and Yue regions. There are many rivers and wetlands in the Jiangnan region, and the rural women often walk barefoot in the water. Li Bai found this to be interesting, and so composed "The Maiden upon the Washing Stone" in imitation of a local folksong:

> Jade complexion of the Ye Stream maiden,
> Dark brows and red rouge powder.
> A pair of golden teeth clogs;
> Two feet white as frost.

A young girl like a flower, with a complexion of jade and faint rouge makeup, bare feet in sandals by the stream: The description is like a painting.

Li Bai continued on to Yangzhou, where he stayed for a while. By this time, Li Bai had left home for two or three years. Even though there are very few poems in his collection in which he misses his family, he did often miss home. In "Thoughts on a Quiet Evening," he said:

> Before my bed, I look at the moonlight;
> Believing it to be frost on the ground.

《闻王昌龄左迁龙标遥有此寄》中末两句说："我寄愁心与明月，随风直到夜郎西。"真可谓情深意长。

吴越风景秀丽，文化发达，山山水水留下了众多六朝名士的足迹。李白游山玩水，写了许多诗篇，赞美吴越山水。

吴越女子十分可爱，她们所唱的民歌十分动听，诗人模仿民歌写了不少作品。如《越女词五首》之二、三曰：

> 吴儿多白皙，好为荡舟剧。
>
> 卖眼掷春心，折花调行客。
>
> 耶溪采莲女，见客棹歌回。
>
> 笑入荷花去，佯羞不出来。

剧，即游戏，嬉戏；耶溪，即越中若耶浮溪。诗中写出了吴越女子多情可爱的风貌。江南地区多水，民间妇女常是临流濯足，诗人看得很新鲜，于是仿照当地民歌作《浣纱石上女》诗，曰：

> 玉面耶溪女，青蛾红粉妆。
>
> 一双金齿屐，两足白如霜。

年轻姑娘如花似玉，淡淡的妆扮，光着脚穿着凉鞋走向溪水边，描写如画一般。

李白接着去了扬州，并在那里住一段时间。此时，诗人离开家乡，已有两三年的时间，虽然李白诗集中留存的思亲诗极少，但他还是会时常想念家乡，《静夜思》曰：

> 床前看月光，疑是地上霜。

Raising my head, I gaze at the bright moon;
Lowering my head, I miss my hometown.

In a mere twenty characters, he is able to express the emotions of the traveler longing for home. This deeply moving poem is very popular. Most children in China today are able to recite it from memory.

After roaming about Wu (Jiangsu) and Yue (Zhejiang), Li Bai returned to Hubei. When he left home, he probably brought quite a large amount money, but by this time, it was all depleted. On the one hand, Li Bai's lifestyle was quite extravagant and costly. On the other hand, he was chivalrous and gallant, and liked to give out money. He once said: "In life, friends are dear / What need is there for gold and coin?" ❶ For this reason, he often used his money to help friends in need. By this time, his funds were depleted, and he had to scrounge together enough money to bury Wu Zhinan. Life must have been difficult as he rambled about Hubei for a long time.

Between Anlu County and Yingshan County in Hubei Province today, there is a small mountain called Mount Shou. Li Bai once retired to this mountain. Approximately when he was roaming about Yangzhou, Li Bai made friends with a District Defender named Meng. It was a Tang practice to call District Defender "*Shaofu*" (Official). Official Meng wrote an essay titled "On Moving," in which he criticized Li Bai for retiring into this unknown little mountain. Of course, this is a satirical essay, imitating Kong Zhigui's "On Moving to Northern Mountain." In response, Li Bai composed "Letter Written for Mount Shou in Response to Official Meng's 'On moving' ," in which he says that Mount Shou "is a small mountain with no reputation, and no accomplishments to speak of. Looking at these words, is not this too ridiculous?" "The Perfected One Zhuang Sheng often spoke of how the petty quail does not envy the great *peng* bird, and the tip of an autumn fur can compare to Mount Tai. From this perspective, what is the difference between large and small?" As Zhuangzi sees it, there is no difference between a small quail and the great *peng* bird; there is no difference between a very fine fur of a winter undercoat and the lofty Mount Tai. "Let it thus be known that caves are where the virtuous cultivate themselves, for secret treasures are not to be found in forests and springs." True men of virtue can retire to any place. The essay, in the viewpoint of Mount Shou, rebuts Official Meng's criticism, expressing Li Bai's own inclinations and ideals.

After living in seclusion on Mount Shou for a while, Li Bai came to Anlu. South of Anlu is the ancient Yunmeng Marsh. The marsh is large, and it is shrouded in a mystical reputation. The *Chuci* (Songs of the South) and Han

举头望山月，低头思故乡。

短短二十个字，却写出了游子思乡的真情，感人至深，脍炙人口，流传极广，现代中国大多数儿童都会背诵这首诗。

李白漫游吴越后，回到湖北。诗人离开家乡时，可能带了不小的一笔钱，但此时，钱已经用光了。一方面，李白生活豪纵，花费很大。另一方面，他任侠仗义，轻财好施，曾说："人生贵相知，何必金与钱。" ❶ 因此，常拿出钱财来接济他的朋友。此时，钱财已尽，他为吴指南下葬，还是东拼西凑借来的钱。他在湖北一带飘荡了很长时间，可以想见，生活已近窘迫。

在今天的湖北安陆县与应山县之间有一座小山叫寿山，李白曾经在这里隐居过。大约在漫游扬州的时候，他认识了一位姓孟的县尉，唐人习惯称县尉为少府，孟少府写了一篇"移文"，责怪李白何以隐居在这座不知名的小山之中。当然，这是模仿孔稚圭的《北山移文》而写的调侃文字。李白于是写作《代寿山答孟少府移文书》，回应孟少府。文中以为，说寿山"小山无名，无德而称焉。观乎斯言，何太谬之甚也"！"达人庄生常有余论，以为尺鷃（yàn）不羡于鹏鸟，秋毫可并于太（泰）山。由此而谈，何小大之殊也"！在庄子看来，小鸟尺鷃（yàn）与鹏鸟没有区别，很细的毫毛与高高的泰山也没有什么不同。"乃知岩穴为养贤之域，林泉非秘宝之区"，高士隐居在什么地方都可以。文中以寿山的口吻反驳孟少府的责难，说明自己的志向和做人的理想。

他在寿山中隐居一段时间之后，来到安陆。安陆的南边就是古之云梦泽，范围很大，富有神奇色彩，楚辞与汉赋中经常

---

❶ 李白《赠友人》。

❶ Li Bai, "Presented to a Friend."

rhapsodies mention it; Sima Xiangru describes it in detail in "Rhapsody of Sir Vacuous." Li Bai said: "Upon reading my fellow countryman Xiangru's great stories of Yunmeng, saying 'there are seven marshes in Chu,' I came to see it." He originally intended to travel about Yunmeng, but he quickly married the granddaughter of Xu Yushi and settled down. In "Letter to Anzhou Administrator Pei," he wrote: "I received an audience with Sir Xu, who betrothed his granddaughter to me, and so I have settled here for three years already." Xu Yushi was the son of the high official Xu Shao of the Early Tang period. Xu Yushi had at one time held the office of Grand Councilor, but died in 679, almost fifty years before Li Bai married in 727. Xu family had obviously already passed their prime.

Miss Xu came from the family of a Grand Councilor, though, and so was of an elevated position. Li Bai was just a wanderer, and so he said that he "married into" the Xu family. In China, there is a special term for such a marriage: *zhuixu*. It is sometimes refered to as "reverse marriage." Since the Shang and Zhou Dynasties, China has been a patrilineal society. The Shang Dynasty began to establish ancestor worship, and since the Western Zhou period, the patrilineal moral system has been firmly embedded into the Chinese psyche. Women were subservient to men, and the status of women was relatively lower. Men were the head of the household, and maintained the ancestral line and the inheritance. When a woman married, she married into her husband's family, then gave birth to children and did house chores. Such distinction of male and female roles was considered normal. Generally speaking, a man who married into a woman's family was met with scorn. In fact, it was mostly only men from impoverished and lowly backgrounds who would marry into their wives' families. Li Bai was deeply affected by Central Asian culture, though, and so was not such a traditionalist. He seemed to be unaffected by marrying into the Xu family and taking on the role of the Xu family son-in-law.

For one thing, after roaming about Wu and Yue, Li Bai was in dire financial straights, and by marrying into the Xu family, at least his financial difficulties were resolved. In his "Preface to Seeing off My Nephew Duan at Jing Pavilion in Autumn to Travel to Mount Lu," Li Bai wrote: "I retired to wine in Anlu, dawdling away ten years." The implication of this statement is that he accomplished nothing during these ten years, but he could at least drink wine, so his life was stable.

Li Bai wrote a poem titled "For My Wife," in which he wrote: "Three hundred and sixty days / Day after day, drunk as mud / Even though you are Li Bai's wife / How is it different from being wife of the Chamberlain for Ceremonials?" This refers to a historical allusion: The Eastern Han Chamberlain for Ceremonials Zhou Ze was once lying ill in the Hall of Purity.

提到，司马相如在《子虚赋》中盛称云梦泽。李白说："见乡人相如大夸云梦之事，云'楚有七泽'，遂来观焉。"他本想漫游云梦，但很快却与许圉（yǔ）师的孙女结婚，并定居下来。《上安州裴长史书》中说："许相公家见招，妻以孙女，便憩迹于此，至移三霜焉。"许圉师是唐初高官许绍的儿子，曾做过宰相，仪凤四年（679）卒，距离开元十五年（727）李白结婚之时已过去快五十年了。许家显然已过了最为显赫的时候了。

但许小姐毕竟出身相门，地位比较高。李白只身漂泊，于是到许府中去成婚，自称"就婚"相府。这种状况，中国称之为"赘（zhuì）婿"，即俗语"倒插门"的女婿。商、周以来，我国就建立了父系社会，商代初步形成了宗法制度，西周以后以父系为中心的伦理观念深入人心。男尊女卑，妇女的地位相对较低。男子顶门立户，维持一姓相承的血统，继承家财，接续宗祀；妇女结婚，嫁到丈夫家，生儿育女，操劳家务，男女角色的这种区别被视为理所当然。一般情况下，男子入赘到妻子家里，会受到轻视。事实上，大都只有家境贫穷、地位低下的男子才会选择入赘。李白深受西域文化的影响，传统观念比较淡薄，似乎并不在意到许府去做上门的女婿。

再有一点，李白游历吴越之后，陷于窘迫，与许氏结婚，至少在经济上可以解决一些问题。李白《秋于敬亭送从侄耑游庐山序》中说："酒隐安陆，蹉跎十年。"言下之意，定居安陆后的十年并没有什么成就，但至少可以喝上酒，日子还算安稳。

李白有《赠内》一首，诗曰："三百六十日，日日醉如泥。虽为李白妇，何异太常妻？"这里有一个典故：东汉太常卿周泽，主管礼乐祭祀，有次病卧于斋宫中，妻子念其老病，前去

His wife was concerned, and so went to visit him, but Zhou Ze took her presence as infringing upon the purity of the hall. In a fit of rage, he threw her in prison. Li Bai enjoyed drinking wine, and was often quite inebriated. He was concerned that he did not give her enough of his attention, and so wrote this poem to her in jest. This shows that their relationship must have been harmonious.

Li Bai enjoyed drinking wine, and was able to drink more than the average person. When he drank, his style was extraordinarily unrestrained and frank. In his "Song of Xiangyang," he wrote: "In one hundred years, thirty-six thousand days / In one day, I must drink three hundred cups." Of course, "three hundred cups" is an exaggeration, but this expresses his love of wine. His love of wine and his tolerance for wine are as famous as his poems. He called himself the "Old Drunken Immortal," and Du Fu said of him: "With one hundred pitchers of wine, Li Bai will give off one hundred poems."

When drinking, at the point between inebriation and sobriety, one will often feel as though one is flying in the clouds, as if one were an immortal. This unusually exciting and exhilarating experience cannot be gained from anything else. This may be why, from ancient times to modern, so many people have been so fascinated with drinking. Of course, a poet's unconstrained drinking is different from the average person's excessive indulgences. When average people are drunk, they may laugh or cry, sleep or fight, but they loose their creative abilities, and may even cause disruptions to those around them. Poets and writers, however, are different; inebriation can stimulate their creative talents. When Li Bai was drunk, but perhaps not excessively drunk, his creative juices flowed, and he composed as if possessed by a muse. This is why Du Fu said: "With one hundred pitchers of wine, Li Bai will give off one hundred poems." The drunker he became, the better his poems became. This was not unusual, though. As soon as the great Tang calligrapher Zhang Xu began to drink, he would write cursive calligraphy, yelling as he wrote. Sometimes, he would even dip his hair in the ink and write. (He could be called China's first performance artist.) People called him "Crazy Zhang." Once sober, he would hold up his calligraphy, and upon examination, declare it to be "divine." He could not reproduce such works. Another great calligrapher, Huaisu, also "Drank wine to cultivate his nature / Wrote cursive to express his ambitions." Once intoxicated, he would write on whatever he could get: walls, clothing, utensils, or anything else. For artists, alcohol is a catalyst that elevates their creativity to a level of divine instinct. As for Li Bai, if he did not drink, he would not be the poet Li Bai. It makes sense that, in China, wine and poetry are often interrelated.

探望，周泽却认为妻子冒犯了斋禁，一怒之下将她投入监狱。李白喜好饮酒，常常沉醉不省，诗人担心冷落妻子，故以玩笑的口吻写诗相赠。这说明他们之间感情非常融洽。

李白喜爱饮酒，酒量过人，饮酒的风格特别豪爽。他在《襄阳歌》中说："百年三万六千日，一日须饮三百杯。"三百杯，当然是夸张，不过说出他对酒的嗜好。他的好饮能饮，与他的诗歌一样出名，他自称"酒仙翁"，杜甫称他"李白斗酒诗百篇"。

饮酒之时，处在半醉半醒之间，常有腾云驾雾的感觉，飘飘而欲仙。这种异常兴奋、陶醉的体验是其他东西难以给予的。或许正因此，古往今来，才有那么多热衷于饮酒的人！当然，诗人豪饮与一般嗜酒者不同，常人喝酒，一旦烂醉如泥，或哭或笑，或睡或闹，在精神文化方面很难有什么创造，甚至还会使周围人不快；而诗人作家则不同，沉醉的状态往往更能激发他们的创作天才。李白酒酣，或不至于一醉不起的地步，此时吟诗，文思如泉涌，下笔如有神，所以杜甫称他"斗酒诗百篇"。酒饮得越酣畅，诗写得越好。这种情况不在少数。唐代大书法家张旭，一饮酒就写草书，挥毫大叫，甚至用头发蘸着水墨书写（可以称得上中国最早的行为艺术），人称"张颠"。酒醒之后，端详自己的作品，以为"神异"，不可复得。另一位大书法家怀素，同样也是"饮酒以养性，草书以畅志"。酒酣兴发，逮到什么，就在上面书写。墙壁、衣服、器物，凡是能够写字的，就草书一番。对艺术家而言，酒是催化剂，使他们的创作激情升华，达到出神入化的地步。对于李白而言，不饮酒，恐怕就不再是诗人李白了。在中国，"诗酒"常常联在一起说，实在有道理。

While in Anlu, Li Bai would also occasionally wander to the outlying areas. In Xiangyang, Hubei, he came to know the famous poet Meng Haoran. Meng Haoran was twelve years Li Bai's senior, and was living in seclusion in Mount Lumen. His poems were simple and detached, similar to Wang Wei's. Meng and Wang were often thought of as one school. Although Meng Haoran had served in government, he never had an opportunity to fully achieve his goals, so he spent most of his life in retirement, traveling about. Li Bai admired Meng Haoran, and the two became best friends. Later, while in Jiangxia (modern Wuhan, Hubei Province), Li Bai again met with Meng Haoran, and the two traveled together. After a short time, Meng Haoran left for Yangzhou, and Li Bai wrote a poem to see him off. This is the very well known poem: "Seeing Meng Haoran off to Guangling (Yangzhou) at Yellow Crane Pavilion" :

> My old friend departs west at Yellow Crane Pavilion;
> Fog and blossoms, off to Yangzhou.
> A solitary sail in the distance, at the end of the azure sky;
> All I can see is the Yangtze River flowing into the horizon.

The original location of the Yellow Crane Pavilion, a famous touring site, is in Wuhan City, on Snake Mountain, facing the Yangtze River. Legend says that the immortal Zi'an once rode to this spot on the back of a yellow crane, and so it is now named Yellow Crane Pavilion. This poem is much relished for its beautiful description of the hesitant reluctance of parting. Lu You said of the last two lines: "If one has not traveled by boat over long distances, one cannot understand these lines." He means that anyone who has not traveled along the Yangtze River has no way of imagining and comprehending the marvelous beauty of the last two lines.

We mentioned how the Tang custom of traveling and retiring could expand a poet's perspectives and disseminate his reputation. Besides this, the Tang also had another, more proactive, method of gaining recognition: They would submit their compositions directly to high officials of influence and authority. Upon appreciating the poet's talents, they would recommend the poet to the central court, where they would receive an appointment. This was a common method during the Tang Dynasty. The submitted composition could be a single poem, a rhapsody, or even a collection of one's better works. Sometimes, scholars would even compose short stories, and then copy them onto scrolls which would be submitted to high officials. These were called "xingjuan," or opening scrolls. Just in case the official would forget one's name, the scholar would sometimes copy more compositions and submit them, calling it a "wenjuan," or refresher scroll, just to refresh the official's memory.

在安陆期间，李白有时也在周边的地区云游，在湖北襄阳，他结识了另一位著名的诗人孟浩然。孟浩然大李白十二岁，此时隐居在鹿门山，其诗平淡高远，与王维齐名，并称"王孟"。孟浩然虽然为出仕奔走过，但始终没有一展抱负的机会，一生中大部分时光都是过着隐居漫游的生活。李白对孟浩然怀有敬意，两人结下了深厚的友谊。后来，李白在江夏（今湖北武汉）再次遇到孟浩然，两人一同游赏。不久，孟浩然要东下扬州，李白写诗送别，这就是传诵千古的绝句《黄鹤楼送孟浩然之广陵（扬州）》：

故人西辞黄鹤楼，烟花三月下扬州。

孤帆远影碧空尽，唯见长江天际流。

黄鹤楼故址在今湖北武汉市蛇山上，正对长江，是著名的游览胜地。相传有仙人子安曾经乘黄鹤到此，故名黄鹤楼。此诗脍炙人口，依依惜别之情，俱在言外。陆游说，后两句"非江行久不能知"。意思是说，不常在长江上旅行的人是无法想象、无法体会到两句诗的妙处。

上文我们说到唐人的漫游与隐居，可以扩大诗人的见识，传播美名。此外，唐人还有一种比较主动的做法——"干谒（yè）"，即向达官显贵等各级有权势的人物投赠自己的文学作品，使他们欣赏自己的才能，从而向朝廷推荐，最终获得官职。这在唐代是普遍的做法。投赠的文学作品，可以是一首诗，一篇赋，也可以是自己得意之作的汇集，有时甚至是自己写作的传奇小说，抄录在卷子上，送给高官，这就是"行卷"。过了一段时期，想到高官可能忘了自己的名姓，于是再抄录一些作品投赠上去，谓之"温卷"，让官员重温一下。

While traveling about, Li Bai also did the same as others. In his "Letter to Sir Han of Jingzhou," Li Bai said: "At fifteen, I enjoyed swordplay and meeting lords. At thirty, my compositions were perfected, submitted to ministers." He meant that he had already had audiences with all lords and ministers that he could meet. In 720, before Li Bai had left home, Li Bai had handed his calling card to Su Ting, Administrator of Yizhou, right in the middle of the road. Su Ting met Li Bai with the etiquette due to a commoner, and said to his staff: "This child has talent of a genius, and composes with no rest. Even though his style is not yet mature, but he shows great promise. If he expands his learning, he can become an equal to Xiangru (Sima Xiangru)." ❶

While in Anlu, Li Bai visited the Commander-in-Chief of Anzhou, Ma Zhenghui. The Commander-in-Chief appreciated his compositions, saying: "Most people's compositions are like mountains without mist, like spring without blossoms. Li Bai's compositions are crisp and free, with famous passages and gorgeous phrases, and threads that hook the reader's imagination; they are clear and brilliant, every line moving the reader." Unfortunately, Commander-in-Chief Ma and his colleague, Anzhou Administrator Li Jingzhi, did not help him any.

Administrator Li left his post shortly after, and was replaced by Administrator Pei. There are no clear records of who Administrator Pei was. In his "Letter to Anzhou Administrator Pei," Li Bai wrote: "I have secretly admired your great righteousness for ten years, yet was separated by the clouds and mountains. I had no path to request an audience. Now, my fortunes have met, and I follow in your dust. You have received me and we have spoken eight or nine times." After Administrator Pei arrived, Li Bai met him eight or nine times, and Administrator Pei seemed to have a good impression of him. He did not anticipate, though, that others would intentionally slander him, and Li Bai had no option but to write the long "Letter to Anzhou Administrator Pei," in which he describes himself and his background in hopes that the magistrate does not reject him, but "recalls his former favor, and again grants an audience." Of course, if the Administrator "bursts into anger," Li Bai would "take permanent leave from My Lord, flying off into the distance." In the end, Li Bai wrote: "At which lord's gate can one not tap one's sword?" This is to say, there are many lords and officials, I can go to any one of their gates for retainer. Li Bai was audacious, and could not help expressing his true feelings. It was unlikely, though, that the Administrator, upon reading this, would still be in a good mood. Just as with the others, this letter did not result in anything, and so Li Bai made up his mind to leave and seek his career elsewhere.

李白漫游各地期间，像其他士人一样，均有这类活动。李白《与韩荆州书》中自谓："十五好剑术，遍干诸侯；三十成文章，历抵卿相。""干"，就是干谒，"抵"，在这里就是拜见并投赠自己的作品。言下之意，诸侯卿相能拜会请求的，诗人都努力地去做了。开元八年（720），李白尚未出峡，就曾在道路当中将自己的名片直接递送给当时的益州长史苏颋（tǐng）。苏颋待之以布衣之礼，并对群僚说："此子天才英丽，下笔不休，虽风力未成，且见专车之骨。若广之以学，可以相如（司马相如）比肩也。"❶

在安陆期间，他拜访安州都督马正会，都督很欣赏他的文章，称赞说："诸人之文，犹山无烟霞，春无草树。李白之文，清雄奔放，名章俊语，络绎间起，光明洞彻，句句动人。"但马都督和同僚安州长史李京之，对他实际上并无帮助。

李长史不久就离任了，接替他的是裴长史。裴长史是谁，史无明文。李白在《上安州裴长史书》中说："白窃慕（裴长史之）高义，已经十年，云山间之，造谒无路。今也运会，得趋末尘，承颜接辞，八九度矣。"裴长史来了以后，与李白见面聊天有八九次，裴长史对他的印象似乎还不错。不料，周围的人却恶意诽谤李白，诗人不得不写了长长的一篇书信《上安州裴长史书》，讲述自己的生平与为人，期望长史"终乎前恩，再辱英盼"，不要将诗人拒之门外。当然，如果长史"赫然作威，加以大怒"，李白也会"永辞君侯，黄鹄举矣"。诗人最后说："何王公大人之门，不可以弹长剑乎？"意思是说，王公大人多着呢，我到哪里不可以做一个门客？李白高傲，结尾忍不住要说出心里的话，但要裴长史看到这里，还很高兴，就比较难了。此事同样没有结果，李白决心离开此地，寻求发展。

---

❶ 李白《上安州裴长史书》。

❶ Li Bai, "Letter to Anzhou Administrator Pei."

李白诗意画 金陵风光

Painting according to Li Bai's Poem of " Landscape of Jinling"

四　长安：拔剑四顾心茫然

Chapter Ⅳ　The Capital, Chang'an: Drawing My Sword, Looking in Four Directions, My Heart Is in the Dark

Li Bai lived in Anlu for approximately ten years. Around 732, he decided to seek his fortune in the capital, Chang'an, where he hoped to realize his dream of becoming a minister to an enlightened emperor. Upon leaving Anlu, he passed through Nanyang on his way to Chang'an. Along the way, he met with local officials and made many friends. From this time, most of his activities surrounded occurred traveling to and from Chang'an, Luoyang, and surrounding regions.

Chang'an, the capital of the Tang Empire, was very large, with grand palaces and beautiful gardens. Commerce was also well developed. Not only was Chang'an the political center of the empire, it was also the cultural center. Many famous poets of the Tang Dynasty passed through Chang'an, where they wrote many poems praising the city.

Upon arriving in Chang'an, Li Bai set his sights on gaining the sponsorship of Princess Yuzhen. He moved into Princess Yuzhen's residence on Mount Zhongnan. Princess Yuzhen was the younger sister of Emperor Xuanzong. The princess was very close to her brother, the emperor. Yuzhen was interested in Daoism, and became a nun. She built the Princess Yuzhen Retreat on Mount Zhongnan, near Chang'an. She also enjoyed befriending literati and scholars, and such famous poets as Wang Wei and Gao Shi visited the princess and presented her with poems.

In his poetry, Li Bai refers to the person who arranged for him to live in Princess Yuzhen's residence as Minister Zhang, but we have no way of knowing what his name was. Minister is an honorific. One theory is that Minister Zhang was Zhang Ji. Zhang Ji was the husband of the Imperial Princess Ningqin, and son of the famous poet Zhang Yue. It would have been possible for him to arrange for Li Bai to stay temporarily in the residence of Princess Yuzhen.

It was disappointing that, even though Li Bai lived in the residence for some time, he never had a chance to meet Princess Yuzhen. Li Bai was very frustrated, and so composed two poems entitled "Presented to Chamberlain for the Palace Garrison Minister Zhang While Enduring Rain in the Residence of Princess Yuzhen." It can be difficult to express certain complaints in direct conversation, but in the delicate, or even brusque, artistic language of poetry, such complaints can be easier for the listener to accept. As for the listener, one can hear what one hears, and not hear what one should not hear; the choice is with the reader. As for the speaker, one can say what one can say, and one can also say that which one should not say; this is the authority of the poet. Poetry has its uses. In his poem, Li Bai said: "In the autumn, I sit in the golden hall of

李白居住安陆约有十年的时间，开元二十年（732）前后，他决定到都城长安去谋求出路，实现自己辅佐明君的愿望。诗人离开安陆，经过南阳，向长安进发。一路上，结交地方官员，广交诗友。此后他的行踪主要是来往长安、洛阳以及附近的地区。

唐帝国的首都长安规模宏大，宫殿华美，园林秀丽，商业发达，不仅是全国的政治经济中心，也是文学艺术的中心。唐代许多诗人都到过长安，在那里逗留，并写下了许多歌咏长安的诗篇。

李白来到长安后，试图获得玉真公主的援引。他住进了玉真公主在终南山的一座别墅中。玉真公主是唐玄宗的胞妹，兄妹感情非常融洽。玉真公主好道，后出家，并在长安附近的终南山建造了玉真公主别馆。公主喜欢结交文人雅士，著名诗人王维、高适等均拜访过公主并赠诗。

安排李白住在玉真公主别馆的人，李白诗中称他为张卿，当是玉真公主的丈夫，但他的名字无法知道。卿是尊称。一说张卿即是张垍（jì）。张垍是皇室宁亲公主的丈夫、当时著名的文士张说的儿子，他安排李白暂住在玉真公主的别馆也有可能。

令人失望的是李白在馆中住了些时日，始终没能见到玉真公主。李白内心非常郁闷，于是写了《玉真公主别馆苦雨赠卫尉张卿》二首。有些抱怨的话，在直接交谈中很难说出口，在诗中却可以委婉别致或者略显唐突——也就是相当艺术地说出来，听者比较容易接受。对于听者，可听的听着，不可听的不听，权且当诗读；对于说者，可说的说了，不可说的亦可说，权且是作诗。诗有诗的作用。李白诗曰："秋坐金张馆，繁阴

Zhang / The lush shadows do not open in the daytime / Empty fog hides the rainy scene / Desolate wind arrives as I gaze." Autumn wind and dismal rain, frigid and dark; Li Bai does not say: "I keep waiting for you, Minister Zhang!" He says that, as he gazes for his arrival, a desolate breeze comes. He is very subtle. During his long wait, he had only wine to relieve him of his sorrow: "Drinking along, I try to encourage myself / Who values talent in statecraft?" Li Bai is again very direct, asking him why he does not value someone with such talent as himself. A retainer of the Warring States Period feudal lord Meng Chang named Feng Xuan was ignored, and so he tapped his sword and sang: "Long sword, go back home. There is no fish with my meals here!" Upon hearing of this, Lord Meng Chang began to value him. Li Bai finishes with: "Sir Xie, tapping his sword / No fish, it is such a pity." This is to say, if you do not begin to value me, I will leave.

Li Bai presented a poem, "Lyric on Immortal Yuzhen," to Princess Yuzhen. The poem praised the princess, calling her a true immortal with great cultivation, describing how she ascended Mount Hua, riding on the clouds and vapors, disappearing in an instant. Nonetheless, he did not see any hope. Li Bai also asked other royalty and officials for help, but nothing came of it.

The first time Li Bai entered the capital, he stayed approximately two years, but it resulted in nothing. After that, he traveled around Binzhou and Fangzhou, and composed many poems on themes of being underappreciated and hopeless. In "Presented to a Youth of Xinping," he first recounted the story of the famous Han Dynasty general Han Xin. In his early years, Han Xin endured humiliation: "His body bent as though it had no bones." Despite this, on the inside, "His lofty aspirations had a foundation." These aspirations did not diminish, and in the end, "Upon meeting the grand emperor / He excelled from hence on." Li Bai sighed: "And what of my own situation / Cold and bitter, I sit here still / The long wind enters my short sleeves / My arms are cold as ice." It is not difficult to detect how dire his situation had become, but he never forgot his goals. "When will I ride upon the winds / To fight for that of which I am capable." In "Presented to Guo Jiying," he also wrote: "Ashamed to peck for food with the chickens / I keep company with the phoenixes / One strike, nine thousand yards / I plan on soaring in the purple haze." Despite his down and out situation, Li Bai longed to realize his ambitions, and would not give up his dreams.

He continued to travel about, like a herdsman "following the water and grass," seeking an opportunity. He left the capital and traveled by boat down the Yellow River. Arriving in the Liang and Song region, he visited the Ping

昼不开。空烟迷雨色，萧飒望中来。"秋风凄雨，一片阴沉，李白不说"我一直在苦等你张卿呵"，而是说，我在"望"中等来了阵阵萧飒。说得很含蓄。漫长等待，他只有借酒浇愁："独酌聊自勉，谁贵经纶才？"说得又很直接，意思是说像我这样的满腹经纶的人才，你为什么不重视呢？战国时期孟尝君的一个门客叫冯谖（xuān），颇受冷遇，于是弹着自己的剑唱着："长剑呀，回家吧，在这里吃饭没有鱼呀！"孟尝君于是对他开始重视起来。李白最后说："弹剑谢公子，无鱼良可哀。"那是在说，再这样轻视我，我就离开了。

　　李白又给玉真公主赠诗《玉真仙人词》。诗中对公主热情称颂，说玉真公主真是仙人，西上华山，腾云驾雾，转瞬间就不见了踪影，修炼的功夫很深。但他并没有看到任何希望。李白又向其他的王公大臣请求，但都没有什么结果。

　　李白第一次入京活动，大约持续了两年的时间，但毫无结果。随后游历邠州、坊州等地，写下的诗篇多以不遇知音、深感失意为主题。在《赠新平少年》诗中，他首先回忆汉代名将韩信的故事，韩信早年忍受欺凌，"屈体若无骨"，可是，他内在的"壮心有所凭"，始终没有消失，终于"一遭龙颜君，啸咤从此兴"，成就大业。李白自叹："而我竟何为，寒苦坐相仍？长风入短袂，内手如怀冰。"不难看出，他的境况很差。但他仍然不忘自己的理想，"何时腾风云，搏击申所能？"他在《赠郭季鹰》诗中也说："耻将鸡并食，长与凤为群。一击九千仞，相期凌紫氛。"对于诗人而言，在这种落魄失意的境况下，依然执著于自己的志愿，渴望实现自我的价值，确实难能可贵。

　　诗人到处奔走，席不暇暖，如同牧民"逐水草"一样，寻找用世的机会。他离开京城乘舟自黄河东下，到达梁宋，游览

Terrace at Liang Garden (in modern Shangqiu, Henan Province), where he composed "Song on the Liang Garden" :

> I float upon the Yellow River, leaving behind the palaces of the capital;
> Hanging the sails, I wish to enter the mountainous waves.
> The sky is high and the water broad, as I travel into the distance;
> Visiting ancient sites, I come to Ping Terrace.
> Ping Terrace mourns for the traveler;
> Facing the wine, I compose "Song of Liang Garden."

Thinking of his unknown future, his wife and children, whom he has left behind, and how he was in a strange land, he asked: "The road back west is long; how can I arrive?" He could not help feeling sad. With a turn of the writing brush, though, he continues:

> In fulfilling one's destiny, what time is there for sorrow?
> Better to drink fine wine and climb a tall pavilion.
> A flat headed Hun boy waves a large fan;
> Summer is not hot; I think there is a light breeze.
> A jade platter of red bayberries is laid out for me;
> Wu salt like blossoms, white as snow.
> Holding salt and grasping the wine, I drink it all;
> Do not follow the example of Yi and Qi, serving their own unsullied
reputation.
> The ancients praised and honored their lord Xinling;
> Today, people plow and plant on Xinling's grave.
> ...
> Palaces and courts of the Liang king, where are they now?
> Mei and Sima have left already, not waiting for others.

The palaces of Liang Garden have long since burnt down to ashes, and Mei Sheng and Sima Xiangru, who in their time were valued retainers of the king of Liang, have long since departed the human realm. The Lord Xinling of the state of Wei during Warring States Period was famous throughout the realm, but today, people farm on his grave mound. Those who comprehend fate have no time to feel sorry for themselves, so he might as well just enjoy his wine! At the end of the poem, though, Li Bai still cannot forget his life's goal: "To lie high upon the Eastern Mountain, it is time to arise / If you wish to save the common people, do not be late!" Xie An (alias: Anshi) of the Eastern Jin was a debonair scholar, skilled at statecraft. Because he often had views that conflicted with

梁园遗迹古平台（故址在今河南商丘）。游赏之际，他写下了
《梁园吟》：

> 我浮黄河去京阙，挂席欲进波连山。
>
> 天长水阔厌远涉，访古始及平台间。
>
> 平台为客忧思多，对酒遂作《梁园歌》。

李白想到自己前途未卜，离妻别子，身在异乡，自问"路远西
归安可得"？不禁愁云满布。但诗人笔锋一转，却云：

> 人生达命岂暇愁！且饮美酒登高楼。
>
> 平头奴子摇大扇，五月不热疑清秋。
>
> 玉盘杨梅为君设，吴盐如花皎白雪。
>
> 持盐把酒但饮之，莫学夷齐事高洁。
>
> 昔人豪贵信陵君，今人耕种信陵坟。
>
>
> 梁王宫阙今安在？枚、马先归不相待。

他说，梁园宫殿早已灰飞烟灭，枚乘、司马相如当时都是梁
王的宾客，备受宠幸，如今也早已不在人间。战国时期魏国
的信陵君当年名闻天下，如今人们却在他的墓地上种庄稼。
领悟命运的人哪有时间去发愁呢，还是畅饮美酒吧！但在诗
的结尾处，李白还是念念不忘他的终身志向："东山高卧时起
来，欲济苍生未应晚。"东晋谢安（字安石）风流儒雅，富有政
治才能，但屡屡与朝旨不合，便高卧东山。时人都说："安石不

those of the court, he retired to Eastern Mountain. At the time, people said: "If Anshi is not willing to come out, what will the common people do?" When he was over forty years old, he finally came out and served as general for Huan Wen. In the battle of Feishui, he defeated the enemy, turning the tables. Li Bai compares himself to Xie An, hoping to "save the common people."

In late fall, Li Bai arrived at Luoyang. As usual, he met with disappointment. Luoyang has a famous site called Longmen. Legend says that this is where the Great Yu excavated a hole through the mountain to drain the great floodwaters. Li Bai stayed in the Longmen area until winter. One day, he drank wine and became very drunk in a guesthouse. In the middle of the night, he suddenly awoke, got up, and looked out the window, upon which he saw snow blowing and ice on the river. In a moment of lament, he composed "Expressing My Intentions After I Awoke One Winter Evening Drunk While Staying in a Guesthouse in Longmen" :

> I came drunk and removed my jade sword;
> Staying in a tavern, sleeping in a fine room.
> In the middle of the night, I suddenly awoke;
> I arose and lit the lamp before me.
> Opening the window and standing up straight;
> Dawn snow, the river ice grand.
> Sadly singing the pains of the cold;
> Melancholy, I suffer my sorrow alone.
>
> ...
>
> And why am I doing this;
> Sighing at the foot of Longmen?
> Wealth and success cannot be anticipated;
> To whom can I write of my sorrows?
> Leave, go away, tears soaking my lapel;
> Raising my voice, singing of Liang Fu.
> The dark clouds should clear of themselves;
> What need have I to seek a true friend?

Du Fu's poems are often melancholy and profound, describing the hardships of life, but Li Bai's poems are bold and uninhibited, describing the luxury. Li Bai, however, also had his down and out days. This poem is very expressive of his true life. In his poem "Twenty-two Rhymes Respectfully Presented to Assistant Director of the Left Wei," Du Fu wrote: "In the morning, I knock on the doors of rich children / In the evening, I follow in the dust of fat horses / Leftover cups and cold roast / All about is the hidden pain of sorrow." Such a scene is

肯出，将如苍生何？"四十多岁，始出任桓温司马。淝水之战，扭转乾坤，克敌有功。李白自比谢安，渴望着能像当年的谢安那样，实现"济苍生"的梦想。

深秋时节，李白到达洛阳，依旧是报国无门，前景暗淡。洛阳附近有一名胜叫龙门，传说是大禹疏导洪水时开凿龙门山留下的遗迹。李白在龙门一带逗留到冬天。一日饮酒大醉，宿于客栈，但半夜时分，诗人忽然惊醒，于是起身开窗，寒风阵阵，晓雪河冰。李白无限感慨，作《冬夜醉宿龙门觉起言志》诗：

　　醉来脱宝剑，旅憩高堂眠。

　　中夜忽惊觉，起立明灯前。

　　开轩聊直立，晓雪河冰壮。

　　哀哀歌苦寒，郁郁独惆怅。

　　而我胡为者？叹息龙门下。

　　富贵未可期，殷忧向谁写？

　　去去泪满襟，举声梁甫吟。

　　青云当自致，何必求知音？

杜甫诗歌沉郁顿挫，多写愁苦生活；李白诗歌清雄豪放，好叙奢华场面。然而李白自有与杜甫一样失意落魄的日子，这首诗颇能见出李白生活真实的一面。杜甫《奉赠韦左丞二十二韵》中说："朝扣富儿门，暮随肥马尘。残杯与冷炙，到处潜悲辛。"

seldom found in Li Bai's poems. Du Fu exposes his wounds for others to see. When Li Bai is at the end of his options, he simply says: "The great road is like the blue sky / Only I have no way out." When he is not able to go any further, he just says: "Wishing to cross the Yellow River, it is jammed with ice / Ready to climb Mount Taihang, it is covered in snow." Right after that, though, he continues to sing in a voice full of optimism and hope: "The strong wind will break the waves sometime soon / Raise the cloud sails, and mount the broad sea." He believes that there will be a day when he can ride the winds to break through the waves, and he will be able to raise his sails and cross the great sea to reach the shores of his ambitions. How moving it is when the poet smiles through his tears. One cannot help but reread "The Road Is Hard" one more time:

> The golden goblet of clear wine, ten thousand cash a pitcher;
> A jade platter of rare delicacies, worth ten thousand coins.
> Lower the cup and stop the chopsticks, not able to eat;
> I pull my sword and look around, heart in a panic.
> Wishing to cross the Yellow River, it is jammed with ice;
> Ready to climb Mount Taihang, it is covered in snow.
> In leisure, come to fish on the azure stream;
> Then ride a boat to the ends of the dreamy sun.
> Difficult is the road, difficult is the road;
> Many forks in the road, where am I now?
> The strong wind will break the waves sometime soon;
> Raise the cloud sails, and mount the broad sea.

While drifting between the two capitals, Li Bai retired to Mount Zhongnan near Chang'an, and to Mount Song near Luoyang.

It has already been mentioned that, in preparing to gain positions in government, Tang scholars obtained favorable reputations by living in seclusion. This was an ancient tradition. Since the Han Dynasty, scholars in secluded retirement have received offers from the court and risen to high positions. Zhuge Liang lived in seclusion in Longzhong in his early years. He was called the "hidden dragon," and Liu Bei "three times visited his thatched hut." Three times, Liu Bei went to Zhuge Liang's place of seclusion and asked him to come down from the mountain. Later, the two worked together flawlessly, becoming an unforgettable legacy in the history. In the Liang Dynasty, Tao Hongjing lived in seclusion on Mount Mao. Liang Emperor Wu frequently approached him for advice on government. He gained the reputation of being the "minister in the mountain." These legends still served

李白诗中很少这样说。杜甫揭开创伤让别人看。李白走投无路，只是说："大道如青天，我独不得出。"诗人寸步难行，只是说："欲渡黄河冰塞川，将登太行雪满山。"紧接着，又唱出充满信心与期待的歌声："长风破浪会有时，直挂云帆济沧海！"他相信，总有一天能够乘长风破万里浪，挂上云帆，横渡沧海，到达理想的彼岸。诗人含泪的笑容多么让人感动！不能不把他的《行路难》读一遍：

> 金樽清酒斗十千，玉盘珍羞直万钱。
>
> 停杯投箸不能食，拔剑四顾心茫然。
>
> 欲渡黄河冰塞川，将登太行雪满山。
>
> 闲来垂钓碧溪上，忽复乘舟梦日边。
>
> 行路难，行路难。多歧路，今安在？
>
> 长风破浪会有时，直挂云帆济沧海！

李白奔波于两京期间，曾在长安附近的终南山和洛阳附近的嵩山隐居。

上文已说到，唐代的士人往往通过隐居生活，获得良好的名声，从而为进入仕途做好准备。这是很古老的传统。汉代以来，就有隐逸之士接受朝廷的徵辟而骤登大位的故事。诸葛亮早年隐居隆中，人称"卧龙"，刘备"三顾茅庐"——三次前往诸葛亮的隐居之所，请其出山，其后君臣相得如鱼水，成为历史上的佳话。梁代陶弘景隐于茅山，梁武帝屡屡遣使前往，咨询朝政，时号"山中宰相"。这些故事在唐代仍然有示范作

as models during the Tang Dynasty. The selection of officials during the Tang Dynasty put great value on the reputations of the candidates. Recluses were pure and unsullied. They looked lightly upon fame and fortune. It was natural that they were favored by both the court and the populace. There were many who came from the mountains and into the court. Of course, there were many kinds of recluses, including those who only wished to be carefree in the mountains and forests, not willing to step foot in the court. There were also those who falsely lived in retirement, only pretending to be recluses, although they were filled with desire for fame and fortune. Lu Cangyong used living on Mount Zhongnan to gain a reputation and become a high official in court. Later, he pointed to Mount Zhongnan and said to Sima Chengzhen: "There is great pleasure to be there." Chengzhen laughed, saying: "As I see it, it is but a shortcut to officialdom." Retirement became but a tool for seeking power and salary. For most scholars, though, retirement was to cleanse one's body and soul, cultivate one's spirit, and obtain a good reputation. Confucius said: "If you are employed, go out and do; if abandoned, then retire in seclusion." If one has the opportunity, then one should be an official and realize one's dreams and ambitions. If one does not have the opportunity, "then one can role it up and save it in one's heart," quietly cultivating oneself. Scholars of ancient times knew this very well.

While living in seclusion on Mounts Zhongnan and Song, Li Bai wrote many poems describing the natural scenery. Mount Song is a sacred site for Daoism. There are many Daoist temples on this mountain. Li Bai's good friend Yuan Danqiu lived on Mount Song. He had just built a new residence, and invited Li Bai and his family over several times. Yuan Danqiu came from an aristocratic family, and originally had great aspirations for participating in the official examinations and building a political career. After failing the examinations, he became interested in the teachings of the *Laozi* and the *Zhuangzi*, and studied the techniques of immortality. When Li Bai came to Yuan Danqiu's residence, Yingyang Mountain Resort, he found the environment to be very nice, surrounded by beautiful peaks, with clouds and cliffs reflecting off each other. In his poem "Written on Yuan Danqiu's Yingyang Mountain Resort," he wrote: "To roam with the immortals, I cross the Ying River / And visit the recluse, Sir Yuan / Suddenly, I loose the desire for common life / Only wishing to be with the overwhelming cliffs." The environment in the mountains was pure and beautiful, and Li Bai truly wished to retire there, never again minding his ambitions to serve society. In the end, though, he decided to first accomplish a grand career, and only then retire.

用。唐代选拔官员十分看重候选人的名声，隐士洁身自好，淡泊名利，自然受到朝野的推重，其中不乏从山林步入庙堂的例子。当然，隐士有多种，其中确有只想逍遥于山林之中而不愿迈入官场一步的隐士；也有虚伪的人借隐居来装样子，骨子里利欲熏心，但却假装恬淡，优游于林泉之间。卢藏用隐于终南山，成名出山，在朝廷做到很高的官。日后，他指着终南山对司马承祯说："此中大有嘉趣。"承祯讥笑说："以仆视之，仕宦之捷径耳。"隐居仅仅成了谋取利禄的工具。对于多数士人而言，隐居是洁身自好、提高素养、获得良好声誉的正常途径。孔子说："用之则行，舍之则藏。"有机会，就去做官，实现自己的理想；没有机会，"则可卷而怀之"，默默地修行。古代读书人都清楚这个道理。

李白在隐居嵩山与终南山时，写下了不少描写自然风光的诗篇。嵩山是道教圣地，上有很多著名的道观。李白的好友元丹丘就住在山中，新置别业，屡次邀请李白及其家人前来。元丹丘出身官宦之家，本有用世之心，积极参加科举考试，落第之后，喜好老庄的清净无为之学，潜心钻研神仙方术。李白来到元丹丘的别业颖阳山居，此处群山连绵，云岩掩映，环境极佳。诗人《题元丹丘颖阳山居》诗云："仙游渡颖水，访隐同元君。忽遗苍生望，独与洪崖群。"山中环境，清静优美，李白真想隐居此地，再也不提拯济苍生的志愿。但最后，他还是想在干出一番惊天动地的事业之后再来隐居。

After living in seclusion at Peach Blossom Cliff for a while, he again began to travel. In 734, he passed through Xiangyang, where he composed "Letter to Sir Han of Jingzhou," in which he introduced himself to Han Chaozong, Administrator of Xiangyang. Han Chaozong liked to recommend young scholars for official positions. Many talented scholars worked under him. At the time, there was a saying: "Students do not wish to be enfeoffed duke of ten thousand households / they only wish to meet Han of Jingzhou once." In his letter, Li Bai wrote:

> I have heard it said among scholars throughout the realm: "Students do not wish to be enfeoffed duke of ten thousand households / they only wish to meet Han of Jingzhou once." What causes people to respect and admire you to this extent? Is it that you are like the Duke of Zhou, spitting your food and pulling your hair so that the great heroes of the realm come rushing to you? Once they ascend to your household, their reputations grow ten times. Thus, the scholars who lie like dragons and are leisurely as phoenixes all wish to base their value on Your Highness. I hope that Your Highness does not spoil them with riches or ignore them in the cold. Among the three thousand guests, there is a Mao Sui. If you allow me to break out, I will be your person.

Mao Sui was a self-introduced retainer of Lord Pingyuan of Zhao during the Warring States Period. Lord Pingyuan said that virtuous gentlemen are like awls in a sack. The point of the awl will instantly poke through the sack and become visible, yet you have been in my household for three years and have not yet shown your abilities. Mao Sui responded, saying that is because you have not yet placed me in sack. Had you placed me in a sack, I would have pushed through and revealed myself long ago. Later, he did indeed bring great honor to the state of Zhao. It was said of Mao Sui that "his three-inch tongue can match for one million warriors." ❶ Li Bai was full of self-confidence, and saw himself as equal to Mao Sui, soon to reveal himself. He then continued to say:

> I am a commoner of Longxi, stranded in Chu and Han. At fifteen, I enjoyed swordplay and meeting lords. At thirty, my compositions were perfected and submitted to ministers. Even though I am not fully seven feet tall, I have the ambitions of ten thousand men. Noblemen and grand officials all recognize my righteousness. How dare I not commit this true mind of the ancients to Your Highness? The works of Your Highness equal the divine, and Your actions move the heavens and

　　李白在桃花岩隐居了一段时间后，再次出游。开元二十二年（734），他路过襄阳，撰写了著名的《与韩荆州书》，拜会大都督府长史兼襄阳刺史韩朝宗。韩朝宗喜好提拔青年，许多有才能的人都愿意到他的府下做事，当时就有"生不愿封万户侯，但愿一识韩荆州"的说法。李白文中说：

　　　　白闻天下谈士相聚而言曰："生不用万户侯，但愿一识韩荆州。"何令人之景慕一至于此耶！岂不以有周公之风，躬吐握之事，使海内豪俊奔走而归之，一登龙门，则声誉十倍。所以龙盘凤逸之士，皆欲收名定价于君侯。愿君侯不以富贵而骄之，寒贱而忽之，则三千宾中有毛遂，使白能颖脱而出，即其人焉。

毛遂是战国时期赵国平原君的门客，曾自荐于平原君。平原君说：贤士处世，譬如锥子装在囊中，锥尖立刻就能刺破布囊而露出来。但你来了三年，没有看见你有什么作为。毛遂说：那是因为没有把我装入囊中，早使我处于囊中，乃脱颖而出。后来他果然为赵国争得了很大荣誉。人们都说毛遂"三寸之舌，强于百万之师"❶。李白把自己看成是将会脱颖而出的毛遂，充满自信。诗人接着说：

　　　　白陇西布衣，流落楚汉。十五好剑术，遍干诸侯；三十成文章，历抵卿相。虽长不满七尺，而心雄万夫。王公大臣许以气义。此畴曩（nǎng）心迹，安敢不尽于君侯哉！君侯制作侔神明，德行动天地，笔参造化，学

---

❶《史记·平原君列传》。

❶ *Shi Ji* (*Records of the Grand Historian*), "Biography of the Lord Pingyuan."

earth; Your compositions examine creation, and Your scholarship examines heaven and man. I hope that Your Highness opens your heart, and does not use common standards. If necessary, invite me to a banquet and engage me in theoretical discussion, or submit me to a ten-thousand word examination while riding on horseback. The scholars of the realm look at the orders of Your Highness when composing, and Your judgement in their actions. If one can pass Your Highness's valuations, one is a fine scholar. Why then would Your Highness not spare a foot of space before You to allow me to raise my brows and expel my breath, to rise above the white clouds?

Han Chaozong was famous for valuing scholars, so Li Bai went to extremes to praise his moral actions and literary compositions. He also said that Han needed only to invite him to a banquet and listen to his expositions, or allow him to write poems and compositions, and he would instantly recognize Li Bai's talent. Li Bai also called Han Chaozong the leader of all scholars, saying that if one is able to pass Han's "valuations", "one is a fine scholar" and one's worth will increase one hundred times. Why then would Han of Jingzhou be concerned over a small official position and not allow Li Bai to "raise my brows and expel my breath, to rise above the white clouds?" In the end, though, Li Bai did not gain the recommendation of Han Chaozong.

In 735, Li Bai was already thirty-five years old when he accepted the invitation of his intimate friend Yuan Yan, and traveled north to Taiyuan. The two crossed over Mount Taihang and arrived in Shanxi. Yuan Yan's father was the Administrator of Taiyuan at the time, and Li Bai stayed with the Yuan family, where the host was very hospitable: "Jade cup and extravagant food on a green jade table / Allowed me to be drunk and satiated, with no desire to return home." After eating and drinking his fill, Li Bai had no intention of returning home. He traveled together with Yuan Yan, visiting all of the famous locations: "Often going out to the west of the city wall / The flowing water of the Jin Shrine is like emerald jade / Floating a boat and playing in the water, the pipes and drums sound / Fine waves like dragon scales, reeds on the bar are green." He was still excited when he later recalled this trip in "Remembering a Trip from Before, Sent to Adjutant Yuan."

Not much later, Li Bai returned to Anlu.

At the end of the Kaiyuan administration, Li Bai's wife, whose family

究天人。幸愿开张心颜，不以长揖见拒。必若接之以高
宴，纵之以清谈，请日试万言，倚马可待。今天下以
君侯为文章之司命，人物之权衡，一经品题，便作佳
士。而君侯何惜阶前盈尺之地，不使白扬眉吐气，激
昂青云耶？

韩朝宗以好士著称，李白极力称赞他的道德文章，并说只要他
设宴款待，听其清谈，或者让自己赋诗作文，立刻可以看出自
己的才能。又称他是士林宗主，士子一旦经过他的评价"品题"，
"便作佳士"而身价百倍，那么，韩荆州何必在乎一个小官的
职位，而不使李白"扬眉吐气，激昂青云"呢！但最终，李白
还是没有获得韩朝宗的推荐。

　　开元二十三年（735），李白已经三十五岁。应挚友元演邀
请，他北游至太原。两人一起翻越太行山来到山西。元演之父
时任太原府尹，李白就住在元家，主人招待得很热情："琼杯
绮食青玉案，使我醉饱无归心。"李白酒足饭饱，简直不想回
家了。他们游览各处名胜："时时出向城西曲，晋祠流水如碧
玉。浮舟弄水箫鼓鸣，微波龙鳞莎草绿。"李白后来在《忆旧
游寄谯郡元参军》诗中追忆此事时，兴致仍然很高。

　　不久，李白返回安陆。

　　开元末，夫人许氏不幸去世。李白与许氏生有一子一女：

name was Xu, passed away. Li Bai and his wife had two children, one boy and one girl. His son's name was Boqin, and his daughter's name was Pingyang. The names Li Bai chose for them were very unusual. They each had special implications, either implying that they came from the west, or that they came from the Li clan. The eldest son of the Duke of Zhou was named Boqin, but Li Bai could not have intended to compare his family to that of the Duke of Zhou's when naming his son. This is something of a riddle. The Duke of Zhou's son Boqin was also named *li* (carp), which is a homophone of *li* (logic) or Li, Li Bai's family name. Li Bai's son's name "Boqin" thus implies that he belongs to the Li clan. Boqin's nickname was Mingyuenu (Bright Moon Boy), and Li Bai's little sister was called Yueyuan (Round Moon). These were both rather unusual names. The ancients believed that, since the sun rises in the east and the moon rises in the west, the moon represents the west. "Round Moon" and "Bright Moon" both represent reminiscence of Central Asia. "Nu" originally meant servant boy, but nicknames of the Southern Dynasties often used the *nu* character, and so it became a term of endearment. "Mingyuenu" therefore meant the lad from Central Asia.

Li Bai's name for his daughter, Pingyang, was also quite unusual. The Han Emperor Wudi met the dancing girl Wei Zifu at his older sister Princess Pingyang's house. Wei Zifu later gained favor through her dancing, and finally became the empress. Later generations thus used "Pingyang" to refer to girls who are good dancers. In ancient times, the social status of singers and dancers was relatively low, and they were looked down upon by scholars and the gentry. It was therefore quite unusual for Li Bai to name his daughter "Pingyang." Li Bai was deeply influenced by the culture of Central Asia, and loved singing and dancing. He often mentioned the beauty and musical skills of Central Asian entertaining girls. Such references were frequent and sincere, far surpassing such references by other poets of his time. One cannot underestimate the implications of his naming his daughter "Pingyang."

As Li Bai had married into the Xu household, he could not stay in their household after his wife died. He brought his two children to the Qi and Lu regions (modern Shandong area), and lived in Rencheng and Shaqiu (near modern Jining, Shandong Province). It is unimaginable to let drunken, wild, and uninhibited Li Bai take care of two young children. Li Bai lived with a young woman named Liu, and then with a woman from Eastern Lu, asking them to take care of his children. He even had a son with the latter, whom he named Poli. Later, he married a woman named Zong.

儿子名伯禽，女儿叫平阳。李白为孩子取名非常特别，都有一定的寓意，或寓来自西方之意，或寓姓李的意思。周公长子叫伯禽，但李白不大可能给儿子取名伯禽，而自比儒家圣人周公。这里有点像谜语，伯禽名鲤，谐音"理"或"李"字。李白之子名"伯禽"，暗含着姓氏"李"字。伯禽的小名叫明月奴，李白妹妹叫月圆，都十分奇特。古人以为，日出于东，月生于西，月象征着西方。"月圆"、"明月"都包含着对出生之地西域的怀恋。"奴"本是奴仆的意思，但南北朝人的小名多用"奴"字，于是成了昵称。明月奴即指从西方来的小家伙。

李白给他的娇女取名平阳，也十分别样。汉武帝在他的姐姐平阳公主家中，遇见了舞姬卫子夫。卫子夫后以歌舞得宠，最终成了皇后，后世即以"平阳"表示能歌善舞的女子。中国古代，歌舞艺人的地位较低，受到士大夫的轻视。李白给女儿取名"平阳"，自然少见。李白深受西域文化的影响，热爱音乐歌舞。他在诗中经常提到胡姬的美貌和乐技，出现的频率之高，态度之热烈，远远超过其他同时代的诗人。他为女儿取名"平阳"，也就不足为怪了。

妻子去世，李白作为赘婿，难以在许家再住下去了。他带着两个孩子，到了齐鲁（今山东一带），在任城和沙丘（今山东济宁附近）居住过。让痛饮狂歌、豪放不羁的李白照料两个年幼的孩子，简直不可想象。李白先后与一个女子刘氏以及东鲁当地的妇人同居，请其照顾孩子。还与后者生有一子，取名颇黎。后来，李白再娶宗氏女。

During this period, Li Bai lived in retirement on Mount Culai with Kong Chaofu, Han Zhun, Pei Zheng, Zhang Shuming, and Tao Mian. At the time, they were known as "the six recluses of Bamboo Creek." Mount Culai was a famous mountain for recluses. At the time, a famous scholar, Wang Xiyi, lived in retirement there. When Tang Emperor Xuanzong came to review this area, he held audience with Wang Xiyi. The emperor had a very pleasant conversation with this ninety-year-old recluse, and even appointed him Erudite of the National University. Even though Mount Culai was remote, it was located along a major thoroughfare between the capital and Shandong, and so recluses could gain notoriety throughout the empire quickly.

Li Bai spent some time in retirement and some time roaming about, waiting for that one life-altering change in fortune. He told his friend: "We have each not yet met with the lord / So plan on living on wild greens for a long time / The rare sword lays hidden in the jade case / Rusting and tainted by the mold / Thus allow the foolish in the world / To look lightly upon me as dirt and ash / One day, the climbing dragon leaves / Where will the frogs and toads be?" ❶ Many compositions from this period displayed expressions of dissatisfaction at not receiving recognition of his talents: "The Chu person did not recognize the phoenix / And bought a mountain chicken for a high price" ❷; "The state of Lu, but a cup of water / Cannot contain a scale that crosses the sea / Zhongni is not respected / Not to say a common person / White jade is exchanged for a catty of rice / Gold is spent on a yard of kindling" ❸; "The Song man could not differentiate jade / The people of Lu thought little of Qiu from the east." ❹ The man from Chu did not know what a phoenix looked like, and ended up buying a wild chicken for a high price to present to the king of Chu. The king of Chu was moved, and rewarded him with ten times the cost of the wild chicken. The man from Song did not know what valuable jade looked like, so when he found a common piece of quartz, he treated it as a treasure. The people of Lu did not know to respect the true sage, Confucius, and treated him as only Qiu from the eastern family, calling him a lost dog. The fools of the world do not value such a talent as myself, looking down on me as dirt and ash. One cannot know how many times the poet was ignored or maltreated for him to be so indignant.

这期间，李白曾与孔巢父、韩准、裴政、张叔明、陶沔（miǎn）等隐于徂（cú）徕（lái）山，时称"竹溪六逸"。徂徕是逸人栖隐的名山，当时一位高士王希夷就隐居在这里。唐玄宗巡游到此，曾接见王希夷。皇帝与九十多岁的隐士谈得很开心，拜他为国子博士。可知徂徕山虽然僻静，但位处京师与山东的要道，故隐者的声名颇能上达天听。

李白时而栖居山林，时而辗转各地，等待着那个根本不知道会不会降临的命运转折。他与朋友说："与君各未遇，长策委蒿莱。宝刀隐玉匣，锈涩空莓苔。遂令世上愚，轻我土与灰。一朝攀龙去，蛙黾（mǐn）安在哉！"❶ 此时许多作品都充满着怀才不遇的哀叹："楚人不识凤，重价求山鸡"❷；"鲁国一杯水，难容横海鳞。仲尼且不敬，况乃寻常人？白玉换斗粟，黄金买尺薪"❸；"宋人不辨玉，鲁贱东家丘。"❹ 楚国人不认识凤凰，高价买了一只山鸡，献给楚王，楚王深受感动，赏赐给他十倍山鸡的价钱。宋国人不晓得宝玉，得到一块燕石，如获至宝。而真正的圣人孔子，鲁国人却不知道尊重，视为东家丘，称为丧家犬。世上愚蠢的人也不知道赏识我的才能，把我视为土与灰。诗人如此激愤，真不知道受到了多少冷遇！

---

❶ 李白《酬张卿夜宿南陵见赠》。
❷ 李白《赠从弟冽》。
❸ 李白《送鲁郡刘长史迁弘农长史》。
❹ 李白《送薛九被谗去鲁》。

---

❶ Li Bai, "Presented in Thanks to Minister Zhang When Spending the Night in Nanling."
❷ Li Bai, "Presented to My Cousin Lie."
❸ Li Bai, "Seeing Lu Regional Administrator Liu off to Be Transferred to Be Hongnong Administrator."
❹ Li Bai, "See off Xue the Ninth as He Left Lu After Being Slandered."

李白画像

Portrait of Li Bai

五　翰林：我辈岂是蓬蒿人

Chapter V　Hanlin Academy: Am I but a Man of the
　　　　　　Wilds?

In 742, Li Bai finally received good news: Emperor Xuanzong invited him to Chang'an to be in the Hanlin Academy.

Li Bai was extremely excited, and departed immediately for the capital, composing "Leaving My Children in Nanling to Leave for the Capital" as he left:

> White wine freshly mature, retired to the mountains;
> Yellow chickens peck at grain, perfectly plump in the fall.
> I call the boy to cook the chickens, and prepare some white wine;
> Sons and daughters laugh and smile, pulling at my clothes.
> Singing loudly to bring on inebriation, wishing to comfort myself;
> I rise to dance as the sun goes down, struggling to give off light.
> Canvassing the thousand chariots, I regret it could not have been earlier;
> Grab my whip and mount my horse, departing for the long journey.
> The foolish woman of Kuaiji underestimated Maichen;
> I too leave home, going west to enter Qin.
> Raising my head to the heavens, I laugh as I exit the door;
> How could I have been a man of the wilds!

It was the fall harvest, and the newly fermented white wine was beginning to give off its fragrance, and the yellow chickens were growing plump. It was a perfect time to make merry with good wine and fine food, so he called on the houseboy to prepare a feast as his children laughed and tugged at his clothes. Singing loudly, drinking himself into a frenzy, he could not help himself from getting up and dancing into the night. The joy and excitement in the poem communicates the exhilaration of the poet as he was about to depart for the capital. The poet longed to exercise his talents and fulfill his lifelong ambitions. This day has finally arrived! But Li Bai was already over forty years old, and he could not help feeling "regret that it could not have been earlier." He could not wait to grab his whip and jump on his horse to leave immediately. He then mentions the story of Zhu Maichen. Zhu Maichen was a poor scholar of the Han Dynasty who relied on selling firewood for a living. By the time he was over forty years old, his wife looked down upon him and demanded a divorce. Zhu Maichen pleaded with his wife, saying: "I will certainly become rich and successful by the time I reach fifty. I am now

天宝元年（742），李白终于迎来了喜讯：唐玄宗下诏，请他到长安供奉翰林。

李白万分高兴，急忙进京，临行前作《南陵别儿童入京》一诗：

> 白酒新熟山中归，黄鸡啄黍秋正肥。
>
> 呼童烹鸡酌白酒，儿女嬉笑牵人衣。
>
> 高歌取醉欲自慰，起舞落日争光辉。
>
> 游说万乘苦不早，著鞭跨马涉远道。
>
> 会稽愚妇轻买臣，余亦辞家西入秦。
>
> 仰天大笑出门去，我辈岂是蓬蒿人！

时值秋熟季节，新酿的白酒开始飘香，黄鸡长得肉满膘肥，正好美酒佳肴欢喜一番。于是召唤童仆置办酒席，小儿女则嬉笑着牵扯他的衣衫。高歌欢唱，豪饮沉醉，情不自禁欢快起舞，直到日落山头。诗中描写的欢快热闹的场景，淋漓尽致地表达了诗人将赴京城的狂喜。诗人渴望着自己的才能能够得到发挥，实现多年来的雄心壮志。这一天终于到来了！然而李白已经四十多岁，不能不使他感到"苦不早"，真恨不得提鞭跨马立即启程。接着诗人提到了朱买臣的故事。汉代朱买臣家贫好学，靠卖柴度日，直到四十多岁还没有发迹，妻子轻视他，提出离婚。朱买臣劝妻子说："我五十岁一定会富贵，现在已经四十

already over forty, so you need only wait a little longer. I will certainly repay you in the future." His wife did not listen, and left him. Later, Zhu Maichen did become a high official. Li Bai's literary talent was second to none, and he had great ambitions, yet over the years of roaming north and south, destitute and forlorn, the women with whom he lived looked down upon him, just as Zhu Maichen's wife did. Finally, he was received by the emperor, and was headed west to Chang'an. "Raising my head to the heavens, I laugh as I exit the door," Li Bai expresses his joy and optimism.

Why was Li Bai so lucky this time? Why did the emperor suddenly think of recruiting him? There are different explanations. One explanation is that a friend of Li Bai, the Daoist priest Wu Yun, was invited to the court, and he recommended Li Bai to the emperor, Xuanzong. This story does not fit the historical records, though, so it is not reliable. Another explanation is that Princess Yuzhen recommended him. Yet another saying is that Li Bai's reputation had traveled throughout the realm, and so the emperor called him for a palace audience. In "Petition to Self Recommend to Vice Censor-in-chief Song," Li Bai said: "In the early years of the Tianbao administration . . . my reputation reached the capital. His Highness heard of it and was pleased, and so called me for a palace audience." In "Preface to *The Collected Works of Li Taibai*," Wei Hao said that Li Bai's invitation to be a Hanlin academician was due to the recommendation of Princess Yuzhen. Wei Hao was a strong admirer of Li Bai, and much of his information came directly from Li Bai, so the saying that Princess Yuzhen recommended him is the most believable. Of course, the emperor's decision could have been influenced by other factors. Later, in "Given to Revenue Manager Cui Wen Kunji," Li Bai said: "Before, I did not ingratiate myself / With staff and umbrella, I entered Qin to the west / The climbing dragon mounts the nine heavens / Becoming one of the heavenly constellations." "I did not ingratiate myself" means he did not curry favor through others, but relied solely on his own reputation when he was recognized by the emperor. He was very satisfied with this. This is also the most admirable quality of Li Bai's personality.

Li Bai was extraordinarily excited, and saw this as an opportunity to "canvass the thousand chariots." He thought that he could rely on his own talent to influence the ruler and his ministers to realize his dream of "defining the world and clarifying the boundaries." He believed that the age of the Warring States ministers-errant had returned.

This time, Li Bai came to the capital with a different social status. Looking about, he found everything to be new and exciting. Many of his later

多岁了，再忍耐些时日，将来一定好好报答你。"妻子不听，离开了朱买臣。后来买臣果然做了高官。李白文才盖世，抱负远大，然而此前南北奔波，失意落魄，同居的妇人就像朱买臣的妻子一样轻视他。如今自己终于得到皇帝的礼遇，西入长安了。"仰天大笑出门去"，生动地写出了诗人的喜悦和对前途充满的希望。

李白此时为什么如此幸运，皇帝怎么会突然想起来要徵召他呢？说法不同。一说是李白的一位朋友吴筠道士，被召入京，于是他就在玄宗面前推荐李白。但这与传记记载不合，故不太可信。一说是玉真公主推荐。一说是李白名播海内，玄宗于是便殿召见。李白在《为宋中丞自荐表》中说："天宝初……名动京师，上闻而悦之，召入禁掖。"魏颢《李太白集序》中说李白入京为翰林供奉，出于玉真公主所荐。魏颢是李白的崇拜者，记载的事迹多出自李白自述，故玉真公主推荐一说最为可信。当然，玄宗的决定可能还受到其他方面的影响。李白后来在《赠崔司户文昆季》诗中说："惟昔不自媒，担簦西入秦。攀龙九天上，忝列岁星臣。""不自媒"的意思是没有钻营，完全凭借自己的名声而得到皇帝的重视，他对这一点很满意。这也是李白人格中最为可贵的地方。

李白异常兴奋，将这次进京完全看做是"游说万乘"的机会，以为凭着自己的才能，一定可以说动人主，实现"寰（huán）区大定，海县清一"的理想。他相信，战国游说之士纵横驰骋（chěng）的时代又来临了。

此时，李白是以新的身份来到京城，看着四周的景象，处处使他感到耳目一新。他后来的诗作中对此多有描述。《赠从

poems describe this time. The first poem of "Presented to Cousin Zhiyao, Governor of Nanping" says:

> The Son of Heaven of the Han family drove a team of horses;
> A scarlet chariot on the road to Shu, to welcome Xiangru.
> The nine levels of heavenly gates opened to the sage;
> One look at the dragon's face, spring blossomed throughout the
> Four Seas.
> In the Red Court, left and right , all called "Long Life! "
> Greeting the enlightened ruler, receiving the heavy burden.
> The Hanlin holds the brush, face full of anticipation;
> The Chimera Pavilion is lofty and towering; who can see it?
> Receiving favor, I initially enter the Silver Terrace Gate;
> Writing documents alone in Golden Bell Palace.
> The dragon foal, carved stirrup, and white jade saddle;
> Ivory bed, damask seat cushion, and golden trays.
> Those who, back then, laughed at my humble lowlyness;
> Now come and request meetings, happy to interact.

In "Presented to Recluse Yang After the Carriage Left Hot Springs Palace," he wrote:

> One day, the ruler brushes me away;
> Broken heart flows red, my bosom is snow.
> Suddenly receiving the brilliant sun's reflected rays;
> Straight up to the white clouds, I sprout wings.
> Having the honor to accompany the phoenix chariot, exiting the
> Crane Capital;
> Mounted on a flying dragon, with heavenly colt horse.
> Aristocrats and officials put on faces;
> With golden seal and purple ribbon, they come to see me.
> Back when we first met, one after another;
> In a few words, we are friends; we had only the lord.
> Wait until I have done my best to repay my enlightened ruler;
> And then we will hold hands, lying on white clouds.

When Sima Xiangru entered Chang'an from Chengdu, he wrote on the city gate: "If I am not riding a scarlet chariot with a team of horses, I will not pass through you again." Later, he did receive the favor of the emperor, and was continually employed. Now, Li Bai had also received the recognition of the emperor and entered the Hanlin Academy, just like Sima Xiangru. The Hanlin

弟南平太守之遥二首》其一：

> 汉家天子驰驷马，赤车蜀道迎相如。
> 天门九重谒圣人，龙颜一顾四海春。
> 彤庭左右呼万岁，拜贺明主收沉沦。
> 翰林秉笔回英盼，麟阁峥嵘谁可见？
> 承恩初入银台门，著书独在金銮殿。
> 龙驹雕镫白玉鞍，象床绮席黄金盘。
> 当时笑我微贱者，却来请谒为交欢。

《驾去温泉官后送杨山人》曰：

> 一朝君王垂拂拭，剖心输丹雪胸臆。
> 忽蒙白日回景光，直上青云生羽翼。
> 幸陪鸾辇出鸿都，身骑飞龙天马驹。
> 王公大人借颜色，金章紫绶来相趋。
> 当时结交何纷纷，片言道合唯有君。
> 待吾尽节报明主，然后相携卧白云。

司马相如从成都初入长安，题市门曰："不乘赤车驷马，不过汝下也。"后来，果然受到皇帝的宠信，不断得到重用。李白如今也像司马相如一样受到朝廷的垂顾，入侍翰林。翰林院在

Academy was in the Silver Terrace Gate, which is why Li Bai said "Receiving the favor, I initially enter the Silver Terrace Gate." The academicians work in the Golden Bell Palace, and receive fine food, drink, clothing, and transportation. All those who previously looked down on Li Bai now came to see him. Why is it that a person's status could change over night? It was because he received the recognition of the emperor. In "On an Autumn Evening in the Eastern Tower of Shanfu, I See My Cousin Kuang off to Qin," he said: "The palaces of Chang'an are in the nine heavens / This place I once passed through while a close official." Now, he held a position next to the emperor, riding on a high horse, following the emperor's carriage in and out of the capital. In those times, this was certainly a great honor. Unlike most scholars, though, he did not become overly greedy despite the splendor and glory before his eyes. The poet wanted to wait until "I have done my best to repay my enlightened ruler." After giving service to his country and the people to repay the emperor for recognizing his talents, he would retire to the mountains and forests.

Li Bai's compositions also went through a great transition at this time. In the past, he was but a commoner, and could write whatever he felt like writing. Now, he was the servant of the emperor, and the contents of his compositions naturally included life in the palace.

For example, from the title of the poem "In Retinue at Yichun Garden, Commanded to Compose a Song About the Fresh Green of the Willows and the Many Songs of the Young Birds at Dragon Pond," it is obvious that this poem was written specifically at the command of the emperor. Besides this poem, others such as "Composed While in Retinue Overnighting at Warm Spring Palace" are all related to palace life. In "Meeting an Old Friend," he said:

> In the Han emperor's garden of the Changyang Palace;
> Upon return, he boasts of the game in Central Asia.
> Yang Xiong, as a humble retinue;
> Presents a rhapsody with magnificence.
> Shake the heavenly brush with vigor;
> Receive the honor of being bestowed an imperial robe.
> Meeting you, Sir, submitting it to the enlightened ruler;
> Another day, we will together ascend in flight.

He compares the Tang Emperor Xuanzong to the Han Emperor Wudi, hoping that he can be like Sima Xiangru and Yang Xiong and receive the appreciation of the emperor through his literary talent.

Li Bai's literary talent was extremely strong, and his compositions were

银台门内，所以李白说"承恩初入银台门"，又在金銮殿中撰稿著书，饮食车马都有极好的待遇。当年那些轻视自己的人，甚至王公大人都主动前来交往。为何一夜之间身份地位会有这么大的变化？只因得到了天子的徵召。《单父东楼秋夜送族弟况之秦》中说："长安宫阙九天上，此地曾经为近臣。"他现在成了天子身边的人，骑着高头大马随着皇帝的车驾出入都城，这在那个时代，无疑是极大的荣耀。不过，不同于一般士人，即使荣华富贵就在眼前，他也没有过分的贪心，诗人想到的是"尽节报明主"，在报效国家、服务社会以感激皇帝的知遇之恩之后，就归隐山林。

李白的创作如今也发生了巨大的变化。过去他只是平民百姓，想写什么就写什么；现在却是皇帝的侍臣，他吟咏的内容自然包含宫廷生活。

如《侍从宜春苑奉诏赋龙池柳色初青听新莺百啭歌》，诗题写得很清楚，这是奉了皇帝诏令专门写的诗歌。此外《侍从游宿温泉宫作》等诗都与宫廷生活有关。《逢故人》诗云：

汉帝长杨苑，夸胡羽猎归。

子云叨侍从，献赋有光辉。

激烈摇天笔，承恩赐御衣。

逢君奏明主，他日共翻飞。

他把唐玄宗比作汉武帝，希望自己也像司马相如、扬雄一样，以文学才华博得天子的赏爱。

李白的文学天赋极高，作品受到了整个朝廷特别是皇帝

praised by the entire court, especially the emperor.

This year, while the emperor and his Consort Taizhen were appreciating the palace peonies, the emperor called the palace musicians, the Pear Orchard Disciples, and the famous musician Li Guinian to perform. Holding a clapper in hand and conducting the palace musicians, Li Guinian began to sing. The emperor said: "When appreciating beautiful flowers and accompanying my concubine, how can we listen to old lyrics?" He thereby ordered Li Guinian to take a "Golden Flower Letter" to Li Bai, inviting him to compose a new song.

Li Bai enthusiastically accepted the order, and immediately submitted three songs to the tune of "Clear and Fair Melody." Even though he had not sobered completely from his drinking the night before, he still managed to easily compose:

> The clouds make one think of the gown, the blossoms make one
> think of the face;
> The spring breeze brushes the railing, the dew thick on the flowers.
> If the group of jade had not met on the mountain,
> They would have met on jade terrace under the moon.
>
> One red flower, dew congealing the fragrance;
> Clouds and rain on Mount Wu, heart broken with longing.
> Might I ask, in the Han palace, whom this resembles?
> The enchanting Feiyan, in her new rouge.
>
> A beautiful flower and a great beauty both bring each other great
> joy;
> Often receive the smiling attentions of the ruler.
> Relieving the limitless regret of the spring breeze;
> The deep fragrance north of the pavilion, leaning on the railing.

All three poems are describing the beauty of Consort Taizhen. The first line of the first poem, "The clouds make one think of the gown, the blossoms make one think of the face," is especially charming and delicate. It has become known as "Taibai's delightful realm." As soon as the poems were completed, Li Guinian rushed them back to the emperor. The emperor ordered the Pear Orchard Disciples to tune their instruments, and Li Guinian began to sing. Consort Taizhen's face lit up. With a seven-jewel glass cup full of fine Central

的推崇。

这年宫中牡丹花开，玄宗与太真妃赏玩之际，特别召集宫中乐器演奏者以及当时著名的音乐家李龟年表演歌曲。李龟年手捧檀板，指挥梨园众乐手，就要开唱，皇帝说："赏名花，对妃子，怎么能用旧的歌词呢？"于是命李龟年拿着"金花笺（jiān）"，宣赐李白，让他创作新的乐章奉上。

李白欣然承旨，立进《清平调》词三首。尽管昨夜醉酒还没有完全醒来，但他还是一挥而就：

　　云想衣裳花想容，春风拂槛露华浓。
　　若非群玉山头见，会向瑶台月下逢。

　　一枝红艳露凝香，云雨巫山枉断肠。
　　借问汉宫谁得似？可怜飞燕倚新妆。

　　名花倾国两相欢，长得君王带笑看。
　　解释春风无限恨，沉香亭北倚阑干。

三首诗都是形容太真妃之美貌，特别是开首一句"云想衣裳花想容"，风流旖旎（yǐnǐ），别致婉转，一向被称为"太白佳境"。诗写成之后，李龟年赶紧呈上。皇帝立即命梨园弟子调试琴弦管笛，李龟年即开始演唱。太真妃容光焕发，手持七宝玻璃盏，

Asian grape wine, she led the singers in song. The emperor was also enraptured, and played his jade flute in accompaniment. As each verse came to an end, he would prolong the beat to allow Consort Taizhen to draw out her voice and be even more expressive. When Consort Taizhen finished singing, she at once drank her cup of wine, gathered her scarf, and gave the emperor a deep and earnest curtsy. The emperor and consort were extremely impressed by Li Bai's lyrics.

Such opportunities were actually not so rare. One day, while the emperor was enjoying a performance by courtiers, he said to Gao Lishi: "On such a beautiful occasion, how can one make due with only flutes and strings? We ought to have songs with lyrics of a genius poet. Only then will the glory of this occasion go down in history." He then ordered Li Bai to be summoned. At this time, Li Bai was inebriated at a friend's home. After being carried to the palace, he stumbled in, barely able to bow. He was ordered to compose poems. Two palace attendants prepared brush and ink, and laid out silk for him to write on. Li Bai took hold of the brush and composed ten poems without a moment of hesitation. His writing was strong and vital, like the flight of dragons and dance of phoenixes, and the meter and structure of the verses were perfect. Here are the second and third verses of "Lyrics for Palace Music" ❶ :

> The willows are a golden delicate color;
> Pear blossoms are white fragrant snow.
> In the jade tower nest emerald parrots;
> In the perl court hide mandarin ducks.
> Chosen songstresses accompany the carved carriage;
> Delicate songs drift out of the bed chamber.
> In the palace, who is number one?
> Feiyan in Zhaoyang Palace.
>
> Kumquats are Qin trees;
> Grapes come from the Han palace.
> Blossoms of haze complement the dusk sun;
> Strings and winds intoxicate the spring breeze.
> The short flute, a dragon singing in the water;
> The long flute, a phoenix descending from heaven.
> The ruler enjoys many entertainments;
> In return, shares with all directions.

Soft with rich fragrance, sumptuous and extravagant   with strict meter, these poems are of a very different style from Li Bai's common poems. They display

满斟西域葡萄酒，欣然领唱，皇上也兴致益然，吹起玉笛伴奏。每曲将尽，又延长节拍，好让太真妃拖起长腔，唱得更加尽情尽兴。太真妃唱罢，将杯盏中的美酒一饮而尽，收起绣巾，再给皇上郑重地拜上一拜。皇帝与妃子对李白的歌词极为赞赏。

这样的机会并不少。一日，玄宗与宫人演奏音乐，对高力士说："对此良辰美景，娱乐怎么能仅仅靠吹笛弹琴呢？应该有配上天才词人的歌词演唱，那才足可以夸耀后世。"于是命令赶紧将李白召来。这时，李白已在一个王府里醉酒不起，好不容易把他扶到宫中，拜舞颓然，只能勉强行礼。即命赋诗。于是，两个内臣准备笔墨，铺陈绢帛于前。李白取笔抒思，毫不停顿，十篇立即就写成了。所书笔迹龙飞凤舞，酣畅有力，诗句对偶格律，无不精绝。《宫中行乐词》十首其二、三曰❶：

柳色黄金嫩，梨花白雪香。

玉楼巢翡翠，珠殿锁鸳鸯。

选妓随雕辇，徵歌出洞房。

宫中谁第一？飞燕在昭阳。

卢橘为秦树，蒲桃出汉宫。

烟花宜落日，丝管醉春风。

笛奏龙鸣水，箫吟凤下空。

君王多乐事，还与万方同。

软浓香艳，富丽豪华，格律谨严，不同于李白平时所作歌行一类的风格，表现出诗人多方面的创作才能。这些作品浓艳精巧，

---

❶《宫中行乐词》十首，《李白集》中现存八首。

❶ Of the ten verses of "Lyrics for Palace Music," only eight are extant in the *Collected Works of Li Bai*.

the poet's multifaceted talents. Because these verses are so sumptuous and delicate, some critics believe they did not come from Li Bai's hand, but the textual evidence proves that they are the works of Li Bai. As Li Bai was a literary attendant to the emperor, he had no choice but to change his style and follow the "Palace Music" style.

Emperor Xuanzong once visited the White Lotus Pond. He was in a good mood, and so called on Li Bai to compose a "preface," in which Li Bai should use a beautiful literary genre to record the visit of the emperor. At this time, Li Bai was drunk in the Hanlin Academy. The emperor had Gao Lishi support Li Bai onto the boat. Later, in "Song of the Eight Drunken Immortals," Du Fu wrote: "The Son of Heaven called him to come, but he would not board the boat / He called himself a drunken immortal." He was probably referring to this occasion. Palace courtiers sprayed water in Li Bai's face to help sober him. As Li Bai sobered slightly, he picked up the brush and wrote out "Preface to the Blossoming of the White Lotus" in one stream, with no corrections or changes.

While in the Hanlin Academy, Li Bai gave free reign to his artistic inhibitions. There is even a rumor of Li Bai "scripting a response to the Tubos."

The Tubos had occupied the stone fortress at Qinghai. The Tang court suspected that they had the intention of rebelling. Shortly thereafter, the Tang court received a message from the Tubos, but it was in language of Tubo, and did not include a Chinese translation. This action suggested a challenge. The Tubo ambassador delivered a letter from the Tubo alliance, but not one official in the court could read this letter. He Zhizhang suggested Li Bai to the emperor, and so Li Bai was summoned to the central court. After Li Bai finished reading the letter, he translated its meaning to the emperor. He then translated a response as dictated by the emperor. This response shocked the Tubo ambassador. As Li Bai's family lived in Central Asia for a long time, and had close ties to the Hun and Qiang, Li Bai was competent in the written languages of other ethnic groups, and so was able to "script a response to the Tubos."

At the time, there was a popular story about Gao Lishi removing Li Bai's boots. Legend has it that the emperor ordered Li Bai to compose some lyrics, but Li Bai was already too drunk. Taking advantage of his drunken state, he raised his feet and told Gao Lishi to remove his boots. Gao Lishi was the emperor's eunuch. Under normal circumstances, eunuchs might not object to removing Li Bai's boots, but Gao Lishi was not an average eunuch. He was highly trusted by the emperor, and was very powerful. When the Emperor Suzong was still Heir Apparent in the eastern palace, he called Gao Lishi Big

所以有论者以为不是李白的作品。但有多方面的版本证据说明它们确实为李白之作。李白作为皇上的文学侍从，这类诗歌必然要随俗而变，随题而变，切合"宫中行乐"的主题。

唐玄宗曾游白莲池，兴致极高，于是召李白作"序"，即用一种优美的文体将皇帝游赏的经过记录下来。此时，李白在翰林院中饮酒，已经大醉。皇帝令高力士扶着李白登舟。后来杜甫在《饮中八仙歌》中说："天子呼来不上船，自称臣是酒中仙。"说的应当就是这件事情。宫人在李白的脸上喷洒些凉水，好让他酒醒。李白稍稍清醒，即挥笔撰《白莲花开序》，文不加点，顷刻而成。

李白在供奉翰林期间，洒脱不群，文笔富丽，充分发挥出他天才横溢的一面，据说还有"草答蕃（bō）书"之事。

吐蕃曾经占领青海的石堡城，唐朝怀疑其有不臣之心。很快，朝廷接到吐蕃的书信，可是，书信只有蕃文，没有汉文副本。这种形式暗含着挑衅的意味。蕃邦使者送达书信，可是满朝文武官员，却没有一个能读懂蕃书。贺知章向玄宗推荐李白，于是召李白上殿。李白看罢，转述文意，并根据皇帝旨意，拟写答复吐蕃的书信，这让蕃邦使者非常惊讶。李白家族长期居于西域，与胡、羌等民族联系密切，故李白能通晓异族文字，"草答蕃书"。

当时社会上还流行着高力士脱靴的故事。传说玄宗命李白撰写乐词，可是李白已经喝了酒，乘着酒不醒，抬起腿，令高力士把他的靴子脱掉。高力士是玄宗的宦官，一般情况下，宦官未必不能为李白脱靴，可是高力士不是一般的宦官，极受玄宗的宠信，权势很大。肃宗在东宫做太子时称其为二兄，诸王

Brother. All princes and princesses called him Grandpa, and spouses to the princesses called him Grandfather. The Grand Councilor at the time, Li Linfu, was also very respectful toward him. Li Bai, though, insisted that Gao Lishi remove his boots. Gao Lishi had no choice but to remove his boots. ❶

Li Bai enjoyed drinking, and enjoyed traveling. One day, he left the capital to go to nearby Mount Hua, to the east. When he arrived at Huayin County, as he passed by the county *yamen* (the office of the county magistrate), the magistrate just happened to be hearing legal cases. Li Bai had been drinking all the way, and was quite inebriated by this time. He was riding on a donkey, and without knowing what he was doing, he rode right into the *yamen*. When the county magistrate saw this, he was quite upset. Here he was hearing cases, and this person suddenly burst in. He ordered Li Bai to be apprehended and brought to the courtroom. When Li Bai arrived in the court, he said nothing. The county magistrate raised his voice and asked:

"Who are you, and how dare you be so insolent?"

Li Bai answered: "Allow me to write a deposition to tell you who I am." The county magistrate had a clerk prepare paper and brush. Li Bai did not write his name, but wrote only:

> I once received the dragon towel to wipe my mouth, the imperial hand to serve me soup, Lishi to wipe my boots, and the honored consort to hold my ink stone. I am permitted to ride a horse past the gate of the Son of Heaven, yet I am not permitted to ride a doneky in Huayin County.

The meaning of this is that the emperor used his handkerchief to wipe my face, the emperor himself used a small spoon to mix my soup, Gao Lishi removed my boots, and Imperial Honored Consort Lady Yang has held my ink stone while I wrote. When the county magistrate saw this, he turned pale with shock, and rushed to get up and ask for forgiveness: "I don't know that Hanlin Academician Li has arrived. I should have come out to welcome you." He did his best to keep Li Bai to stay, but Li Bai refused. He mounted his mule and rode off.

These stories are somewhat exaggerated, and they may stretch the truth, but they do show us Li Bai's special status at the time. We can refer to a poem by Li Bai's friend Ren Hua. In "Miscellaneous Writings Sent to Li Bai," he wrote: "New poems are transmitted by the mouths of the palace people / Fine lines do not leave the mind of the Great Ruler / Riding on a heavenly horse with much spirit / Seeing off the flying swan together with the bold and noble / Receiving honor, summoned many times /returning from a summons, you are

公主均称之为阿翁，驸马辈则呼之为爷，当时的宰相李林甫对他也十分敬畏。可是，李白却硬让高力士为他脱靴。高力士无奈只得脱去李白的靴子。❶

　　李白好饮酒，好游赏。一日离开京城，到京城附近东面的华山游玩。来到华阴县，路过县衙门（县官办公的地方）的时候，县官正在里面判案。李白一路豪饮，此时已是醉醺醺，骑着小毛驴，不知不觉地进了县衙门。县官一看，我这正在审理案件，怎么突然闯进来一个人，很是恼火，吩咐手下将来人押到堂上。李白到了堂上也不说话。县官大声说道：

　　"你是什么人，岂敢这样无礼？"

　　李白说："让我来写供词，告诉你我是何人。"县官让手下的准备纸笔。李白并不写上自己的姓名，只写道：

　　"曾得龙巾拭唾，御手调羹，力士抹靴，贵妃捧砚。天子门前尚容我走马，华阴县里不许我骑驴。"

　　那意思是说，皇帝用手巾为我擦过脸，皇帝亲自用小勺为我搅匀羹汤，高力士为我脱靴，杨贵妃为我捧砚台。县官一看，大惊失色，赶紧起身谢罪："不知道李翰林到此，有失远迎。"竭力挽留李白，李白谢绝，重新跨上毛驴走了。

　　这些故事虽然不免有些夸张、附会的成分，但可以看出李白当年的特殊身份。这可以对照李白的友人任华的诗歌，其《杂言寄李白》曰："新诗传在宫人口，佳句不离明主心。身骑天马多意气，目送飞鸿对豪贵。承恩召入凡几回，待诏归来仍

---

❶ 参见李肇《国史补》卷上、段成式《酉阳杂俎》前集卷十二《语资》。

❶ See Li Zhao, *Guoshi bu* (*Addendum to the National History*), volume 1; Duan Chengshi, *Youyang-zazu* (*Miscellaneous Morsels from Youyang*), first volume, juan 12, "*Yuzi*."

still half drunk." This poem says that Li Bai's poems and lyrics received the welcome of those in and out of the court. The several times he was summoned to court, he was partially drunk, just like in the legends.

Li Bai was able to exercise his literary talent, and his work received the respect of all levels of the court, yet he did not feel completely satisfied, because he had still not realized his greatest ambition.

When Li Bai was summoned to the capital, he was assigned to the Hanlin Academy. Early in his reign, the Emperor Xuanzong established the Hanlin Academy, and later he also established the Institute of Academicians. The academicians in the Institute of Academicians were solely responsible for drafting imperial orders and decrees. In other words, they drafted documents for the emperor. Their position was more important. Li Bai's position was as Hanlin Academician Awaiting Orders, also called Hanlin in Attendance. Even though people were in the habit of referring to them as Hanlin Academicians, they were not the same as the academicians in the Institute of Academicians. They were not responsible for drafting documents. They were only scholars of extraordinary literary skills, and were the emperor's literary attendants.

When Li Bai departed his homeland, he established a great ambition, to "elucidate the doctrines of Guan [Zhong] and Yan [Ying], and execute their wisdom, hoping to assist my lord, defining the world and clarifying the boundaries." In other words, he planned to assist the emperor in realizing the political ideal of bringing peace to the empire. He also dreamed of becoming a person like Taigong, Guan Zhong, or Zhuge Liang: They started out in the lower levels of society. Once they were recognized by the enlightened ruler, they followed him out of the mountains to reveal their great plans and establish an immortal accomplishment. Now, though, being a literary attendant, Li Bai had no opportunity to explicate the policies of Guan Zhong or Yan Ying, or to discuss measures to reform society. He could find no hope of realizing his grand ambition.

Of course, literary attendants were not forbidden from participating in government; take for example Li Bai's countrymen Sima Xiangru and Yang Xiong. Even though they received the appreciation of the emperor through their literary works, they also influenced policy. Xima Xiangru was especially active in government when he quelled the ethnic minority groups of the southwestern region. Li Bai desired to be like Sima Xiangru, to gain access to the emperor through his literature, and then advance to participating in government. In his poem "Expressing My Emotions, Presented to Drafter Cai Xiong," he wrote: "Meeting with a sagely great ruler, I dare speak of success

半醉。"诗中说到李白的诗歌受到举朝上下的欢迎，几次待诏都如同传说的那样带着醉意。

李白的文学才能得到发挥，受到朝廷上下的尊重，但他并没有感到完全的满足，因为他最大的理想仍然没能得以实现。

李白被召入京，在翰林院任职。玄宗即位之初，设翰林院，后来又别置学士院，学士院的翰林学士专掌诏令文诰，即代理皇帝撰写各种文诰，职位比较重要。而李白此时的职位是翰林待诏，或称翰林供奉，尽管人们习惯上仍称翰林学士，但事实上不同于学士院中的学士，并不专门职掌诏令的撰写，他们只是艺能方面的杰出之士，是皇帝的文学侍从之臣。

李白离开家乡时就立下大志，将"申管晏之谈，谋帝王之术。奋其智能，愿为辅弼，使寰区大定，海县清一"，即辅佐皇帝实现天下太平的政治理想。他也一直渴望成为像太公、管仲、诸葛亮那样的人物，起先生活在社会下层，一旦明主慕名垂顾，他们随之出山，大展宏图，建立不朽的功业。但现在，作为文学侍从，他根本无法与皇帝讲论管仲、晏婴的治国之道，商讨社会改革的各种措施，根本看不到实现远大理想的任何希望。

当然，文学侍从并非不能从政，如李白家乡的先辈司马相如、扬雄等人，虽以文学博得帝王的好感，但都能影响政治，特别是司马相如，曾奉使安抚西南地区的少数民族，在政治上很有作为。李白渴望着能像司马相如那样，因文学得以亲近皇帝，并进一步参与政治。他在《书情赠蔡舍人雄》一诗中说：

and failure." He actually imagined being able to discuss ideas of the success and failure of states with the sagely and enlightened emperor.

Unfortunately, the court needed only to utilize Li Bai's literary talent. Even worse, though, was that the court was no longer able to accept a genius such as Li Bai. There were a few reasons for this.

Even though Li Bai's literary genius was recognized by all throughout the court, and he personally received much preferential treatment from the emperor, this inevitably caused jealousy among some. Within the magnificent palace, there was always open strife and veiled struggle. It was not long before Li Bai was the target of slander. In his "Clear and Fair Melody," Li Bai used the Han Dynasty Zhao Feiyan to refer to Consort Taizhen, intending only to praise her beauty. Li Bai did not expect Gao Lishi to use this to attack him, saying that as Zhao Feiyan came from a lowly family and had affairs with court attendants, Li Bai's reference to Zhao Feiyan must have deeper meanings. Li Bai received less favor after this. In his "Chant on the Jade Pot," Li Bai wrote: "Even though the noble lord loved pretty eyebrows / There is no stopping the jealousies in the palace from killing people." "Pretty eyebrows" refer to a beautiful woman. The end results of palace romances are often the same. This expression by Li Bai was not made lightly. After scholars waiting in attendance in the Hanlin Academy received the favor of the emperor, they would usually receive an official title, such as Wang Shuwen of the middle Tang period, who received the title of "in waiting for chess." Wang Pi "began in the Hanlin Academy in waiting for calligraphy." After he received the recognition of the Emperor Dezong, he was assigned the duty of imperial tutor in the eastern palace, and from there advanced to higher position. Li Bai remained as Hanlin Academician Awaiting Orders, attending to the emperor. He did not receive an official title. The court only recognized his literary talent, but did not believe he had the potential to be a high official.

Li Bai's style was elegant, and his nature was conceited. He stood out in a crowd with his unique character, attracting the attention of others. When He Zhizhang (alias Jizhen), guest of the Heir Apparent at the time, met Li Bai in Chang'an, he called Li Bai an exiled immortal, and pawned a gold turtle he wore as an accessory to buy wine to drink together with Li Bai. In the first of two poems titled "Facing Wine, Remembering Supervisor He," Li Bai wrote: "There is a wild guest from Siming / Debonair He Jizhen / On first meeting in Chang'an / He called me the exiled immortal." He Zhizhang, alias Jizhen, was a famous poet during the Tang Dynasty. He was much older than Li Bai, so it was quite unusual that he could so admire Li Bai. He Zhizhang had held the

"遭逢圣明主，敢进兴亡言。"他确实想象着能够对圣明的皇帝谈论国家兴亡的道理。

但朝廷此时只需要利用李白的文学才能，更糟的是，朝廷已经无法容纳李白这样的天才了。说起来，大致有几方面的因素。

李白杰出的文学天才虽然赢得了朝廷普遍的赞赏，他本人也得到皇帝的许多优待，但这势必会引起一些人的忌妒。华丽的宫廷里总是充满着各种明争暗斗，李白不久就遭到谗言的诋毁。李白的《清平调》中曾以汉代的赵飞燕来比拟太真妃，本意只是称赞太真美丽而已，不料，高力士以此挑拨，说赵飞燕出身下贱，而且与宫奴私通，诗中用赵飞燕来形容太真妃，含有影射之意。李白随之受到冷落疏远。其时他作有《玉壶吟》一诗，曰："君王虽爱蛾眉好，无奈宫中妒杀人。""蛾眉"指美女，才子与美女在朝廷中的命运往往极为相似。李白的这一感叹恐怕不是泛泛而言。士人待诏翰林，在得到皇帝亲幸之后，往往都加上正式的官衔，如中唐时期的王叔文"以棋待诏"；王伾"始以书待诏翰林"，得到德宗赏识之后，使人东宫任侍读、侍书之职，然后步步升迁，进入较高的职位。李白则始终以翰林待诏的身份供奉左右，没有授予正式的官职，朝廷只认可他的文学天赋，并不认为他具备大臣的才干。

李白风度飘逸，天性高傲，在众人之中自有超凡的气质而格外引人瞩目。时任太子宾客的贺知章（字季真）在长安见到李白，就称他为谪仙人，并解下自己佩戴的金龟来换酒，与李白一道共饮。李白《对酒忆贺监二首》其一说："四明有狂客，风流贺季真。长安一相见，呼我谪仙人。"贺知章，字季真，唐代著名的诗人，比李白年长许多，但对李白却能这样推崇实

position of Director of the Palace Library, so people referred to him as "Director of the Palace Library He," but in his poem, Li Bai referred to him as "Supervisor He." Zhizhang was open-minded, and came from Siming, Zhejiang Province. He called himself the "wild guest of Siming," so Li Bai wrote in his poem "there is a wild guest in Siming." Due to He Zhizhang's praise, Li Bai's reputation as an "exiled immortal" spread throughout the capital like wildfire. Li Bai valued this moniker, as in many ways, an exiled immortal matched his self-image quite well. Being an exiled immortal was not only about the pursuit of an idealistic state of having "the style of an immortal, bones of a Daoist." It was also about transcending the mundane matters, just as Ren Hua described in his poem: "Seeing off the flying swan together with the bold and noble." In the Wei Dynasty of the Three Kingdoms period, Ji Kang* wrote: "Seeing off the flying swan / Hands strumming the five strings." Ji Kang was by nature arrogant, and did not bow to authority. By saying Li Bi looks up at a departing swan, Ren Hua's poem not only infers Li Bai's attitude toward the aristocracy, raising his head and looking over them, but also implies Li Bai's appreciation and continuation of Ji Kang's spirit. Unfortunately, Li Bai had not spent much time in the court, and his incessant arrogant and self-important personality was not easily accepted by the other officials in court.

Although Li Bai indulged in wine and games, he was very serious about government. In his mind, becoming a government official was not for personal glory and wealth, but to realize political aspirations, to serve the ruler in pacifying the realm. As soon as he accomplished his goal, he would retire to the country, where he would live a life of simplicity in seclusion. Mundane glory had no place in Li Bai's mind, but such values could not be applied to the political realm. Although Li Bai had to submit poems and letters to different officials in search of a chance to enter the government when he was a commoner, once he arrived in the capital, he revealed his true self. He refused to ingratiate himself with the established powers to secure his own political future. He retained his individual personality. Those who refuse to curry favor in order to remain in the bureaucracy, yet still wish to have some influence in the political realm, will never succeed.

One more important reason was Li Bai's lack of understanding of the internal workings of the empire. Before entering the capital, Li Bai was after all only an external observer of the court. After being established in the Hanlin Academy, he had an insider's understanding of the court. It was easy for him to see the conflicts and chaos underneath the prosperity of the Tang Dynasty. In

属难得。贺知章曾任秘书监，人称"贺秘监"，李白诗题中称"贺监"。知章性情旷达，家乡在浙江四明，自号"四明狂客"，故李白诗中称"四明有狂客"。经过贺知章的褒奖，李白"谪仙人"的称号在京城迅速传播开来。李白十分看重这一称号，在很大程度上，谪仙人就是李白自我想象的形象。谪仙不仅在于具有"仙风道骨"，对理想境界的向往，同时也表现出对世俗的一种超越态度，正像任华在诗中所描写的那样："目送飞鸿对豪贵。""目送归鸿，手挥五弦"，是三国曹魏时嵇（jī）康的诗句。嵇康天生傲骨，不事权贵。任华的诗句既包含着李白用仰望飞鸿、仰面朝天的方式来对待王公贵戚，又寓含着李白对嵇康精神的赞许与继承。但诗人初入宫廷不久，始终保持傲然独立、锋芒毕露的个性，很难为周围的官员所容。

李白虽然纵酒嬉戏，但对政治却十分真诚。在他想来，进入仕途，并不是为了个人的荣华富贵，而是为了实现政治理想，辅助君王实现天下太平，一旦功成名就，自己就退身江湖，隐居山林，过着平淡简朴的生活。所以，世俗的荣华在李白的心目中并没有地位。但这种价值观念在官场上是行不通的。如果说，李白在布衣之时，为了进入仕途还不得不向各种官员投诗献赋，那么进入京城之后，李白就显现出了自己的本色，他不肯为自己的官运前程而向权贵们献媚，始终保持独立的人格。不肯趋炎附势的人要想继续留在官场中，还想在政坛上发挥重要的影响力，那是很难的事情。

还有一个重要的原因，在于李白对于王朝内部的认识。未进京前，李白对于朝廷毕竟是一个局外人的观察，而供奉翰林之后，对朝廷就有了一个内部的了解。他不难发现，大唐帝国的盛世外表掩盖着某种矛盾冲突以及不合理的现象。他

---

* Also Romanized using an alternate pronunciation as Xi Kang.

his poem "Song of the Calling Marsh, Presented to Gentleman Summoned to Officer Cen," Li Bai wrote: "The chickens group together and fight for food / The phoenix flies alone and is without peers / The gecko laughs at the dragon / The fish's eye is mistaken for a pearl / Mother Mo* wore brocade / While Xi Shi* carried firewood / To shackle Chao and You* to government / How is that different from having Kuilong* labor in the dust and dirt?" This was a world in which the virtuous and foolish were inverted, and right and wrong were reversed. When Li Bai encountered the dark side of the imperial court, he felt helpless and disgusted. The beautiful hopes and aspirations he brought into the capital were finally shattered.

Li Bai enjoyed drinking wine. Du Fu wrote "Song of Eight Immortals of Drink," in which he described him: "With one hundred pitchers of wine, Li Bai will give off one hundred poems / Asleep in a tavern in the market of Chang'an / The Son of Heaven called him to come, but he would not board the boat / He called himself a drunken immortal." When he was summoned to court, Li Bai was often very inebriated. Being such, it would be very difficult for him to be a minister with important administrative responsibilities. In his poem "Reading in the Hanlin Academy, Describing My Aspirations to the Collected Virtuous Ones," he said of himself: "I am originally a scattered person." He indulged in wine and was unrestrained, not concerned with details. This kind of personality could not interact very well with the restrained and dogmatic order of the officials' world.

After being slandered, his political dreams could not be realized, and Li Bai could not remain in Chang'an. In the spring of 744, Li Bai submitted a request to return to the mountains. The Emperor Xuanzong granted his request and bestowed a grant of money upon him. He then left the capital.

He was an optimistic person, and did not complain, nor did he like to compose sad poems. He rarely revealed the sad side of his emotions. Many years afterwards, he said in reflection: "As I was about to leave / Plentiful tears soaked my official cap tassels." ❶ One can imagine how disappointed he must have felt as he was leaving the capital.

在《鸣皋歌送岑徵君》诗中说："鸡聚族以争食，凤孤飞而无邻。蝘蜓嘲龙，鱼目混珍。嫫母衣锦，西施负薪。若使巢、由桎（zhì）梏（gù）于轩冕兮，亦奚异乎夔（kuí）龙鳖（bié）蹩（xiè）于风尘？"这是一个贤愚易位、是非颠倒的世界。李白接触到了王朝内部灰暗的一面，感到无奈与厌恶，他在进京之前怀的美好理想和希望终于破灭。

李白好酒，杜甫作《饮中八仙歌》描述："李白一斗诗百篇，长安市上酒家眠。天子呼来不上船，自称臣是酒中仙。"奉诏之时，李白常是酩酊大醉，这样就很难担当有重要的行政事务需要处理的职事官。李白《翰林读书言怀呈集贤诸学士》诗中自称"本是疏散人"，嗜酒狂放，不拘小节，这种性格恐怕很难应对官场上的繁文缛节和死板规程。

李白受到谗毁，自己的政治理想无法实现，长安已经不是他能留下的地方了。天宝三载（744）春天，李白上书请求还山，玄宗准许了他的请求，赐给他一笔钱财。就这样，他离开了京师。

他为人乐观开朗，不作苦吟，也不太爱写苦愁的诗。内心忧郁悲伤的一面，他很少亮出来。事后多年，他回想起来，只是说："临当欲去时，慷慨泪沾缨。"❶ 可以想见，诗人离开京城之际，内心还是充满着酸楚。

---

* Mother Mo, the consort of the Yellow Emperor, said to be very ugly.
* Xi Shi, a famous beauty of the Spring and Autumn period.
* Chao and You, Chao Fu and Xu You were recluses of the mythical Emperor Yao's time.
* Kuilong, a minister in the Yao's government.

❶ 李白《经乱离后天恩流夜郎忆旧游书怀赠江夏韦太守良宰》。

❶ Li Bai, "After the Rebellion, I Left Houtian'en and Wound up in Yelang, Reflecting upon Past Travels, Expressing My Emotions to Governor of Jiangxia Wei Liangzai."

李白醉酒图

Painting of drunken Li Bai

六 知己：幽梦谁与适

Chapter VI Close Friends: My Deep Dreams, with
Whom Can I Share

Li Bai spent less than two years serving in the Hanlin Academy. Once his dreams of fulfilling his political ambitions had been shattered and he left the capital, some of his "solicitous" friends disappeared. Those best friends of yesterday now have become strangers behind closed doors. Many years later, when Li Bai recalled in reflection, he was still quite hurt: "One day, I took leave due to illness, and wandered the rivers and seas / Of those I knew in former days, how many still remain / Before, they often greeted at the door, but afterwards, the door is closed / Friends today change tomorrow." ❶ At a time like this, to meet a true friend is truly moving. In this case, Li Bai made friends with another great poet of the Tang Dynasty—Du Fu.

After leaving the capital, Li Bai arrived in Luoyang, where he met Du Fu. For two great poets to meet was like two meteors coming together in the vast night sky; it was truly rare. The famous poet and scholar Wen Yiduo described their meeting as "The sun and the moon in the sky bumping into each other," which means that the meeting is as important as that of Confucius and Laozi in ancient Chinese history. ❷

At the time, Li Bai was forty-four years of age, and Du Fu was thirty-three. In their travels together, drinking wine and composing poems, they became dear and fast friends.

Du Fu had been rushing about Luoyang for two years to no avail, and was very disappointed. Li Bai had just come out of the Hanlin Academy, "escaping from the golden chamber" to head to the mountains and forests. Both had been through different experiences, but they were in similar states of mind. Du Fu's poem "Presented to Li Bai" said: "Marquis Li had the complexion of the golden chamber / You escaped to attend to your secluded endeavors / We also had our travels to Liang and Song / And had just planned to gather jade grass*." Upon first meeting, they were very happy, and planned on exploring Daoism together. Mount Wangwu was not far to the northwest of Luoyang, and there was a famous Daoist temple headed by the Daoist master Hua Gaijun on the mountain, so why not go there to gather jade grass?

Fall arrived, and Li Bai and Du Fu both finished their business at hand and honored their appointment. They rode a small boat across the roaring rapids of the Yellow River and headed straight for Mount Wangwu.

Mount Wangwu is on the border between modern Shanxi and Henan

　　算起来，他供奉翰林，前后不到两年。如今他在政治上渴望施展雄才大略的梦想完全破灭了，而离开京师后，原先一些"殷勤"的朋友也没有了踪影，昨天还信誓旦旦为知己，今日已是关门谢客陌路人。多年之后，李白回想起来，仍然很伤感："一朝谢病游江海，畴昔相知几人在？前门长揖后门关，今日结交明日改。" ❶此时遇到真心交往的朋友，那真是让人感动！而这位知心朋友正是唐代另一位伟大诗人——杜甫。

　　李白离开京师，到了洛阳，不久就遇见了杜甫。两位伟大诗人相逢，就仿佛广阔的夜空中两颗遥远的行星能够相遇，实在太难得了！著名诗人与学者闻一多形容他俩的会面是"青天里太阳和月亮走碰了头"，他说，大概除了孔子与老子见面，在中国古代恐怕再也没有比此意义更重大的会面了。 ❷

　　当时李白四十四岁，杜甫三十三岁，两人一道游历，饮酒赋诗，结下了深厚的友谊。

　　杜甫在洛阳奔波了两年，什么结果也没有，抑郁不欢，而李白刚从翰林出来，"脱身金闺"，向往山林。两人经历不同，然而心境有相似之处。杜甫有诗《赠李白》曰："李侯金闺彦，脱身事幽讨。亦有梁宋游，方期拾瑶草。"初次见面十分愉快，两人相约一道寻仙访道。王屋山就在洛阳西北不远的地方，那里有著名的道士华盖君住持的道观，何不就此到那里一游，撷拾瑶草？

　　秋天到了，李、杜两人各自忙完手中的事情，如期赴约。他们乘着一叶小舟渡过了怒涛汹涌的黄河，直奔王屋山。

　　王屋山在今天的山西与河南交界处，是济水的发源地，山

---

❶ 李白《赠从弟南平太守之遥二首》其一。
❷ 闻一多《唐诗杂论》。

❶ Li Bai, first poem of "Two Poems Presented to Govenor of Taiping, Cousin Zhiyao."
❷ Wen Yiduo, *Miscellaneous Essays on Tang Poems*.
* Jade grass was a legendary medicinal herb.

Provinces, and is the source of the Ji River. The mountain is very steep and high, and the forests are thick. There are many Daoist temples on the mountain, making it an important Daoist site. They followed treacherous mountain paths, slowly climbing upwards, "looking back every three steps, and sitting down every five." They frequently stopped to rest and look around at the beautiful scenery: "Thousands of rocks but no people, millions of valleys silent" ; "Wind in the pines and water over the rapids, the sounds harmonizing to the season." ❶ Off in the distance, they could see the blue tiled rooftop of a Daoist temple and white grass rooftops of huts reflecting in the dense forest. The quiet Daoist temple appeared to be even more remote. Grass up to the knees and closed gates, the two found it to be odd. After calling for a while, an elder finally came out, but the elder was not Hua Gaijun. Rather, he was Hua Gaijun's senior disciple, Old Lu. Old Lu told the poets that Hua Gaijun had already ascended to the land of the immortals. The two poets were disappointed. Old Lu was moved by the sincerity of the two, and so took them in to see the temple, and even open the cultivation chamber of Hua Gaijun, which had been locked for a long time, allowing them to pay their respects.

After taking their leave of Old Lu, they began their journey throughout the regions of Liang and Song.

Liang and Song are the names of ancient states. In the Tang Dynasty, they were also known as Bian and Song, referring to Bianzhou and Songzhou. Bianzhou is the area of modern Kaifeng City, Henan Province, and Songzhou is the area of Shangqiu City, Henan Province. The names of the two places have often been confused throughout history. Shangqiu is the ancient city of Suiyang. After King Wu of the Zhou overthrew the Shang Dynasty, he enfeoffed this land to the older brother of King Zhou of Shang, and named it Song. Han Emperor Wendi enfeoffed Kaifeng to his son Liu Wu, Prince Xiao of Liang, and named it Liang. He was later moved to Shangqiu, but was still called Liang. Shangqiu City therefore has several names: In the Han and Six Dynasties periods, it was called the State of Liang or Commandary of Liang; during the Sui and Tang Dynasties, it was named Songzhou. Kaifeng, not far from Shangqiu, was known as Greater Liang during the Sui and Tang Dynasties. Liang and Song were both very near, and their names were frequently changed, resulting in the confusion. When the Prince of Liang was in Shangqiu, he worked on many projects and left behind many historical sites.

It just happened that the poet Gao Shi was in this area, and met with Li Bai and Du Fu. The three traveled together, drinking their fill and singing their hearts out, climbing high and reflecting on history, and sharing their most

势巍峨，树木繁茂，多有道观，为道教胜地。他们沿着崎岖的山路，拾级而上，"三步回头五步坐"，不时地停下来休息，并环顾欣赏四周一片秋景："千岩无人万壑静"；"松风涧水声合时。" ❶ 远远就看见道观青青的屋瓦和几间白茅草屋掩映在丛丛秋树之中，平日冷清的道观此时更加显得寂静。蒿草没膝，院门虚掩，两人觉得奇怪。呼唤了半天，才有一位长者出来。但长者并不是华盖君，而是华盖君的大弟子卢老。卢老告诉诗人，华盖君已经仙去。两位诗人好生失望。卢老为两位求访者的虔诚所打动，带着二人在道观中游览，还特意打开了封锁已久的华盖君修行炼丹的静室，让他们凭吊致意。

告别卢老，他们开始了梁、宋之游。

梁、宋都是古代国名，唐代又称汴、宋，分别指汴州与宋州，汴州在今河南开封市一带，宋州在今河南商丘市一带。但两地名称历史上经常相混。商丘，古代是睢阳古城。周武王灭商，将商纣王的庶兄微子启封在那里，称之为宋。汉文帝起初将儿子梁孝王刘武封在开封，称为梁，但后来迁到商丘，仍称为梁。这样，商丘市一带就有不同的名称：两汉、六朝时称为梁国、梁郡；隋唐时代称为宋州。距离商丘不远的开封，隋、唐时期通称为大梁。梁、宋地缘相近，多次改称，故多相混。梁王在商丘，大兴土木，传下了很多名胜古迹。

正巧，诗人高适也在此地活动，与李、杜相遇，于是一道游赏。三人同行，一路上，开怀畅饮，纵情高歌，登高怀古，

---

❶ 杜甫《忆昔行》。

❶ Du Fu, "Recalling a Former Trip."

intimate thoughts. They came to know each other well, and built strong friendships.

Liang and Song of the Tang were still quite prosperous: "In the cities are ninety thousand households / High beams reflecting through the thoroughfares." The high buildings and wide courtyards were dense throughout the cities, with wealthy households within earshot of each other. The population was dense and economy thriving. Especially prominent were the widely dispersed avenues and canals which passed by, allowing for extremely convenient water and land transportation. Du Fu described it as "ships and carts reaching half of the world." Because it was an ancient region, many ancient traditions remained. The lifestyles of the rich and powerful families were still extravagant, much as they were during the times of the Prince of Liang. Large numbers of guests, staff, and itinerant scholars filled the halls of the aristocracy. Poem, wine, song, and dance were accompanied by laughter and merriment. The culture of traveling men of chivalry, or knights-errant, was quite popular in this region. In a poem, Du Fu described it as: "With white blade, avenging the unrighteous / Gold as if non-existent / Killing a man in the red dust / Repayment in this moment." ❶ This sort of fashion was especially attractive to Li Bai.

In his later years, Du Fu recalled his travels with Li Bai and Gao Shi to Shanfu Terrace in his poem "Earlier Travels" : "In earlier days, with Gao and Li / In the evening, we climbed Shanfu Terrace / Cold growth among the stone tablets / Wind from ten thousand miles blows clouds this way." Shanfu Terrace was Fu Zijian's Lute Terrace, located in the ancient Shanfu City, one kilometer south of modern Shan County, Shandong Province. Fu Zijian was from the state of Lu during the Spring and Autumn Period, and was a disciple of Confucius. He was known for his moral conduct, and later became the magistrate of Shanfu. He was accomplished at governing and educating the populace through ritual and etiquette, and he played the lute. He was able to govern Shanfu without ever leaving his court. It was as if he had the manner of the Daoist "governing through inaction." Gao Shi was on familiar terms with Governor Li of Songzhou and Magistrate Cui of Shanfu County. Governor Li had recently renovated Lute Terrace, so Gao Shi composed a poem for him, in which he praised the renovation as being an implementation of Fu Zijian's administration.

Governor Li and Magistrate Cui were very happy to meet these great poets, especially Li Bai, former Hanlin Academician and honored guest of the emperor. They invited the three to hunt in the nearby Mengzhu Marsh.

互诉衷肠，彼此间有了更多的了解，也加深了情谊。

唐时的梁、宋仍然十分繁华，"邑中九万家，高栋照通衢"，城中高楼广阁，鳞次栉比，富室大户，遥遥相望，人口稠密，经济繁荣，尤为突出的是，通衢大道分布很广，又有广济渠经过，因此水陆交通都十分便捷，被杜甫称为"舟车半天下"。正因是老地方，古代的遗风留存不少。豪门望族生活奢华，与过去梁王时候的情形差不多。显贵的门下云集着众多的宾客幕僚、游说之士，朱门之中，诗酒歌舞，欢声笑语，此起彼伏。当地游侠之风炽盛，杜甫在诗中形容道："白刃仇不义，黄金倾有无。杀人红尘里，报答在斯须。"❶这种风气特别适合李白的个性。

杜甫晚年《昔游》中回想此时与李白、高适游单父台时说："昔者与高李，晚登单父台。寒芜际碣石，万里风云来。"单父台即宓（fú）子贱之琴台，在今山东单县城南一里远的故单父城中。宓子贱是春秋时鲁国人，孔子的弟子，有德行，后来做了单父宰，善于用礼乐来教化、引导百姓，故能弹鸣琴，身不下堂而单父治，不用离开办公的地方就把单父治理得很好。看起来，很有点道家"无为而治"的气度。高适熟悉宋州的李太守和单父县的崔县令，李太守新近重建琴台，所以高适写诗留赠，称赞太守能够再造琴台，实行宓子贱之政。

李太守、崔县令见到这几位大诗人，特别是曾受过皇上优遇的前翰林待诏李白，十分高兴，邀请三位诗人在附近的孟渚泽一带打猎。本来就爱好游猎的诗人当然欣然答应。太阳刚刚

---

❶ 此段引诗均见杜甫《遣怀》。

❶ See Du Fu, "Dispatching My Heart" for all quotations in this paragraph.

Enjoying hunting, the poets naturally accepted. As the sun rose and the wilds were still covered in a thin veil of mist, the hunters had already set out astride horses with bows strung, galloping over the hunting grounds: "Darting off astride a prized colt / Carved bow stretched tight with a singing string / Falcon high, Lu grass pale / The fox and hare, so fat and tender / Hiding, we race after / Going out the eastern gate into the fields / In one sweep, the wilds empty / Calling and yelling by the mounts." ❶ Hearing only the sound of the bow strings and the rushing of the arrows, one saw the dead fox and slain hare. In an instant, bird and beast dispersed, and the wilds were desolate. They hunted until the dusk before they called the hunt to an end. They all carried the yields of the hunt back to the city, where they held a banquet in Shanfu's Eastern Pavilion. Each presented their quarry, which they roasted and accompanied with wine. What a lively scene. The governor called upon two singing girls to perform for the drinking and feasting guests. With their sleeves flowing with the dance, they were like immortals. With conversation and laughter, the guests drank their fill, not dispersing until dawn of the following day.

Later, the three parted ways. Gao Shi wrote in his poem "In Song, Parting with the Three Gentlement, Zhou, Liang, and Li" : "Sir Li is a hero in his heart / Boldness is his nature." Gao Shi admired Li Bai very much, and his hesitation to part with his new friend is evident in this poem. "Boldness" is a word of praise, describing his singular integrity and obstinacy. Gao Shi felt that Li Bai's arrogance and individuality was completely spontaneous; it was just in his nature. From external appearance to his behavior, Li Bai made a very unique impression on people. When Wei Hao saw him in Guangling, he said "his pupils were firey, wide open like those of a hungry tiger. He was often well-dressed, debonair and generous." His eyes were brilliant and full of spirit. In his later years, Du Fu composed "Expressing My Emotions," in which he remembered his experiences during this period: "I remember being with Gao and Li / Discussing literature as we entered the tavern / The two gentlemen had great ideas / Meeting me, their expressions were happy / After some wine, we climbed Chui Terrace / Reflecting on the past, we looked out at Pingwu." It is evident that they enjoyed themselves very much, and that they got along very well together.

In 745, Du Fu accepted the invitation of Qizhou Adjutant Li Zhifang to come to Qizhou (modern Jinan, Shandong). There were many places of interest in Qizhou, including Mount Li and Daming Lake. The scenery of beautiful lakes and lovely mountains has always made favored destinations for scholars to gather. Li Zhifang built a pavilion at the foot of Mount Li and by the banks of Daming Lake

升起，原野还飘荡着薄薄的晨霭时，这队打猎的人就已经结伴携徒，跨马控弦，在猎场上奔驰开了，"骏发跨名驹，雕弓控鸣弦。鹰豪鲁草白，狐兔多肥鲜。邀遮相驰逐，遂出城东田。一扫四野空，喧呼鞍马前"❶。只听到阵阵弦响，嗖嗖箭发，就看到兔死狐亡。顷刻之间，鸟兽走散，四野空荡荡。打猎直到日暮黄昏才收场。众人扛着猎物，回到城里，就势在单父东楼置酒设宴，各献所获，炮炙佐酒，好不热闹。太守召来两位官妓表演歌舞，为诸位助着酒兴。长袖飘舞，姿态若仙，欢声笑语，夜阑酒酣，直到第二天清晨，大伙这才兴尽而散。

其后三人分道东下。高适有《宋中别周梁李三子》诗，其中云："李侯怀英雄，肮脏乃天资。"高适对李白颇为倾慕，诗中表达朋友之间惜别之情。"肮脏"为褒义词，形容人的挺拔不俗、刚直倔强。高适认为李白傲然独立的风姿，完全出之于自然，天性如此。李白为人，从仪表到作风，都能给人以不同寻常的感受。魏颢在广陵见到他时，云是"眸子炯然，哆如饿虎。或时束带，风流酝藉"，说李白目光炯炯有神，风度翩然。杜甫晚年作《遣怀》诗，追忆这段经历："忆与高、李辈，论交入酒垆。两公壮藻思，得我色敷腴。气酣登吹台，怀古视平芜。"可见他们的游赏非常尽兴，彼此间的交情也非常融洽。

天宝四载（745）杜甫应齐州司马李之芳的邀请来到齐州（今山东济南）。齐州的名胜很多，有历山、大明湖等等，湖光山色，景致绝佳，向来是士人云集的好去处。李之芳在大明湖畔、历山之下新建一亭子，取名历下亭。邀请诸位朋友坐在亭

---

❶ 李白《秋猎孟渚夜归置酒单父东楼观妓》。

❶ Li Bai, "After Returning from Hunting in the Fall at Mengzhu Marsh, Viewing Singing Girls at a Banquet in the Eastern Pavilion of Shanfu."

and named it Lixia (At the Foot of Li) Pavilion. He invited his friends to sit in the pavilion, backs to the mountain, facing the lake, and take in the beautiful scenery. With wine in hand and the breeze in their faces, they shared their friendship. It must have pleased not only the senses, but also the mind. Beihai (modern Yidu, Shandong) was not distant from Qizhou, and Li Zhifang's great uncle Li Yong, who was the Governor of Beihai at the time, also came to Qizhou.

Li Yong was a famous literatus and calligrapher of the Tang Dynasty. His father, Li Shan, wrote the famous commentary on the *Zhaoming Wenxuan*. Li Yong was bold and extravagant. He indulged in hunting and leisure, with little attention to details. He was fierce and ardent, and had a strong sense of right and wrong. During Empress Wu's reign, he would argue and debate in court, causing many people great concern for his safety. Li Yong responded to their concern, saying: "How can I establish my legacy if all I do is agree and say yes?" The reputation of his compositions and calligraphy spread throughout the empire. Li Yangbing called him the "immortal of writing."

Everyone gathered in Lixia Pavilion, where they recited poems and sang songs while feasting and drinking, having a wonderful time. Li Bai composed "There Was a Brave Woman in Donghai," in which he wrote:

> Official Li of Beihai;
> Submitted flying essays to the heavenly court.
> Abandoning offense and warning of the customs;
> The sweat aroma spreads to Cangying.

He strongly praised Li Yong. Du Fu wrote: "To the right of the sea lies this ancient pavilion / In Jinan, famous scholars are plenty." These lines have been passed down through the ages. Today, this couplet is written on Lixia Pavilion (modern name is Guest Pavilion) in the calligraphy of He Shaoji of the Qing Dynasty, except that the two characters for "Right of the sea" have been changed to "At the foot of Li."

In the fall of this year, Du Fu went to Yanzhou. Li Bai still had family living in Ren City of Lu Commandary (modern Jining, Shandong), and also had some farmland nearby. Li Bai had been wandering for many years when he returned home. He invited Du Fu to come. When the two again met, they came to know each other even better. They drank together, chatting into the wee hours, singing, traveling, and visiting friends. They became true friends.

One autumn day when the sky was clear and the air was crisp, Li Bai remembered Hermit Fan, who lived in the nearby mountains, "in a leisurely garden, cultivating deep grace." He went together with Du Fu on horseback to visit Mr. Fan.

中，背山面水，尽揽幽胜，把酒临风，共叙朋友情谊，实在是赏心悦目，心情舒畅。北海（治在今山东益都）距离齐州不远，李之芳的族祖李邕时任北海太守，也来到齐州。

李邕是唐代著名的文学家、书法家。父亲李善是《昭明文选》有名的注家。李邕性豪侈，驰猎纵逸，不拘细行，性格刚烈，嫉恶如仇。武后时在朝廷上抗言争辩，人多为之担心，李邕答道："唯唯诺诺，我的名声怎么能在后世流传呢？"他的文章与书法的名声传布天下，李阳冰称他是"书中仙手"。

诸人聚于历下亭中，摆酒设宴，吟诗酬唱，相得甚欢。李白作有《东海有勇妇》，诗中云：

北海李使君，飞章奏天庭。

舍罪警风俗，流芳播沧瀛。

对李邕极为称赞。杜甫有诗曰："海右此亭古，济南名士多。"此为后人传诵的名句，如今的历下亭（今名客亭）上还有清人何绍基所书此联，只是"海右"二字改成了"历下"。

这年秋天，杜甫到兖（yǎn）州去了。李白一直有家小寄住在鲁郡的任城（今山东济宁），附近还有一些田地。在外游历好几年，李白回到家中。他邀请杜甫前来。两人重逢，有了更多的了解，情同手足，一起把酒豪饮，相对促膝夜话，或谈天，或高歌，或登览，或访友，彼此真正成了知音。

一日秋高气爽，李白想起来在附近山中"闲园养幽姿"的范居士，于是与杜甫一道，骑上马，寻访范氏去了。

Many years earlier, Li Bai visited Mr. Fan's place of seclusion, but this time, he did not know which way to go. They rode back and forth several times before they found a path with cocklebur growing along the side. Li Bai was in a hurry, and suddenly fell off his horse and went head first into the cocklebur. Cocklebur is a member of the family asteraceae. The broad leaves are serrated, and the fruits have a hard shell with barbs which stick to clothing. When Li Bai fell into the cockleburs, his hair, beard, and clothing were covered with burs. The two laughed loudly, and then continued on their way. Recluse Fan was very hospitable, and led the poets in by their arms, set out wine, and commenced to drink with his old friends. They did not eat other delicacies of the mountains. They ate only a large dish of stir-fried cocklebur sprouts. Li Bai incorporated this experience into a poem in later years. The title of the poem is very interesting: "Seeking Recluse Fan North of Lu City, I Fell into a Patch of Cocklebur; Written upon Seeing Fan Serving Wine and Plucking Cocklebur."

Du Fu also wrote a poem, "Seeking Recluse Fan the Tenth Together With Li the Twelfth." In the poem, he not only described this experience of visiting a friend, but also described the friendship of the two poets. As they spent more and more time together, Du Fu came to better understand Li Bai. Not only did he appreciate Li Bai's outgoing boldness, but also praised his poetry: "Sir Li has fine verses / Often similar to Yin Keng." Yin Keng was a Southern Dynasties poet who was known for his expertise in five-character poems. His style was refined and delicate, often describing scenery. He was very popular in his time. Du Fu praised Li Bai's poetry as already attaining the state of mind of the ancients. "I am also a guest east of Meng / And love you as a brother / In drunken slumber, we share an autumn blanket / Holding hands, we wander by day." East of Meng refers to the region of the Lu Commandary. These few animated lines portraying the friendship of these two poets have been repeated through the ages.

Li Bai still could not forget his fascination with Daoist cultivation, and often brought Du Fu along to visit Daoist masters. Du Fu became interested, and influenced by Li Bai, studied quite seriously. "East of Meng, we traveled to the old recluse / Still recalling the joy of shared aspirations / Serving Teacher Dong / Today I am alone and desolate." Many years later, in "Former Travels," Du Fu, "alone and desolate," remembered the joys he shared with Li Bai as thcy studicd Daoist cultivation techniques under Master Dong beside the alchemy furnace.

The two poets finally parted, Du Fu returning to Chang'an, and Li Bai

　　范氏的隐所，李白好几年前来过，但这会儿出了城，才发现茫然不知该走哪条路，两匹马在荒坡上来来回回转了好几圈，才走上一条路边长有苍耳的小道。李白走得急，一下子从马上摔了下来，一头扎进苍耳堆里。苍耳是一种有刺的菊科植物，宽大的叶子上布满了锯齿，结的果实叫苍耳子，壳硬，还带着刺，很容易粘在人的衣服上。诗人倒在苍耳丛中，头发、胡子和衣服上都粘着苍耳果子。两人大笑不已，重新骑马上路。范居士殷勤好客，把臂将诗人们引进屋里，摆上酒水，与老友畅饮。不吃别的山珍海味，而是一盘可口的炒苍耳苗。这段经历，李白后来写进了诗里，诗题很有趣：《寻鲁城北范居士，失道落苍耳中，见范置酒摘苍耳作》。

　　杜甫也作有《与李十二白同寻范十隐居》一诗，诗中不仅记叙了此次访友的经历，也记录了两位诗人真挚的友情。随着两人相处日久，杜甫对于李白也越来越了解，不仅欣赏他的豪爽，也推崇他的诗歌："李侯有佳句，往往似阴铿。"阴铿是南朝诗人，擅长五言诗，风格清丽，长于写景，为时所重。杜甫称赞李诗已经达到了古人的境界。"余亦东蒙客，怜君如弟兄。醉眠秋共被，携手日同行。"东蒙即是鲁郡一带。这几句生动地描写两位大诗人之间的友情的诗句，历来为人们所称道。

　　李白还是忘不了修道炼丹，常常带着杜甫寻访附近的真人炼师。杜甫很感兴趣，受李白的影响，他学得还挺认真。"东蒙赴旧隐，尚忆同志乐。伏事董先生，于今独萧索"，过了很多年，"独萧索"的杜甫在《昔游》诗中还是把与李白等人跟随董炼师在修行静室、炼丹炉旁参悟学习的经历看成一大乐事。

　　两位诗人要分别了，杜甫要去长安，李白要去吴越。杜甫

going to Jiangnan in the east. In "Presented to Li Bai," Du Fu wrote: "Mad drink and wild song, passing the days / High flying and domineering, heroes for whom?" Li Bai also composed "Seeing off Du Fu the Second at Eastern Stone Gate of Lu Commandary" to give as a souvenir. The emotions are very moving:

> How many more days of drunken farewells?
> Climbing to Bianchi Terrace.
> When will the road at Stone Gate,
> Again see the golden goblets used?
> Autumn waves descend upon the Si River;
> Sea view illuminates Mount Culai.
> Tumbleweed, each one's own way;
> So finish the cup in hand.

At this, the two poets each went their own way, never again to meet face to face. Nonetheless, the two poets did exchange poems. Li Bai longed for his younger poet friend: "Missing you upon the Wen River / Boldly setting myself on the southern journey." ❶ In Chang'an, Du Fu too longed for Li Bai, as expressed in "Missing Li Bai on a Spring Day" :

> Bai's poems are beyond comparison;
> Soaring ideas have no peers.
> Fresh and novel, like Commander Yu;
> Elegant and remote, like Adjutant Bao.
> North of the Wei, trees in spring;
> Jiangdong, clouds at dusk.
> When, over a cup of wine;
> Can we again analyze literature?

After a period of "In drunken slumber, we share an autumn blanket / Holding hands, we wander by day," Du Fu had an even deeper understanding of Li Bai. He praised Li Bai's ideas as being soaring and flowing, exceptional and superior, and his poetry as reaching a state of being "beyond comparison." Worthy of noting is that Du Fu accurately captured the characteristics of Li Bai's poetry: fresh and novel, elegant and remote. In the poem, "Commander Yu" refers to the Northern Wei literatus Yu Xin of the Northern and Southern Dynasties period. He was skilled at poetry and metrical prose. His works were novel and elegant, but in his later years, his style turned desolate and somber. "Adjutant Bao" refers to the Southern Song Dynasty literatus Bao Zhao, who specialized in *yuefu* ballad poems. His seven character ballads were especially

《赠李白》曰："痛饮狂歌空度日，飞扬跋扈为谁雄？"李白也写了《鲁郡东石门送杜二甫》诗为杜甫送行，情意深长，颇为动人：

> 醉别复几日？登临遍池台。
>
> 何时石门路，重有金樽开？
>
> 秋波落泗水，海色明徂徕。
>
> 飞蓬各自远，且尽手中杯。

两位诗人从此各奔东西，再也没能见面。但两人还有诗歌来往，李白想念自己的这位年轻朋友："思君汶水上，浩荡寄南征。"❶ 杜甫在长安也思念起李白，《春日忆李白》曰：

> 白也诗无敌，飘然思不群。
>
> 清新庾开府，俊逸鲍参军。
>
> 渭北春天树，江东日暮云。
>
> 何时一樽酒，重与细论文？

经过一段"醉眠秋共被，携手日同行"的生活，杜甫对李白的理解更深了。他称颂李白情思飘然流宕、卓异不凡，称赞他的诗歌已经到了"无敌"的境界。值得注意的是，杜甫准确地抓住了李诗的特点：清新、俊逸。诗中"庾开府"即南北朝北周的文学家庾信，擅长诗赋、骈文，作品清新艳丽，晚年风格转为苍凉沉雄。"鲍参军"即南朝宋时的文学家鲍照，长于乐府诗，特别是七言歌行写得酣畅感人，风格俊逸，影响很大。杜甫认为李诗清新有如庾信，俊逸类似鲍照，颇能把握李白诗歌

---

❶ 李白《沙丘城下寄杜甫》。

❶ Li Bai, "Sent to Du Fu While Beneath the Shaqiu City Wall."

uninhibited and moving. His elegant and remote style had far-reaching influences. In describing Li Bai's poems as fresh and novel like Yu Xin's, yet elegant and remote like Bao Zhao's, Du Fu captured the characteristics of Li Bai's poetry very well. Not only was Du Fu Li Bai's good friend, but also the greatest fan of his poetry. The distance between these two geniuses was very close.

At the time, Du Fu was in Chang'an, which is on the banks of the Wei River, and so is called "North of the Wei," and the scenery "North of the Wei, trees in spring." At the time, Li Bai was in the Jiangsu and Zhejiang region, which is called "Jiangdong." Du Fu imagined that the scene there was "Jiangdong, clouds at dusk." These two lines appear ordinary, but they are innovative: Du Fu, North of the Wei, misses the distant Li Bai. He raises his head and gazes off to the distance, and sees the spring trees north of the Wei stretching off into the horizon. At the same time, he imagines that Li Bai in Jiangdong is also missing him, and when Li Bai raises his head to gaze off into the distance, he sees a sky full of dusk clouds floating off into the western sky. "Spring trees and dusk clouds" has since become a common phrase depicting the longing between two friends.

Li Bai also understood Du Fu very well. It is said that he once wrote a poem titled "Given to Du Fu in Jest":

> Atop Fanke mountain, I meet Du Fu;
> Wearing a rainhat at high noon.
> I ask him why he has become so thin since I last saw him;
> "It is due to my earlier struggles to write poems."

Some suspect that this poem is not actually by Li Bai, but the description of Du Fu in this poem is quite vivid, saying that because it is so difficult for Du Fu to write poems that he has become too thin. It really does capture the characteristic of Du Fu. Li Bai was elegant and remote, not concerned with formalities. When his creativity flowed and his brush was in hand, one pitcher of wine would yield one hundred poems. Yet when Du Fu wrote poems, his attitude was stern, picking and choosing each word and phrase. In the second half of his life, when he understood that his ambitions would not be realized, his life's goal became to make his "collected poems last long throughout the world." He directed all of his energies into composing poetry, putting all of his heart and soul into it, demanding beauty and perfection. Du Fu was very serious about composing poetry. He himself said: "If the words do not shock people, I will not rest until death" ("The Waters of the River Are Like the Sea, So I Causally Describe It"). When the two great poets, each with a strong

的特点。杜甫不仅是李白的知己，也是李白诗歌的知音。两座高峰之间的距离总是最短。

杜甫此时在长安，长安在渭水边，故称"渭北"，景色是"渭北春天树"；李白此时所在的江浙一带，称为"江东"，杜甫想象他此时所见的情景是"江东日暮云"。两句看似平淡，却有新意：渭北的杜甫思念远方的李白，抬头远望，渭北一天春树伸向远方；他同时想象着江东的李白也正在想念自己，李白举目遥望，满天暮云止飘向西天。"春树暮云"后来就成了表达朋友思念的成语。

李白也很理解杜甫。据说他曾有一诗《戏赠杜甫》，诗曰：

饭颗山头逢杜甫，头戴笠子日卓午。

借问别来太瘦生，总为从前作诗苦。

有人怀疑此诗是伪作，但诗中描写杜甫形象颇为生动，说杜甫由于"作诗苦"而"太瘦生"，可谓是抓住了杜甫的特点。李白天才俊逸，不拘约束，诗思泉涌，援笔立就，斗酒诗百篇；而杜甫作诗，态度谨严，字斟句酌，中年之后，心中抱负难望成就，于是便将"诗卷长留天地间"作为自己的人生目标，倾注全身心力集中于诗歌创作，呕心沥血，力求尽善尽美。杜甫作诗用心良苦，自称"语不惊人死不休"（《江上值水如海势聊短述》）。两位具有强烈个性的大诗人相处在一起时，各自创作上的特点就更加鲜明了。对照自己下笔如注

personality, interact together, their individual personalities become even more evident. Compared to his own free flowing style of composition, Li Bai was able to even more clearly see Du Fu's quality of "the struggle to write poems." In this light, Li Bai was also Du Fu's true friend.

Although their personalities were very different, and their poetic qualities were also unlike, the intellectual worlds of Li Bai and Du Fu were very similar. They both exhibited bold, uninhibited, forthright, and obstinate strength. This was the foundation of their friendship. Geniuses in the world of poetry were often lonely, but Li Bai and Du Fu were born in the same time, and were able to meet and know each other. It was truly good fortune that they could become intimate friends.

的写作，李白更能清楚地看到杜甫的"作诗苦"的特点。从这方面说，李白也是杜诗的知音。

李、杜个性不同，诗风各异，但是，两人深层的精神世界中却极为相似，颇有相通，都具有一种雄放、张扬、坦荡、执著的强大力量，这是他们彼此成为知己的基础。诗国的天才常常寂寞孤独，但李、杜同生于一个时代，又能相遇、相识，彼此成为知己，确实很幸运。

李白的友人、唐代另一位大诗人杜甫画像
Portrait of Du Fu, a friend of Li Bai and
another great poet in the Tang Dynasty

七　彷徨：一生傲岸苦不谐

Chapter VII　Doubt: A Life on the Lonely Bank,
Suffering not Assimilating

Li Bai basically spent ten years, from 744, when he left Chang'an, to the outbreak of the An-Shi Rebellion in 755, wandering about. In "Expressing My Feelings, Presented to Drafter Cai Xiong," he wrote: "One day, I went to the capital / Ten years, I was a guest in Liang Garden." Liang Garden was in Kaifeng. He uses it here only to refer to the place where many people get together. In "Seeing Yang Yan off to Eastern Lu," he also wrote: "Once I parted from the golden court of magnificence / I wandered away by the banks of the Yangtze River." Likewise, he used "Yangtze River" to refer to his wandering about in the wilds.

During this period of time, his life consisted mainly of singing aloud and drinking without inhibition, seeking immortals and visiting Daoists, roaming about mountains and wandering along rivers.

While wandering through the regions of Bian and Song, through the introduction of a friend, Li Bai was initiated into the Daoist priesthood and became a formal Daoist. In "Roughly Creating the Elixir of Longevity, Presented to Liu Guandi," he wrote: "If I cannot roam in the golden court / I wish to be a guest in the Jade Court." This means he does not wish to be an imperial official any longer, but is committed to cultivating Daoist longevity techniques, desiring to achieve the realm of the gods and immortals. In "Composed upon Parting with the Gentlemen of Guangling," he said: "Working the elixir expends much fire / Picking herbs exhausts the mountains and rivers." He hurried about, practicing techniques and collecting medicinal herbs, hoping to extend his life and achieve longevity.

The poet would look out over the sea at the dawn mists, waving his hands: "Raising my hands, for what do I wait / The carriage of the blue dragon and the white tiger." ❶ What is he waiting for? He is hoping for a carriage drawn by a blue dragon and a white tiger and driven by a true immortal to appear.

He was standing at a cliff, looking out at the distance, where clouds and mist tangled and turned. The emerald green mountains on the other side appeared to be floating in the air. How much he wished for a multicolored rainbow to support a heavenly bridge: "If the immortals love me / They will raise their hands and wave at me." ❷ How much he wished for immortals to actually appear before him and wave at him.

Poets always have rich imaginations, but to be obsessed with fantasies of immortality, Li Bai had a much richer imagination than the usual poet. How many poets have to work hard to express their imagination, but Li Bai's supernatural realms of imagination and fantasy flow like the incoming tide.

从天宝三载（744）离开京城长安，到天宝十四载（755）安史乱爆发，这十年时间，李白基本是在各地漫游。他在《书情赠蔡舍人雄》中说："一朝去京国，十载客梁园。"梁园在开封，诗人此处不过是借"梁园"指称各地宾客云集之处而已。《送杨燕之东鲁》亦曰："一辞金华殿，蹭（cèng）蹬（dèng）长江边。"同样借"长江"之名，泛指浪迹江湖。

这段时期，高歌痛饮、寻仙访道、游览山水仍是他生活的主要内容。

李白在汴宋一带漫游时，经友人介绍，他在一座道观中正式举行入道的仪式，至此成了一名正式的道士。他《草创大还赠柳官迪》中说："不向金阙游，思为玉皇客。"意思说，他现在不再想做官，而是热衷于修道炼丹，渴望达到神仙的境界。《留别广陵诸公》中亦说："炼丹费火石，采药穷山川。"他奔走忙碌，炼丹采药，期望延年益寿。

诗人早晨遥望海边的朝霞，挥动着双手："举手何所待？青龙白虎车。"❶他在期待什么呢？他渴望着真的有仙人所乘的青龙白虎车出现。

他站在山崖上，遥看远方，云烟缭绕，对面青山苍翠，仿佛飘浮在空中。他多么希望能有五色彩虹，架起天桥："仙人如爱我，举手来相招。"❷仙人真的出现在他的面前，挥手召唤。

诗人总是充满想象，可是李白要比一般的诗人更加热衷于想象，沉溺于仙境的幻想之中。多数诗人写诗，不得不绞尽脑汁，发挥想象，然而李白的想象、梦幻般的情境、超越现实的

❶ 李白《早望海霞边》。
❷ 李白《焦山望松寥山》。

❶ Li Bai, "In the Morning, Gazing at the Clouds over the Sea Horizon."
❷ Li Bai, "At Mount Jiao, Gazing at Mount Songliao."

They take hold of him and cannot be shaken, so he has no choice but to describe them in poem. His poems are recreations of the fantasies in his mind. They are also his main method of satisfying his never resting spirit.

While in Shandong, Li Bai remembered the landscapes of Zhejiang. He was moved and agitated, and composed the famous long poem "Chant on Roaming Mount Tianmu in a Dream, Left as a Souvenir," in which he wrote: Of the immortal realms of the sea, there is Yingzhou, all around which, the waves are endless. Yet it is nowhere to be found. Mount Tianmu, in Zhejiang, may be shrouded in cloud and mist, yet one can climb it and roam about on it. It is rumored that, while hiking on Mount Tianmu, which is near the Shan River (in modern Xinchang County, Zhejiang), people have heard the song of the heavenly mother (*tianmu*), from which the mountain was named. Mount Tianmu is not high, but within Li Bai's imagination, "Tianmu reaches the heavens, all the way to the sky / Its force challenges the Five Sacred Mountains, overshadowing Chicheng / Tiantai, fourty-eight thousand yards / Almost collapses in comparison, leaning to the southeast." He says that the force and presence of Mount Tianmu exceeds that of the Five Sacred Mountains, and Mount Tiantai appears to be falling over at the feet of Mount Tianmu. The poet continued, saying:

> I wish, because of this, to dream of Wu and Yue,
> In one night fly past the moon in Mirror Lake.
> The moon in the lake shines on my shadow,
> Sending me to Shan River.
> The abode of Sir Xie is today still extant,
> The Lu River ripples, the gibbon calls are clear.
> Sir Xie clogs on my feet;
> I climb the white cloud steps.
> Half way up the cliff, I see the sea sun;
> In the sky I hear the heavenly rooster.
> A thousand cliffs and ten thousand turns, the road unsure;
> Distracted by flowers, leaning on a rock, suddenly it is dark.
> Bears roar and dragons call, the thunder of a cliff spring;
> Majestic deep forests, ahh, shocking layered peaks.
> The clouds are dark, ahh, about to rain;
> The water rippling, ahh, forming mist.
> Thunder piercing;
> Hills and peaks collapse.

景象却如潮水般涌来，魂牵梦萦，挥之不去，不得不诉之于诗歌。诗歌成了他脑海中幻境再现的形式，也是他满足因幻境而激动不已的心灵的主要手段。

在山东时，李白再次想起越中山水，他激动不已，写下了著名的《梦游天姥吟留别》长诗，诗中说：海上仙境有瀛洲，四周波涛茫茫，但却无处可寻求。越中天姥山，依稀掩映在云霞，却可登山攀岩去旅游。越中剡溪附近的天姥山（今浙江新昌县境内），传说登山人曾听到过仙人大姥的歌唱，因而得名。天姥山并不高，但在李白的想象中，却是"天姥连天向天横，势拔五岳掩赤城。天台四万八千丈，对此欲倒东南倾"。说天姥山的气势超过了五岳，而天台山看起来仿佛倾倒在天姥山的脚下。诗人接着说：

　　我欲因之梦吴越，一夜飞度镜湖月。

　　湖月照我影，送我至剡溪。

　　谢公宿处今尚在，渌（lù）水荡漾清猿啼。

　　脚着谢公屐，身登青云梯。

　　半壁见海日，空中闻天鸡。

　　千岩万转路不定，迷花倚石忽已暝。

　　熊咆龙吟殷岩泉，栗深林兮惊层巅。

　　云青青兮欲雨，水澹澹兮生烟。

　　列缺霹雳，丘峦崩摧。

The stone gate to the heavenly grotto,
Opens with a crash.
Dark and deep, no end to be seen;
Sun and moon shine upon the gold and silver terrace.
Rainbow for robes, ahh, wind for a horse;
The lords of clouds, ahh, come down, one after the other.
Tigers beat zithers, ahh, phoenix circling the carriages;
People of immortality, ahh, lined up like reeds.

The poet dreamt that he was in the landscape of the Wu and Yue region. In the reflected light of the moon, he flew over Mirror Lake, and arrived at the banks of Shan River. The residence of the Southern Dynasties poet Xie Lingyun was clearly still there, but he heard only the gurgling of the flowing water nearby and the calls of the mountain gibbons. Wearing mountain clogs designed by Xie Lingyun, he climbed his way up the mountain path. Half way up, he saw a red sun rise up from the ocean and heard a rooster crowing to announce the dawn. As the stone path wound its way upward, the poet rested against a stone next to a patch of flowers. Suddenly, the valley turned dark, almost as if dusk had descended. The poet shivered as he heard the sound of a mountain waterfall and the roars of bears and calls of dragons echoing in the deep and dark forest and against the valley walls. Black clouds rolled in and mist rose from all directions, almost as if a mountain storm were approaching. Suddenly, a crack of thunder pealed and rocks from the peaks fell. The stone gate of a heavenly grotto opened with a roar. A powerful ray of light pierced through, and the blessed land of the heavenly grotto dazzled the eyes. The gold and silver terrace was brilliant, almost as if the sun and moon shone together. He saw divine immortals descending, the "lord of the clouds" floating over, wearing rainbows for robes and driving the long wind for horses. Tigers and leopards strummed lutes and zithers for him, and phoenixes drive his chariot. Crowds of immortals disseminated about ... yet, when the poet woke up, the mist cleared before his very eyes, and the immortals were nowhere to be found. The poet concludes with the lament:

Worldly pleasure is also like this:
The myriad matters, from times ancient, are as the easterly flowing
waters.
Parting with you, Sir, ahh, when will you return?
Let then a white deer go in the green valley;
Soon I will ride it to visit the famous mountains.

洞天石扉，訇（hōng）然中开。

青冥浩荡不见底，日月照耀金银台。

霓为衣兮风为马，云之君兮纷纷而来下。

虎鼓瑟兮鸾回车，仙之人兮列如麻。

诗人梦见自己来到吴越的山水之间，在月光的映照下，飞过镜湖，来到剡溪边。南朝诗人谢灵运当年的住处分明还在，只听见附近流水潺潺，山猿清啼。脚穿着谢灵运当年特制的登山木屐，沿着山路拾级而上。走到半山腰处，看见一轮红日正从海上升起，还听见天鸡高唱报晓。石径蜿蜒向上，诗人在花丛边倚石休息。忽然山谷变得昏暗起来，仿佛暮色降临。诗人不寒而栗，只听岩泉飞湍之音，熊咆龙吟之声，震荡在幽深的密林之中，回响在峡谷山崖之上。乌云涌动，水雾四起，好似山雨欲来。突然间，霹雳震响，峰峦岩石为之崩落。洞天的石门，轰然打开。一道强烈的光线直射出来，洞天福地之中光亮耀眼，金银台金碧辉煌，仿佛日月同时照耀。只见神仙纷然而下，"云之君"以彩虹为衣，长风为马，飘然而来。虎豹为之鼓琴弹琴，凤鸾为之驾车回旋，成群仙人排布得密密麻麻……可是，等到诗人惊醒，眼前烟霞四散，仙人也杳无踪迹。诗人最后感慨：

世间行乐亦如此，古来万事东流水。

别君去兮何时还？且放白鹿青崖间，须行即骑访名山。

How can I lower my brow and bend my waist to serve the
aristocrats,
    Causing myself unhappiness?

The poet is not willing to compromise by bowing to those powerful aristocrats.
He wishes to ride a white deer to visit the famous mountains and lead a
carefree and unrestrained life.

He gathered his luggage and set off on new journeys. He passed through
Yangzhou and Jinling, and ended up in Zhejiang. He climbed Mount Tiantai,
and prepared to again visit He Zhizhang. He Zhizhang's home was in Siming,
near modern Shaoxing. He held Li Bai in great esteem, calling him the "exiled
immortal," for which Li bai was grateful. A few years earlier, when He
Zhizhang returned home, Li Bai wrote "Seeing Guest He off to Return to
Yue" as a souvenir. When Li Bai arrived at He Zhizhang's home, he
discovered that He had died shortly after returning home. Li Bai composed
"Facing Wine, Remembering Supervisor He" in eulogy:

> There is a wild guest from Siming;
> Debonair He Jizhen.
> On first meeting in Chang'an;
> He called me the exiled immortal.
> Before, he loved the thing in the cup;
> Today, he is the dust beneath the pine.
> At the place where he exchanged his golden seal for wine;
> I remember, tears soaking my kerchief.

Li Bai left Zhejiang, setting off on his return journey to settle down in Jinling.
His life in Jinling can reveal very well his contradictory and confused
emotional world. Before he was admitted to the Hanlin Academy, Li Bai had
great ambitions, planning to achieve great things, and then retire to the
mountains and forests. During this time, his life's goals were very clear, and
even though he met with many disappointments, he still kept his goals in sight
and maintained a cheerful disposition. Two years in the central court, though,
not only brought him glory and firmly established his reputation as a poet, but
also tore down his youthful aspirations, proving to him that his political
ambitions could never be attained. After leaving the capital, he fell into
desolation and lost his direction. Drinking and singing, taking courtesans out
roaming, seeking immortals and studying Daoism, all could not settle his
restless soul. He sang in deep melancholy:

安能摧眉折腰事权贵，使我不得开心颜。

诗人不愿委曲求全，折腰逢迎那些权贵们，而是想骑着白鹿游访名山，过着无拘无束、悠闲自得的生活。

诗人收拾行囊，开始了新的漫游。他经过扬州、金陵等地，最后到达越中。他登天台山，又准备拜访贺知章。贺知章家在四明，即今浙江绍兴一带，他非常赏识李白，称之为"谪仙人"，李白对此十分感激。几年前，贺知章还乡时，李白作《送贺宾客归越》一诗送别。李白来到贺知章家，得知他回乡不久就病逝了。诗人作《对酒忆贺监》，凭吊友人：

四明有狂客，风流贺季真。

长安一相见，呼我谪仙人。

昔好杯中物，今为松下尘。

金龟换酒处，却忆泪沾巾。

李白离开越中，启程回返，在金陵停留下来。金陵时期的生活，颇能显现出他矛盾、迷茫的内心世界。供奉翰林之前，李白胸怀大志，一心期望能够成就大业，然后归隐山林。这一时期他的人生目标非常明确，虽然多次遭遇挫折，但他始终充满自信，保持乐观的情绪。但两年多"近臣"的生活，一方面给他带来了荣耀，确立了他的诗歌创作的重要地位，另一方面却摧毁了他早年的理想，他所期望的政治成就根本不可能实现。离开京城，他陷入迷茫的境地，失去了人生的方向。尽管他饮酒高歌，携妓出游，寻仙访道，但这些似乎都不能使他躁动不安的心灵得以平静。他沉郁地唱道：

A life on the lonely bank, suffering not assimilating;
Favor distant, recommenders have toiled, my ambitions are mostly
distorted.
Yan Ling gave standing greetings to the Han Son of Heaven;
What need to hang one's sword and serve the jade dais.
Success in one's career is not worth valuing;
And failure is not worth grieving.
Han Xin was humiliated to be compared to Jiang and Guan;
Mi Heng was ashamed to associate with butchers and bar hands.
Don't you see Li of Beihai?
Where are his valor and heroism today?
Don't you see Minister Pei?
His grave mound is overgrown with weeds three yards tall.
From youth I already wanted to go to the five lakes;
Seeing this, I certainly keep the bells and vessels distant. ❶

He lashed out at the benighted government; fame and fortune, glory and riches, all are fleeting things. One needs not busy oneself over such external glory. He might as well lead the secluded life that he longed for since his early years.

However, in the chaos and turmoil, he still had one last fleeting illusion. Climbing Phoenix Terrace in Jinling, he sang:

On Phoenix Terrace, the phoenix roams;
The phoenix leaves and the terrace is empty, but the river flows on.
The path to the Wu palace is overgrown by grass and flowers;
The robes and caps of the Jin Dynasty have become ancient
mounds.
Three Hills half fallen, beyond the blue sky;
Two rivers divided in the middle by White Egret Isle.
Drifting clouds can always block the sun;
That Chang'an is not visible makes one sad. ❷

The Eastern Wu of the Three Kingdoms period and the Eastern Jin Dynasty established their capitals in Jinling. What was formerly the capital now has only ruins of palaces, with weeds overgrowing the small pathways. Of the debonair characters of yore, nothing is left today but the grave mounds all about. The poet stood on Phoenix Terrace, gazing off toward Chang'an. Chang'an is where the court was. The "sun" represents the emperor. Drifting clouds have blocked the sun and Chang'an cannot be seen. This reveals the poet's concern for politics. After having left Chang'an, Li Bai drifted about the

一生傲岸苦不谐，恩疏媒劳志多乖。

严陵高揖汉天子，何必长剑拄颐事玉阶。

达亦不足贵，穷亦不足悲。

韩信羞将绛、灌比，祢衡耻逐屠沽儿。

君不见李北海，英风豪气今何在？

君不见裴尚书，土坟三尺蒿棘居。

少年早欲五湖去，见此弥将钟鼎疏。 **❶**

他抨击昏暗的时政，功名利禄、荣华富贵都是转瞬即逝的东西。人生不需要为这种外在的荣誉奔波，还不如去过早年就盼望的归隐生活。

但在纷乱嘈杂、茫然无措之中，他还有最后一丝幻想。他登上金陵凤凰台，吟唱道：

凤凰台上凤凰游，凤去台空江自流。

吴宫花草埋幽径，晋代衣冠成古丘。

三山半落青天外，二水中分白鹭洲。

总为浮云能蔽日，长安不见使人愁。 **❷**

三国东吴、东晋建都在金陵。往日的都城，如今却是宫殿荒芜，花草长满了小径；昔日的风流人物而今也只剩下处处墓冢。诗人站在金陵凤凰台上，遥望长安。长安是朝廷所在，"日"是帝王的象征，浮云蔽日，长安不见，表现出诗人对政治的关注。李白离开长安后，漂泊东西，学道求仙，表面看起来，他已经

❶ 李白《答王十二寒夜独酌有怀》。
❷ 李白《登金陵凤凰台》。
❶ Li Bai, "Answering Wang the Twelfth; With Concerns Drinking on a Cold Night."
❷ Li Bai, "Climbing Phoenix Pavilion in Jinling."

east and west, studying Daoism and seeking immortality. On the surface, he did not appear to have any interest in government, but deep down in his heart, it was not so simple. Of course, two or three years in the Hanlin Academy had caused him great disappointment, and his determination to retire to the hills and woods became even more resolute, but once he settled in the woods and traveled the wilds, he again felt extremely lost. While he was living a life of drinking and singing, he retained a fantasy that would be very difficult to realize. In his roamings, distant from the government, he hid an expectation that the average person could never hold. His youthful ambitions had taken on a much more complex form.

Within his dispirited disillusionment, he embraced one final sliver of hope. Wandering about the wilds, he often thought of his children, "two children are in the east of Lu gate / Since parting, several years have already past." ❶ When friends went back to Shandong, he asked them to look on his family for him:

> My family has settled next to Shaqiu;
> Not returning for three years has only broken my heart.
> When you travel, you have come to know my son Boqin;
> He ought to be driving a small cart and riding a white goat. ❷

Li Bai imagined that, after not returning home for several years, his children must have grown some. They must be driving small carts and riding white goats in play. Once he thought of his children, this mad and unfettered genius poet finally exposed his soft side:

> The Wu mulberry leaves are green;
> The Wu silkworms have already entered their third slumber.
> My family has settled in Eastern Lu;
> Who will plant the fields on the north slope of Mount Gui?
> It is already too late for the spring work;
> And water travel is also hopeless.
> The southern wind blows the returning heart;
> And drops it before the tavern.
> East of the tavern is a peach tree;
> The leaves and branches caress the green mist.
> This tree was planted by me;
> Since I left, it has been three years.
> The peach tree today is already as high as the tavern;
> But my travels have not yet come full circle.

不再对政治抱有什么兴趣了，但他的内心深处，并非如此简单。当然，两三年的翰林经历确实使他对现实政治颇多失望，隐退江湖的想法时而变得很坚决，可是，当他栖身林泉、游历江湖时，又觉得非常失落。在痛饮高歌的生活中，他保持着某种很难实现的幻想；在远离政治的轨迹中，他始终暗藏着某种一般人根本无法期待的期待。早年的理想如今以一种更加复杂的形式出现。

在颓唐无力、萎靡不振之中，他还是怀着最后的真挚。浪迹江湖，他时常想念自己的子女，"二子鲁门东，别来已经年" ❶。有朋友回东鲁，他请求代回家看看：

我家寄在沙丘旁，三年不归空断肠。

君行既识伯禽子，应驾小车骑白羊。 ❷

李白想象着几年不归，儿女都已经长大很多，一定会驾着小车、骑着白羊在玩耍。当他想起自己的孩子时，这位狂放不羁（jī）的天才诗人终于显露温情的一面：

吴地桑叶绿，吴蚕已三眠。

我家寄东鲁，谁种龟阴田？

春事已不及，江行复茫然。

南风吹归心，飞堕酒楼前。

楼东一株桃，枝叶拂青烟。

此树我所种，别来向三年。

桃今与楼齐，我行尚未旋。

❶ 李白《送杨燕之东鲁》。
❷ 李白《送萧三十一之鲁中兼问稚子伯禽》。

❶ Li Bai, "Seeing off Yang Yan to Eastern Lu."
❷ Li Bai, "Seeing off Xiao the Thrity-first to Lu, Also Asking After My Young Child Boqin."

My beautiful daughter's name is Pingyang;
Plucking flowers, leaning next to the peach tree.
Plucking flowers, she sees me not;
Tears fall like a flowing spring.
My young son's name is Boqin;
As tall as his sister.
They walk together under the peach tree;
Patting each other's back , who else will love them?
Thinking of how this has come to pass;
My heart burns daily with sorrow.
I lay out paper to write my distant feelings;
And so I go to Wenyang River. ❶

In 751, at the age of fifty-one, after remaining in Jiangnan for a long time, Li Bai returned to Eastern Lu to be reunited with his children. Shortly thereafter, he returned to Liang Garden to marry the grand-daughter of Zong Chuke.

Zong Chuke was a relative of the Empress Wu Zetian, and was the Grand Councilor three times. His social standing was very high, but he was corrupt and took bribes, using his position for his personal benefit. In the end, he was killed in a political struggle. Li Bai did not seem to mind Zong Chuker's poor reputation, and still married his grand-daughter. They had a happy marriage. When Li Bai met with misfortune, his wife did her best to help him. When his wife wanted to go to Mount Lu to visit the Daoist priestess Li Tengkong, Li Bai was very supportive, and sent her off saying: "The daughter of the councilor to multiple lords / Learns the Dao and loves the immortals." ❷ While wandering about the land, Li Bai wrote many poems to his wife expressing his love. Sometimes, he would even borrow his wife's voice to write poems to himself, imagining how much his wife missed him.

Fall of this year, the Administrative Assistant to the Military Commissioner of Youzhou, He Changhao, came to visit and invite Li Bai to a position under the Military Commissioner. At the time, Youzhou was under the jurisdiction of An Lushan, who had been planning treason for some time. He saw that Xuanzong was getting old and was obsessed with pleasure, and that the court was overrun with treacherous officials. All great powers must come to an end, and so An Lushan began assembling a private army and waiting for an opportunity. In "Presented to Administrative Assistant He Changhao the Seventh," he expressed a desire to join the ranks of the commissioner and fulfill his ambitions, but he had already heard of An Lushan's treasonous plans.

Li Bai decided to first go to the commandary to gain an understanding of

娇女字平阳，折花倚桃边。

折花不见我，泪下如流泉。

小儿名伯禽，与姊亦齐肩。

双行桃树下，抚背复谁怜？

念此失次第，肝肠日忧煎。

裂素写远意，因之汶阳川。 ❶

天宝十载（751），在滞留江南多时之后，五十一岁的李白回到东鲁，与孩子们团聚。不久，他赶到梁苑，与宗楚客的孙女结婚。子女还是留在了东鲁。

宗楚客是皇后武则天的亲戚，曾经三次做宰相，地位很高，但贪赃枉法，依附权贵，后因政治纷争被杀。李白似乎并没有顾忌宗楚客的名声，还是与宗氏女结婚了。婚后，夫妇之间感情很好。李白落难，夫人四处奔走，试图营救。夫人要去庐山寻访女道士李腾空，李白非常赞同，称"多君相门女，学道爱神仙"❷，为她送行。在浪迹天涯的日子里，李白写有很多诗歌赠送妻子，抒写他的眷恋之情；有时又以妻子的口吻来写诗，想象妻子如何思念他。

这一年秋天，幽州节度使幕府判官何昌浩来访，欲邀李白入幕。当时统辖幽州的安禄山久有图谋不轨之心。他看到玄宗年事日高，纵情声色，朝廷奸邪当道，盛极转衰，便暗自招兵买马，等待时机。李白在《赠何七判官昌浩》诗中虽然表达了渴望加入军幕、建功立业的愿望，但此时，他对安禄山图谋不轨，已有所闻。

诗人决定，先到军中了解事实的真相，再作决定，所以还

❶ 李白《寄东鲁二稚子》。
❷ 李白《送内寻庐山女道士李腾空二首》之二。

❶ Li Bai, "Sent to My Two Young Children in Eastern Lu."
❷ Li Bai, Second of "Two Poems Sending My Wife off to Seek the Daoist Priestess Li Tengkong of Mount Lu."

the situation before making his decision, so he still headed north to Youzhou. When he arrived in Kaifeng and prepared to cross the river, he wrote: "To explore the tiger's lair, I head for the desert / Cracking my whip and galloping the horse, I cross the Yellow River." "Tiger's lair" here refers to An Lushan's camp, and "desert" refers to Youzhou.

In the winter of 752, he arrived at Youzhou. Before long, he gained an understanding of matters in the north. In "Song of the Northern Wind," he wrote: "Mount Yan snowflakes large as seat cushions / Flakes blowing down on Xuanyuan Terrace." Mount Yan is next to Youzhou, referring to An Lushan's territory. "Snowflakes large as seat cushions" on the surface describes the frigid cold of the land, and secretly refers to the severity of the crisis. Xuanyuan Terrace refers to the heartland, implying that war is about to come, and that the heartland is threatened. Once Li Bai saw that An Lushan was about to rebel, he was very much concerned, and intended to submit to the court plans to avert the crisis. This never came to be, though, as many others who reported An Lushan's rebellious intentions were sent by the Emperor Xuanzong to Youzhou to be punished by An Lushan. Helplessly, Li Bai could only silently return to the south, eventually arriving at Xuancheng.*

The landscape near Xuancheng was beautiful, and this was also where the Southern Dynasty poet Xie Tiao served. Li Bai liked here very much, and did not want to leave. Li Bai was fascinated by the literary styles of the Northern and Southern Dynasties poets, and especially that of Xie Tiao. He often expressed admiration in poems, such as "Sending off Secretary Shuyun at Xie Tiao Tower in Xuancheng" :

> That which abandoned me and left;
> Yesterday's days cannot be kept back.
> That which has disordered my heart;
> Today's day is troublesome.
> The long wind, ten thousand miles, sends an autumn goose;
> To this I can drink on the tall tower.
> Penglai prose, Jian'an bones;
> In the center, Little Xie again waxes eloquently.
> My heart becomes ever more leisurely, heroic ideas fly away;
> I wish to ascend the blue heavens, and seize the brilliant moon.
> Draw a sword and cut the river, yet the river continues to flow;
> Lift a cup to drown my sorrows, yet the sorrows become even more.

是北上幽州。到了开封，准备渡河，李白写道："且探虎穴向沙漠，鸣鞭走马凌黄河。"此处"虎穴"是指安禄山的老巢，"沙漠"即指幽州。

天宝十一载（752）十月，他抵达幽州，不久，即对北方的情况有所了解。在《北风行》一诗中，他写道："燕山雪花大如席，片片吹落轩辕台。"诗中"燕山"与幽州相邻，指安禄山盘踞之地。"雪花大如席"明写其地苦寒，暗喻当时危机深重。"轩辕台"借指中原，意思是战乱将及，中原危机。李白已经看出安禄山将会谋反，心中十分担忧，打算向朝廷献计献策，提出解决危机的办法。但这件事情并未实行，当时许多通报安禄山谋反的人都被玄宗遣送到幽州让安禄山处置。李白无能为力，只得悄悄南返，最后到了宣城。

宣城附近，水光山色，风景颇佳，又是南朝诗人谢朓（tiǎo）做官的地方，李白十分喜爱这里，流连忘返。李白对魏晋南北朝诗人的文采风流，极为神往，对谢朓的诗歌更是情有独钟，常在诗中表示倾慕，《宣城谢朓楼饯别校书叔云》曰：

> 弃我去者，昨日之日不可留；
> 乱我心者，今日之日多烦忧。
> 长风万里送秋雁，对此可以酣高楼。
> 蓬莱文章建安骨，中间小谢又清发。
> 俱怀逸兴壮思飞，欲上青天揽明月。
> 抽刀断水水更流，举杯消愁愁更愁。

---

* Xuancheng, in modern Anhui Province.

Life on earth does not follow one's wishes;
Tomorrow morning, let the hair loose, and board a small boat.

Xie Tiao had served as the Governor of Xuancheng. There is a tower there, and the local people call it Xie Tiao Tower. This poem is bold and expressive, with little restraint, coming out of nowhere, and gone without a trace; the reader has no option but to just follow along as the poet takes an emotional ride. It begins with all sorts of sorrows and worries, but facing the howling wind and autumn geese, the poet frees his mind and drinks heartily, renewing his state of mind. "Penglai prose" refers to Han literature. As the poet ascended Xie Tiao Tower, he thought of Xie Tiao. From Han literature and the Seven Masters of Jian'an to contemporaneous poetry and prose, Xie Tiao's style was truly the most delicate and extensive. It attracted the reader's attention. In fact, when Li Bai thought of himself, he believed that those extraordinary poets all possessed the grand ambitions to "ascend the blue heavens, and seize the brilliant moon." Just as his emotions reached their climax, the poet again came out with a line from nowhere, saying he draws his sword to cut the river and uses wine to drown his sorrow. Once he points out the hopelessness of consolation, his mood once again drops to rock bottom. In the end, he presents the utterly hopeless answer, which is no answer: "Life on earth does not follow one's wishes / Tomorrow morning, let the hair loose, and board a small boat." The poet disappears into vast serenity.

At this time, Li Bai met a famous admirer who is often mentioned because of his enthusiastic admiration. In 754, Li Bai traveled to Guangling (modern Yangzhou, Jiangsu Province), where he met a young poet, Wei Wan. Wei Wan later changed his name to Wei Hao and retired to Mount Wangwu (in modern Yangcheng, Shanxi Province), and took the name of Recluse of Mount Wangwu. He greatly admired Li Bai, and wished to meet him face to face, and so he followed Li Bai's tracks for two to three years. He rushed to Kaifeng and then to Shandong before hearing that Li Bai had long since gone south. He then followed him to Jiangsu and Zhejiang, but Li Bai had already left that region. He then went to Guangling before finally meeting Li Bai. Li Bai was not exaggerating when he said Wei Hao "Drifted east to the waters of the Bian River / Visiting me three thousand *li* away." ❶ Li Bai found Wei Hao dressed in a Japanese fur coat and in high spirits; Wei Hao found Li Bai with brilliant eyes, debonair and refined. The two got along very well together. The Japanese fur coat Wei Hao wore was a gift of Chao Heng (Japanese name Abe no Nakamaro), a Nara Japanese scholar who traveled to China to study, and later

人生在世不称意，明朝散发弄扁舟。

谢朓做过宣城太守，当地有一座楼，人称谢朓楼。这首诗写得酣畅淋漓，发兴无端，来无踪，去无影，我们只有随着诗人的激情起伏上下。本是各种烦扰、忧愁，但面对长风秋雁，开怀畅饮，诗人的情绪重新振作起来。"蓬莱文章"即指汉代文学。诗人登谢朓楼，联想起谢朓，从汉代文学、建安七子，到近代的诗文，谢朓的风格真是清秀而发越，引人瞩目。实际上，诗人想到了自己，他认为，那些杰出的诗人都具有"欲上青天揽明月"的壮思。正当激情上扬之时，诗人又破空而来一句，抽刀截水，借酒浇愁。一旦点出慰藉的徒然，诗人的情绪再次跌落谷底。最后，在给出了"人生在世不称意，明朝散发弄扁舟"这一无可奈何、不是答案的答案之后，诗人消退在无边的宁静之中。

李白此时遇到了一位著名的崇拜者，崇拜者因为他的热情而每每被后人提起。天宝十三载（754），李白到了广陵（今江苏扬州），遇到一位青年诗人，他就是魏万。魏万后改名魏颢，隐居在王屋山（今山西阳城境内），号王屋山人。他十分仰慕李白，希望能够会面，于是连续两三年，都在追寻李白的游踪。青年人赶到开封，又追到山东，才知道李白早已南下，再寻到吴越，李白却已经离开，直到广陵才得以相见。李白说魏颢"东浮汴河水，访我三千里"❶，并非虚言。李白看魏颢，身著日本裘，精神抖擞；魏颢看李白，更是目光炯然，风流蕴藉。两人相谈，十分投机。魏颢穿的日本裘是日本奈良时代遣唐的留学生晁衡送的，晁衡，原名阿倍仲麻吕，后来一直住在中国。

❶ 李白《送王屋山人魏万还王屋》。

❶ Li Bai, "Seeing Wei Wan, Recluse of Mount Wangwu, off to Return to Mount Wangwu."

remained there. Wei Hao's Japanese coat left a deep impression on Li Bai. Although Li Bai was already fifty-four years old and Wei Hao was very young, the two had the same interests. In their travels together, they got along together very well. Li Bai believed that Wei Hao would become famous sooner or later, and even gave Wei Hao his manuscripts, asking Wei Hao to compile them for him. Later, Wei Hao did pass the Presented Scholar examination and compiled *Li Hanlin Ji* (*Collected Works of Hanlin Academician Li*), and even composed a preface for it. This was Li Bai's earliest compilation of poems, but it is no longer extant. Only the preface remains. The two then shared a boat to Jinling, where they parted. Li Bai said to him: "If the Yellow River does not stop flowing / The white-headed will long miss you." Wei Hao also said: "This parting is not a long parting." ❶ From then on, they did not meet each other any more.

Just as Li Bai was wandering about in Jiangnan, a great civil strife finally broke out.

魏颢穿着日本裘，给李白留下很深的印象。李白此时已经五十四岁，而魏颢则很年轻，但两人志趣相合，一道游览，十分相得。李白相信他今后一定会成名，还将自己的诗文稿交给他，请他编集。后来，魏颢果然中了进士，编好了《李翰林集》，还写了一篇序言。这是李白最早的诗集，但现在已经散佚，只留下那篇序言。两人随后同舟来到金陵，并在金陵分手。李白对他说："黄河若不断，白首长相思。"魏颢也说："此别未远别。"❶ 但两人此后再也没能重逢。

正当李白在江南一带逗留时，一场大内乱终于爆发了。

---

❶ 李白《送王屋山人魏万还王屋》；魏万《金陵酬翰林谪仙子》。

❶ Li Bai, "Seeing Wei Wan, Recluse of Mount Wangwu, off to Return to Mount Wangwu" ; Wei Wan, "Thanking Hanlin Scholar Exiled Immortal in Jinling."

唐代绘画中的宫廷仕女
Court women of the Tang paintings

八　动乱：战鼓惊山欲倾倒

Chapter VIII　Rebellion: War Drums Shock the Hills, Causing Them to Tumble

In his early years, Emperor Xuanzong focused his energies on governing the empire, but in his older age, he believed the empire was peaceful, so he did not pay much attention to government. He entrusted the central government to a few high ministers while he wallowed in pleasure and entertainment. At the time, Li Linfu held the reigns of the government. He had always catered to the emperor's wishes with lips of honey, but he held daggers in his bosom. He often framed the innocent as he eradicated all who disagreed with him. Many of Li Bai's friends and people whom he respected, such as Cui Chengfu, Li Shizhi, and Li Yong, had been either exiled or killed. Li Linfu also obstructed the talented. In 747, Emperor Xuanzong wished to discover talented scholars throughout the empire. To select the most talented, he ordered all talented and able scholars to assemble in the capital to sit for a Special Examination. Fearing that these examinees would reveal his devious wrong-doings, Li Linfu established a multitude of obstacles. In the end, not one single person passed the examination. He submitted a document congratulating the emperor, saying that he had not overlooked any talented scholar in the entire empire. By this time, Xuanzong was already so muddled that he seemed to not even notice the problem.

In 745, Emperor Xuanzong conferred the title of Honored Consort upon Yang Taizhen. Consort Yang's appearance was full and amorous, touching and moving. She was knowledgeable in music, was a good singer and dancer, and therefore quickly received the attention of the emperor, resulting in the saying: "The love of three thousand was all on one person." Consort Yang loved to eat lychees, but this fruit grows only in the southern regions and remains fresh only a few days. For this reason, the emperor ordered the southern regions to rush lychees into the court via express horse relay. The road from the south to the capital in the northwest spanned several thousand miles, and uncountable relay stations were prepared for the express post horses to deliver the lychees. The Late Tang poet Du Mu composed the poem "Passing Huaqing Palace," in which he wrote: "Looking back at Chang'an, the embroidery is in mounds / The thousand gates on the mountain top open in order / One rider in red dust, and the consort smiles / No one knows that it is the lychees arriving." The post horse gallops, the palace gates open, and what is delivered is only the Honored Consort's fruit. Even worse, once she was promoted, she brought along many relatives. Her relatives received various official appointments and enfeoffments. Yang Guozhong was one beneficiary. Yang Guozhong was brash, and enjoyed drinking and gambling. The emperor valued him, and he was quickly promoted to the upper levels of court service. He arrived in the

玄宗早年励精图治，但晚年以为天下太平，对政治无所用心，将朝政交给了几个大臣，而自己则沉溺于声色享乐之中。当时李林甫执政，他一向迎合皇帝的心意，口蜜腹剑，屡兴冤狱，诛锄异己。李白的一些好友和敬仰的对象，如崔成甫、李适之、李邕等，或遭贬，或被杀。李林甫又阻断贤路。天宝六载（747），玄宗欲广求天下杰出之士，命各地有才能的人都到京城参加专门的考试，以获得选拔。李林甫怕这些应试者揭露其奸恶，设置重重阻碍，最后，竟然没有一个人被选中。他上表祝贺皇帝说，朝野上下没有被遗漏的贤才。玄宗此时已经昏愦，丝毫不觉得其中的问题。

天宝四载（745），玄宗册封杨太真为贵妃。杨贵妃姿质丰艳，楚楚动人，熟悉音律，能歌善舞，很快得到玄宗无比的宠爱，所谓"三千宠爱在一身"。杨贵妃喜吃荔枝，可是这种水果产自南方，保持新鲜又不过几天，于是，皇帝命令岭南每年驰驿进贡。从岭南到西北京城有数千里的路程，无数个驿站备马疾驰，传送荔枝。晚唐诗人杜牧有《过华清宫》诗咏其事："长安回望绣成堆，山顶千门次第开。一骑红尘妃子笑，无人知是荔枝来。"驿马疾驰，宫门大开，送来的只是贵妃想吃的水果。更有甚者，一人得道，鸡犬升天。杨玉环的亲戚都纷纷加官晋爵，杨国忠也是其中的获益者。杨国忠生性豪爽，好饮酒，善赌博，深得皇上的赏识，青云直上。他于天宝四载

capital in the fall of 745, and in less than ten years, he became Grand Councilor. He became famous throughout the empire, and held supreme power. These high officials thought only of their own power, glory, and enrichment, with no regard for the crisis the empire was facing. The chaos in the central court during the latter half of Xuanzong's reign was largely responsible for the outbreak of the An-Shi Rebellion.

In the winter of 755, An Lushan, Military Commissioner of the three towns of Pinglu, Fanyang, and Hedong, mobilized his army in Fanyang (in modern Beijing), claiming that he received a secret order to arrest Yang Guozhong. He led an alliance of his own troops and Khitan troops, forming an army of two hundred thousand "sharp infantry and cavalry." He brazenly marched toward Luoyang, dust flying for a thousand *li*, and the clamor of drums shaking the heavens.

The curtain opened on the "An-Shi Rebellion."

An Lushan (705?—757), of multi-racial descent, was from Liucheng of Yingzhou (modern Chaoyang, Liaoning Province). His father was a Hun, and his mother, who was a fortuneteller, was a Turki. By nature, An Lushan was fierce and belligerent. "Galuoshan" was the name of the god of war in Turkic, so he was named Galuoshan. Later, he took the Chinese surname An, and sinified Galuoshan to become An Lushan. An Lushan lost his father at a young age, and roamed about in his youth. As he became an adult, fluent in six Central Asian languages, he became a merchant, conducting trade, and also committing occasional petty thievery. He was finally arrested by the Military Commissioner of Youzhou, Zhang Shougui, for stealing sheep. Zhang Shougui ordered him stripped and prepared to beat him to death. Seeing that he was about to lose his life, An Lushan shouted out: "Doesn't Your Honor wish to defeat the foreigners? Why beat Lushan to death?" Seeing that he was large and strong, and that he did not speak like a common person, the Military Commissioner loosened his ropes and pardoned him of his death sentence. Not much later, he made An Lushan a subordinate commander along with Shi Siming. Shi Siming was also a multi-racial native of Yingzhou. They were both fellow townsmen, had known each other since childhood, and had done business together. An Lushan was big and Shi Siming was skinny. The two were quite diligent in their jobs, and were quickly promoted to assistant generals. An Lushan was cunning, and was good at manipulating people's emotions. Zhang Shougui liked him, and treated him like an adoptive son. An Lushan was once defeated in battle, and according to martial law, should have been beheaded. Zhang Shougui could not bring himself to kill An Lushan, but

（745）的秋天奔赴京城，不到十年的功夫，就做到了宰相，权倾天下，声名显赫。这几位大臣光想到自己的荣华富贵，争权夺利，根本不考虑国家面临的危机。玄宗时代后期朝政的混乱在很大程度上促成了安史之乱的爆发。

天宝十四载（755）十一月，平卢、范阳、河东三镇节度使安禄山以奉密诏讨杨国忠为名，在范阳（治在今北京）起兵。他率领所部以及契丹等盟军，号称二十万"步骑精锐"的大军，烟尘千里，鼓噪震天，浩浩荡荡地向洛阳进发。

"安史之乱"拉开了序幕。

安禄山（705？—757）本是营州柳城（今辽宁朝阳）的混血胡人。父亲胡人；母亲突厥人，以卜为业。安禄山天生勇猛好斗，突厥语中称战神为"轧荦（luò）山"，所以就取名轧荦山。后来冒姓安，谐音轧荦山就叫做安禄山。安禄山从小死了父亲，少年时代浪迹天涯。长大后，能通六蕃语，做起商人，从事中介贸易，时而也做一些鸡鸣狗盗的事情，终于有一次因为盗羊而被幽州节度使张守珪抓住。张守珪令人扒了他的衣服，就要一顿好打，直至杖杀。眼看着命就要没了，安禄山急着大叫："大夫不欲灭两蕃耶？何为打杀禄山！"节度使一看这人长得肥壮，有些模样，说话也不同寻常，于是就给他松绑，免了死罪。不久，让他与史思明一起在手下做了小将。史思明也是营州混血胡人，两人同乡，自幼相识，一同做过生意。安禄山长得肥硕，史思明长得精瘦，两人干得十分卖力，不久升为偏将。安禄山生性狡黠，善揣人情，张守珪很喜欢他，养为义子。有一次安禄山吃了败战，按军法当斩，张

the other generals would not accept him not being killed. Zhang Shougui was in a difficult dilemma, and had no option, so he turned An Lushan over to the capital so the emperor could personally deal with him, hoping that the emperor might take note of his talents and pardon him. Upon first meeting, the militaristic emperor did recognize An Lushan as a rare military talent, and eventually pardoned An Lushan of his death sentence.

After returning to Youzhou, An Lushan was very careful in his dealings. Whenever representatives came from the central court, An Lushan would treat them generously and be sure to bribe them liberally. When they returned to the court, they would always speak kindly of An Lushan. Xuanzong gradually took notice of An Lushan, and after a short time, appointed him as Military Commissioner of Pinglu, then Military Commissioner of Fanyang, and so on. In the Tang Dynasty, the office of Military Commissioner was originally held by civil officials, and the civil officials would then appoint Fan and Han Chinese generals. This not only aided the central government in having direct control over the empire's military forces, but also aided in controlling the actions of the frontier troops. As for An Lushan, though, this was not the case. Now, a Fan general held direct military authority. As his military authority grew, he became increasingly emboldened.

In his later years, Xuanzong became less involved in government affairs, wishing only to have several devoted generals hold the frontier borders for him. For this reason, the emperor placed even more faith in An Lushan, giving him generous gifts and promoting him. In 750, he enfeoffed An Lushan as Prince of Dongping Commandery. The Tang practice of enfeoffing military commanders with princedoms began with An Lushan. An Lushan became increasingly audacious, going so far as demanding that he be appointed Grand Councilor, backing down only after the high ministers objected.

An Lushan was quite obese, saying himself that his belly weighed three hundred pounds. His portly and clumsy appearance frequently gave people the impression of being faithful and honest. Moreover, his witty responses and humorous personality secured for him the admiration of the emperor and those around him. The emperor once pointed at his belly, saying in jest: "What is it you have stuffed in your belly that it is so large?" An Lushan quickly responded: "Nothing but a loyal heart!" Hearing this, the emperor was delighted beyond compare. It was quite difficult to tell whether An Lushan's "appearance of being direct and foolish" was just an act, or if it was his true nature. When the emperor once allowed An Lushan an audience with the Heir Apparent, An Lushan surprisingly did not bow. Only when those around him

守珪不忍杀他，但不杀诸将不服，十分为难，没有办法，只好将安禄山押送京师，让皇帝亲自处置，或许皇帝爱其材力，还能免于一死。果然，好武的皇帝一见安禄山，认为是个不可多得的将才，最终赦免了安禄山的死罪。

安禄山回到幽州后，小心经营，朝中有使者来，他好生款待，并厚赂他们。他们到了朝中每每为安禄山说些好话，玄宗渐渐看重安禄山，不久便任命他为平卢节度使、范阳节度使等。唐朝的节度使起初都是由朝廷的文臣担任，文臣手下再设蕃、汉诸将，这样不仅有利于中央政府直接掌握国家的军事力量，而且也有利于控制边塞的军事行动，但是到了安禄山这里，蕃将直接掌握军权。军权增大，他越发无所顾忌。

玄宗晚年于国事无所用心，只想能有几个效死力的边将，为他守住边疆，因此对于安禄山恩宠有加，不是厚赐，就是加官晋爵。天宝九载（750）赐安禄山爵东平郡王。大唐将帅封王就是从安禄山开始的。安禄山日益骄恣，还提出要任宰相，终因大臣反对，这才罢了。

安禄山体肥无比，自称腹重三百斤，他那肥胖笨拙的外表，常常给人忠实憨厚的印象，再加上应对敏捷，生性诙谐，更是得到皇帝及其周围人的喜爱。皇帝有一次指着他的肚皮开玩笑说："你的肚皮中装着什么东西，弄得这么大？"安禄山反应迅速，应声答道："没有别的东西，只有一片赤心而已！"皇帝听了，无比开心。实在让人难以捉摸，安禄山是装成这种"外若痴直"的样子，还是本来如此。玄宗曾让他见太子，安禄山竟然不拜。旁边的人都拜了，安禄山这才拱手说："臣是

bowed did he raise his hands in greeting and say: "I am a Hun, and do not understand the etiquette of the court. What title does the Heir Apparent hold?" Emperor Xuanzong said: "The Prince is the heir to the throne. After We complete Our infinite reign, he will replace Us, ruling over the land." An Lushan said: "I am truly too stupid. I originally believed that there was only Your Highness. I had no idea there was an Heir Apparent." Only at this time did An Lushan bow to the Heir Apparent. Upon seeing this, the emperor adored An Lushan even more. The Honored Consort Yang was favored by the emperor, and so An Lushan exhausted his abilities to engraciate himself to this imperial consort. On his birthday, the emperor and consort gave An Lushan much valuable clothing, jade, wine, and food. Three days later, An Lushan was summoned to the palace. Lady Yang wrapped An Lushan in a large brocade swaddling cloth and had the palace attendants carry him, saying it was "the Honored Consort's third day washing ceremony of her baby Lu[shan]." When the emperor saw this, he was delighted, and bestowed a washing ceremony monetary gift on Lady Yang, and also bestowed a generous gift on An Lushan. From this point onward, An Lushan could come and go in the palace as he pleased.

Those who have received favor always worry about falling out of favor. An Lushan understood that the emperor was getting old, and once he passed away, not only would he lose all that he presently had, but he would also face certain death. This caused him great trepidation. He originally planned on waiting until the death of Xuanzong to rebel, but it was becoming urgent, and he had no choice but to move up his plans. In the winter, he assembled his troops and began his march toward the throne, washing his path with blood.

Thus began eight years of chaos.

An Lushan's troops basically employed the battle strategies of the nomadic peoples, emphasizing speed, fierceness, and agility. The main force marched straight forward with no circuitous routes and no cover from left or right flanks. They set off from Fanyang and charged straight for Luoyang. Wherever they passed, there was basically no resistance. The troops of the heartland had not seen battle in several decades, and were completely unprepared. Not until they reached the region of Luoyang and Kaifeng in Henan did the rebels meet with some resistance. An Lushan's troops had been fighting battle after battle for many years, and had rich experience in marching and fighting. The local defensive troops of the Tang Empire were completely incapable of defending against the force of the rebel army, and lost battle after battle. One month later, Luoyang fell, and eight months later, Tongguan fell. In

个胡人，不熟悉朝中礼仪，不知太子是什么官？"玄宗说：
"太子就是皇储，朕千秋万岁后，将由他代替朕，君临天下。"
禄山曰："臣实在愚昧，以前只知有陛下一人，不知道还有太
子。"这才拜见太子。皇帝看到这情形，更加喜欢他了。杨贵
妃得宠，安禄山也尽其所能，向这位皇妃大献殷勤。安禄山
生日，皇帝及贵妃送了许多名贵的衣服、宝器、酒食。过了
三天，召禄山入禁中。杨贵妃用锦绣做成大襁褓，裹着安禄
山，使宫人抬着，号称"贵妃三日洗禄儿"。玄宗看了，大
喜，赐贵妃洗儿金银钱，又厚赐安禄山。自此，安禄山便可
以自由出入宫中。

得宠者总是担心失去恩宠。这一点安禄山心里明白，皇上
年事已高，一旦去世，不但会丧失目前所拥有的一切，还会招
来杀身之祸，因此心中十分畏惧。他原计划在玄宗驾崩之后再
举事，可是形势紧迫，只得提前行动。十一月里，他就拉出军
队，开始为自己走向皇帝的宝座，杀开一条血路。

一场持续八年的战乱从此开始。

安禄山的军队基本上是游牧族的军事战术，快速、勇猛、
灵活，主力部队正面进攻，没有迂回，也不用左右侧翼的掩护，
直接自范阳出发，直扑洛阳。所到之处，基本上没有遇到什么
抵抗，中原士卒几十年不见兵甲，毫无准备。直到河南洛阳、
开封一带，叛军才遇到一些抵抗。安禄山的兵马多年来一直转
战南北，富有行军、作战经验，大唐帝国各地的守军根本抵挡
不住叛军的攻势，屡战屡败。一个月后洛阳失守，八个月后潼

the end, even the capital Chang'an could not hold out.

Tang Emperor Xuanzong originally focused his energies on governing the empire. After ascending the throne, he created the greatest period in the Tang Dynasty, elevating the power of the empire to new heights. His political achievements were comparable to those of the Tang Emperor Taizong. In the later years of his reign, though, the emperor became old, and did not concern himself with affairs of the state, pursuing only personal pleasure. By the time he saw An Lushan's troops about to take the capital, he had no option but to make a panicked escape to Sichuan.

On the road to Sichuan, only a few palace guards and close officials remained. They killed Lady Yang and her family in apology to the empire, but they had no way of turning back the tide of the times. Xuanzong struggled the entire way to Sichuan. Upon reaching Lingwu, with the support of the people, the Heir Apparent, Li Heng, established himself as emperor, becoming Tang Emperor Suzong. The new emperor directed the troops on the difficult road to suppressing the rebellion.

At the onset of the An-Shi Rebellion, Li Bai was in Xuancheng. Shortly thereafter, he arrived at Liyang, near Jinling, where he composed "Song of a Fierce Tiger," in which he expressed his concern:

> Banners in riotous profusion in Henan and Hebei;
> War drums shake the mountains to the point of collapse.
> Half the people of Qin are prisoners in the land of Yan;
> The Hun horses however eat Luoyang grass.
> One loss and one failure of the troops at the gates;
> In the morning surrendered, in the evening rebels, the cities of
> Youzhou and Jizhou.
> If the giant turtle is not killed, the waters of the sea will stir;
> If the fish and dragons flee, how will there be peace?
> Much like the battle between the Han and Chu;
> Back and forth, no end in sight.

At the outbreak of the An Lushan Rebellion, the war drums shook heaven and earth. The two circuits of Hebei and Henan (a circuit was an administrative region in the Tang Dynasty) fell, one after the other. In the poem, the troops composed of the brothers of the heartland are refered to as the "people of Qin." Most of them became prisoners of An Lushan's rebel troops, which originated in the area of Yan. Wherever the rebel troops occupied, they would plunder the children and valuables and send them back to Fanyang, making them

关失守，最后，连都城长安也没能保住。

　　唐玄宗本是励精图治的皇帝，即位以后，确实开创了唐朝鼎盛的时代，将国力提高到新的水平，政绩可与唐太宗媲美。但开元后期，皇帝年老，不太操心国事，只贪图享乐。眼看着安禄山军队就要攻陷京城，玄宗只得仓皇出逃四川。

　　在入蜀的路上，禁卫部队和亲近臣僚所剩无几，尽管杀了杨贵妃杨氏一门以谢罪天下，但却根本无法挽回大局。玄宗一路艰辛，逃到四川。而太子李亨此时到达灵武，在众人恳求下，自立为皇帝，后称唐肃宗。新皇帝随即指挥军队开展了艰苦的平乱战役。

　　安史乱起，李白正在宣城，不久来到金陵附近的溧阳，所作的《猛虎行》，表现出对时局的密切关注：

　　　　旌旗缤纷两河道，战鼓惊山欲倾倒。
　　　　秦人半作燕地囚，胡马翻衔洛阳草。
　　　　一输一失关下兵，朝降夕叛幽蓟城。
　　　　巨鳌未斩海水动，鱼龙奔走安得宁？
　　　　颇似楚汉时，翻覆无定止。

安禄山乱起，战鼓惊天动地，河北、河南两道（道，唐时行政区划）相继陷落。多为关中子弟组成的唐军，诗中称为"秦人"，大半成了从燕地发动叛乱的安史军队的俘虏；叛军在各占领区，大肆掠夺子女玉帛，然后送到范阳，皆所谓"燕地囚"。

"prisoners in the land of Yan." The court originally sent Anxi Military Commissioner Feng Changqing to hold the eastern capital of Luoyang. At the time, the elite troops of the Tang were stationed on the frontiers. Not many troops were stationed in the heartland. As soon as Feng Changqing arrived in Luoyang, he opened the coffers to withdraw funds to raise an army of sixty thousand. Considering that this army had no time to train, though, how could they possibly resist the armed cavalry of An Lushan? After several days of bloody battle, Luoyang fell and the rebel troops overtook the area, and so "The Hun horses however eat Luoyang grass." Chang'an was to the west and Luoyang was 400 kilometers to the east, with Tongguan and Shanzhou in the middle. After Luoyang fell to the rebels, Chang'an was in a precarious position. The court then sent Gao Xianzhi to lead an army of fifty thousand and ordered the eunuch Bian Lingcheng to oversee the troops. They set out from Chang'an and made camp in Shanzhou. At this time, Feng Changqing was leading the retreating troops back to Shanzhou. Feng Changqi said that the rebel troops were fierce, and suggested that they retreat to Tongguan to protect Chang'an. As the Tang troops were retreating, the rebel troops caught up with them. The Tang troops fell into chaos. With horses and troops trampling each other, they ran off in disarray. The losses were severe. This is the "one loss" in Li Bai's poem. When the neighboring districts heard the news, they quickly surrendered to the rebel troops. The eunuch Bian Lingcheng submitted a report to the emperor, in which he accused Gao Xianzhi of abandoning several hundred *li* of land in the Shan region and skimming off the food supplies for the troops, as well as withholding gifts from the emperor to the troops. Xuanzong was infuriated, and ordered the two generals to be immediately beheaded. From his appointment to his execution, Gao Xianzhi was in his position for only eighteen days. With all newly enlisted troops, to be able to defend Tongguan was the best plan available, and yet the emperor did not observe the severity of the situation. When people later heard that he killed a great general based only on the word of a eunuch, none failed to sigh. This was the "one failure" in Li Bai's poem. The Tang army used the strategic position of Tongguan to temporarily hold off the rebel army. As the rebel army could not take the mountain pass, they had no choice but to temporarily give it up. It was indeed thanks to Gao Xianzhi that Tongguan could be held. "In the morning surrendered, in the evening rebels, the cities of Youzhou and Jizhou" refers to the Governor of Changshan, Yan Gaoqing. When An Lushan rebelled, all the commanderies in Hebei, "the cities of Youzhou and Jizhou," had surrendered. The only exception was Yan Gaoqing, who mobilized an army in

朝廷初派安西节度使封常清坚守东京洛阳，其时，大唐精锐部队多在边疆驻守，中原没有多少军队。封常清一到洛阳，开府库，取钱财，招募士兵六万人。然而，这些士兵都没有时间训练，如何能抵挡安史的铁骑？血战数日，洛阳沦陷，胡骑充斥郊野，所谓"胡马翻衔洛阳草"。长安在西，洛阳在东，相距400公里，中间是潼关、陕州。洛阳失守，长安危在旦夕。朝廷于是派遣高仙芝将兵五万，命宦官边令诚任监军，从长安出发，驻扎陕州。此时，封常清正率余众，溃退到了陕州。封常清建议，叛军攻势猛烈，不如退守潼关，以保长安。唐军撤退途中，叛军追至，唐军一片混乱，士马践踏，狼狈奔走，伤亡惨重。此即李白诗中所谓"一输"。附近州县闻讯，很快投降叛军。宦官边令诚入奏皇帝，称高仙芝弃陕地数百里，盗减军粮及皇帝赏赐。玄宗大怒，命令军中立斩两员大将。可怜高仙芝自上任到被杀仅仅十八日，手下士兵多为新募，前人称"驱乌合之众，当鸱张之虏"，能够守住潼关已是上策，而玄宗不察当时艰难情势，徒以宦者之一言，而杀干城之将，后人闻此，莫不扼腕叹息！此即李白诗中所谓"一失"。唐军凭借潼关的险势，终于暂时抵挡住叛军，叛军攻不下关隘，只得暂时放弃。能够保住潼关，确是高仙芝之力。"朝降夕叛幽蓟城"，说的是常山太守颜杲卿的事。安禄山反叛，河北诸郡，所谓"幽蓟城"，皆投降叛军，只有颜杲卿起兵抗击叛军。他通告各郡，称唐

opposition to the rebels. He reported to all the commanderies that the Tang army was about to retake Hebei, upon which, seventeen commanderies of Hebei vowed their loyalty to the Tang government. When Shi Siming heard of this, he led an army to attack Yan Gaoqing. As Yan Gaoqing had mobilized his army only eight days ago, they were not prepared to defend the city, and so the city fell in short order. Those commanderies that had vowed their loyalty to the court again surrendered to the rebels. This is what Li Bai meant by "In the morning surrendered, in the evening rebels."

At the time, "the giant turtle was not killed," the seas were churning, the government officials and the populace were escaping in all directions, and the empire was in the middle of crisis. The poet compared this chaotic situation to the period of war between Xiang Yu and Liu Bang at the end of the Qin Dynasty. Why would he think of the struggle between the Han and the Chu? Because that was also a period of great chaos, and Liu Bang relied on two men to conquer the empire, "Liu Bang's survival depended on two ministers" : Zhang Liang and Han Xin. Before these two men met Liu Bang, though, who could have recognized that they had the talent to settle the land and found an empire? Li Bai is concerned with the talent and skills of heroes during chaotic times. He compares himself to Zhang Liang and Han Xin before they were discovered. This is why he continued to say:

> The worthy and the wise are forlorn, and so it has been since ancient times;
> Present day also abandons the scholars of the white clouds.
> I have a plan, but dare not offend a scale of the dragon;
> I hide myself in the southern lands, hiding from the Hunnish dust.
> Precious books and jade sword hang in the high tower;
> Golden saddle and strong steed are dispersed among old friends.
> Yesterday I was but a guest of Xuancheng;
> Pulling on the bell to request an audience with the governor.
> At times, games of luck and gambling can fortify ones happiness;
> Circle the bed three times, and yell as I make a throw.

Li Bai resented that he had great ideas but was abandoned, so he hid himself in the south, taking refuge in Xuancheng, gave his steed to a friend, and tied up his books and sword in a tall tower. He was not satisfied with doing nothing, though, so "pulling on the bell to request an audience with the governor," he visited the local officials in hopes of helping with the fight. In the end, though,

大军即将平定河北，河北十七郡闻讯皆归顺朝廷。史思明得知随即引兵攻颜杲卿，颜杲卿起兵刚刚八天，守城战备不能充分，很快城陷。归顺朝廷的郡县立刻又投降叛军，此所谓"朝降夕叛"。

当时"巨鳌未斩"，四海动荡，官民四处奔逃，国家处于危机之中。诗人将这种天下混乱不定的局势比做秦末项羽、刘邦楚汉相争之时。诗人为什么会想到楚汉相争呢？因为那也是一个天下大乱的年代，而刘邦定天下，主要依靠两个人：张良和韩信，"刘项存亡在两臣"。但是两人未遇刘邦之前，又有谁能看出来他们是安邦定国的大才呢？诗人关注的是乱世当中的英雄奇才，他把自己比做未遇之前的张良、韩信。所以他接着说：

> 贤哲栖栖古如此，今时亦弃青云士。
> 有策不敢犯龙鳞，窜身南国避胡尘。
> 宝书玉剑挂高阁，金鞍骏马散故人。
> 昨日方为宣城客，掣铃交通二千石。
> 有时六博壮快心，绕床三匝呼一掷。

李白自叹怀长策而被弃，只有窜身南国，流寓宣城，骏马赠送友人，书剑束之高阁。但他并不甘心无所作为，仍然"掣铃交通二千石"，拜会地方长官，以求有用武之地。然而多少激愤、

he could convey his indignance and aspirations only through gambling and games.

From this, one can see that not only was Li Bai very concerned about the current situation and had a clear understanding of the state of the conflict, but that the state of the crisis in which the empire now stood was also an important opportunity for the talented and elite to stabilize the realm and put to use their skills and talents. For these reasons, on the one hand, he retired into the deep mountains and avoided the chaos of battle, living in Pingfengdie on Mount Lu, but on the other hand, he hurried here and there, rushing everywhere looking for an opportunity for employment. Although he said: "Henceforth, I leave to fish in the Eastern Sea ❶ " ; yet he also said: "Zhang Liang had not yet left to follow Red Pine (Immortal)." ❷ Although he said: "I am not a person of a peaceful era / So I retire to Pingfengdie" ; yet, he also said: "I can only laugh at my exaggerated boisterousness / Who, oh who, understands the true me?" ❸ He also said: "Upon whom does rectification depend / You, Sir, understand the true me." ❹ He rushed all about seeking employment to serve the empire. In the past, people have accused Li Bai of boisterous exaggeration and drunken excesses while the empire was facing certain disaster. They said there is no comparing Li Bai, who never thought of the common people, to Du Fu, who was sincerely concerned about the fate of the state and its people. ❺ These people have truly misunderstood Li Bai.

无限壮心，只能寄之于赌博游戏之中。

　　从这里可以看出，一是，李白非常关心时局，相当了解战乱的形势。二是，李白认为国家处于危难之中，正是英才俊杰安定天下、施展才能的重要关头。因此，他一方面隐居深山，躲避战乱，他曾上庐山，隐居于屏风叠。另一方面他来去匆匆，席不暇暖，辗转各地，寻找用世的机会。他既说："我从此去钓东海。" ❶ 又说："张良未逐赤松（仙人）去。" ❷ 既说："吾非济代（济世）人，且隐屏风叠。"又说："苦笑我夸诞，知音安在哉？" ❸ 又说："匡复属何人？君为知音者。" ❹ 他奔走四方，求人汲引，以图报效国家。前人有谓李白在国家面临灾难之际，所作诗歌，不过豪侠使气、狂醉于花月之间，对于天下百姓苍生，往往不系于心，与杜甫忧国忧民完全不可同日而语。❺ 这实在是误解了李白。

❶ 李白《猛虎行》。
❷ 李白《扶风豪士歌》。
❸ 李白《赠王判官，时余隐居庐山屏风叠》。
❹ 李白《赠常侍御》。
❺ 参见宋·罗大经《鹤林玉露》。
❶ Li Bai, "Song of a Fierce Tiger."
❷ Li Bai, "Song of the Brave Warrior of Fufeng."
❸ Li Bai, "Presented to Judge Wang; at the Time, I Was Living in Pingfengdie on Mount Lu."
❹ Li Bai, "Presented to Attendant Censor Chang."
❺ See Luo Dajing (Song Dynasty), *Helin Yulu* (*Jade Dew in Crane Forest*).

李太白文集卷第一

草堂集序

宣州當塗縣令李　陽冰

李白字太白隴西成紀人涼武昭王暠九世孫蟬聯
珪組世為顯著中葉非罪謫居條支易姓為名然自
窮蟬至舜七世為庶累世不大曜亦可歎焉神龍之
始逃歸于蜀復指李樹而生伯陽驚姜之夕長庚入
夢故生而名白以太白字之世稱太白之精得之矣
不讀非聖之書恥為鄭衛之作故其言多似天仙之
辭凡所著述言多諷興自三代已來風騷之後馳驅
屈宋鞭撻揚馬千載獨步唯公一人故王公趨風列
岳結軌群賢翕習如鳥歸鳳盧黃門云陳拾遺橫制

李白诗集书影

Picture of Li Bai's poetry

九 入幕: 为君谈笑静胡沙

Chapter IX Service: Talk and Laugh for the Lord,
             Quiet the Hunnish Sands

While Tang Emperor Xuanzong was escaping to Sichuan, he was not aware that his son Li Heng had already established himself as emperor. He continued to give orders to the various princes to suppress the rebellion. He assigned his various sons to subdue the rebels in different regions, ordering armies to battle to quell the rebellion. The Heir Apparent, Li Heng, was assigned "Marshal of Soldiers and Cavalry of the Land," to pacify the northern and northeastern regions, and retake Chang'an and Luoyang to the south. Prince Yong, Li Lin, was responsible for the southern region, Prince Sheng, Li Qi, was appointed the central and southeastern regions, and Prince Feng, Li Gong, ruled over the northwestern jurisdiction. Of the four princes, Prince Sheng and Prince Feng had not yet come of age; the Heir Apparent, Li Heng, was already Commander-in-Chief of the Northwest. In fact, only Prince Yong, Li Lin, led an army. Xuanzong ordered that each prince was permitted to appoint their own cabinets and raise funds, armies, and provisions. This clearly permitted Prince Yong, Li Lin, complete autonomy.

Xuanzong did not hear the news of Suzong's ascension to the throne until thirty days after he gave his orders. In the face of the reality that the heir apparent had already ascended the throne, he had no choice but to acquiesce. However, the order to "the various princes to suppress the rebellion" had already been given, and could not be rescinded.

Prince Yong, Li Lin, was Xuanzong's sixteenth son. As soon as he received the order, he rushed to Jiangling, where he recruited an army of several tens of thousands, established a navy, and sailed down the Yangtze River to Jinling. It appeared as though Prince Yong was preparing to use pacification as an excuse to head north, but he occupied Jinling, where he established a very autonomous government.

The rules of succession during the Tang Dynasty were not yet firmly established. According to tradition, even though the first born son of the official empress was usually established as heir apparent, and thereby also succeeded to the throne, the heir apparent was also frequently abolished. Xuanzong was not the first born of the empress, and he also changed his mind several times before establishing Li Heng as heir apparent. When the An-Shi Rebellion broke out, Li Heng took the opportunity to lead an army north and establish himself as emperor. That he was self-appointed placed the legitimacy of his succession under suspicion. It would take time and further developments before the empire could accept and recognize his status.

Prince Yong, Li Lin, led his army to Jiangling, where he wanted to pacify

　　唐玄宗逃到四川，并不知道太子李亨已经继位，仍下令实行诸王分镇，即让自己的几个儿子分别坐镇各大区域，领兵出战，平定叛乱。太子李亨任"天下兵马元帅"，坐镇北方、东北地区，南取长安、洛阳。永王李璘负责南方区域，盛王李琦分管中部及东南一带，丰王李珙领导西北辖区。四王之中，盛王、丰王并未出阁；太子李亨本在北方统帅；实际上只有永王璘一人出来领兵。玄宗命令，各路诸王可以自行任命官属，自行筹措粮草，这无疑是让永王璘拥有了割据之地。

　　玄宗下达这一诏令三十天以后，才接到肃宗登位的消息。面对太子已经登基的事实，他只有认可。但"诸王分镇"的诏令已经下达，根本无法挽回。

　　永王李璘是唐玄宗第十六子，他接到诏令后，立刻赶到江陵，招募数万将士，组建水师，沿江东下，直抵金陵。永王以平乱为号召，似乎准备北上，然而占据金陵，颇有割据江东之势。

　　唐代皇位的继承并没有十分牢靠的成规。按照传统，虽然是嫡长子立为太子并继位，但太子常有被废的情况。唐玄宗并非嫡长，他所立的太子也是几经变更，最后才立李亨。安史乱起，李亨乘机分兵北上，自立为皇帝。既然是自立，那么他继位的合法性就不是完全没有疑问，他要得到各方的拥戴还需要时间和形势的发展。

　　永王李璘拥兵江陵，他要平定叛乱，建功立业，扩大自

the rebellion and expand his power base. This required that he attract scholars of the land to raise his reputation and prestige. As he headed east under the banner of pacification, Prince Yong aggressively recruited talents and troops. The populace of the Southeast was also anxious to have a resistance army quell the rebellion as quickly as possible, and so many people joined Prince Yong's movement. It was under these circumstances that Li Bai accepted an invitation to become an advisor to Prince Yong.

Ever since Li Bai was "bestowed gold to retire to the mountains" and left the Hanlin Academy to roam the wilds, seeking immortals and visiting Daoists, it may have appeared that he was leading the life of a drunkard, but deep within his heart, he always had a desire to participate in government, and hoped that a miracle would again provide him the opportunity to unleash his talents and pacify the empire.

Li Bai always considered himself a rare person of unusually high ability. In the face of such a severe disaster of the empire, he believed that he had the ability to aid in resolving the great problems and calamities. His experience in the Hanlin Academy, though, made Li Bai understand that it would be very difficult for him to participate in government. He clearly understood that almost no one could understand his aspirations, and almost no one took him seriously. This is why, after leaving the capital, his dreams rarely appeared in his poems as they used to in his early works. He also did not have the desire of his youth to express his ambitions. He rarely spoke of them, choosing to frequently speak of drinking wine and visiting immortals, describing the brilliance of lakes and beauty of mountains. That desire, though, still remained in him. His dreams were still there. They had not yet vanished from that naive heart of him. They were often revealed indirectly. In "On an Autumn Evening in the Eastern Tower of Shanfu, I See My Cousin Kuang off to Qin," he wrote: "Gazing off at the sun over Chang'an / I see not the people of Chang'an / The palaces of Chang'an are in the nine heavens / This place I once passed through while a close official / Day after day / My hair grows white, yet my heart does not change." In "In Lu, I Send off Two Cousins to Take the Examinations in the Western Capital," he wrote: "The frost withers, followed by my hair / Every day, I recall the Palace of Brilliant Light." These both express the deep-seated hidden wishes of the poet.

It was in this emotional state that Li Bai accepted the invitation of the Prince Yong, Li Lin. After Prince Yong mobilized his army and marched east to Xunyang (modern Jiujiang, Jiangxi Province), he sent messengers three times to Li Bai with generous gifts, asking Li Bai to join his government. The

己集团的势力，都需要争取天下名士，以提高声誉与威望。永王李璘一路东下，以平乱为号召，广招贤才，招募将士，而当时东南民众都希望能有一支抗敌的军队，尽早平定动乱，因此不少人都参加到永王的幕下。就是在这种形势下，李白应邀成为永王璘的幕佐。

自从李白被"赐金还山"，离开翰林院后，虽然浪迹江湖，寻仙访道，看似过着今朝有酒今朝醉的生活，但他的心灵深处，却始终向往政治，渴望再度出现奇迹般的机遇，使他得以施展平治天下的才能。

李白一向自视为奇士高人，面对国家深重的灾难，他自信有能力帮助国家解决面临的大问题、大危难。然而，翰林院的经历使李白了解到这种介入政治方式的困难。他清楚地知道自己的梦想，几乎无人能够理解，也几乎从没有人把它当真。所以离开京师以后，他的梦想，已经不像在前期的作品中那样，经常连篇累牍地出现在诗中；他也不像青年时代那样，渴望着抒发自己的理想。他说得很少，他常常说饮酒访仙，说湖光山色，但他的那份渴望还在，他的那段梦想还在，丝毫也没有从他天真的心灵中消失。不过，它们常常通过曲折委婉的方式表现出来。他在《单父东楼秋夜送族弟况之秦》中说："遥望长安日，不见长安人。长安宫阙九天上，此地曾经为近臣。一朝复一朝，发白心不改。"《鲁中送二从弟赴举之西京》中也说："霜凋逐臣发，日忆明光宫。"都表达了诗人内心深处隐藏着的这种愿望。

正是在这种内心状况下，李白接受了永王李璘的邀请。永王璘起兵后，东巡到浔阳（今江西九江），三次派遣使者，重礼请李白出山做他的幕佐。第三位使者是韦子春，曾官秘书

third messenger was Wei Zichun. Wei Zichun once served as Editorial Director of the Palace Library, and was one of Prince Yong's advisors. After Prince Yong's repeated invitations, and seeing as he stated pacifying the rebellion and stabilizing the empire as his reason, Li Bai finally accepted the invitation to join his government. In his poem "Presented to Wei Zichun of the Imperial Library," he also wrote: "If I have not a mind of pacifying the age / What good is there in keeping oneself clean and pure / ... Your discussions of the world are certainly vast and mighty / Deliberations of the sword are scattered like a political strategist / Sir Xie's [actions] were not in vain / He served the whole population / ... In the end, he pacified the society / Accomplishments complete, he left for the five lakes." China has always had the saying that "If successful, one should attend to the world; if unsuccessful, one should attend to one's self." Li Bai felt that if one does not have a mind to pacify the world, what good is there in simply being clean and pure? Li Bai praises Wei Zichun for being learned and eloquent. Discussing the world and deliberating the Dao, Wei Zichun was unceasing, much like Zhou Yan of the Warring States Period, who was known as "Yan, he who discusses the world." Discussing military matters and the sword, he was frank and sure of himself, comparable to the strategists of the Warring States Period. Was Li Bai not speaking of himself? "Sir Xie" is Xie An of the Eastern Jin. Xie An often disagreed with the court, and so he retired to Eastern Mountain. He still held ambitions of ruling the empire, though, and in the end, he came out and served, saving the people of the world. Li Bai uses Xie An to express his own ideals.

That Li Bai joined Prince Yong's government was related to Li Bai having learned stratagem at a young age under Zhao Rui. Stratagem was very common during the battles and warfare of the Warring States Period. When the empire fell into the chaos that was the An-Shi Rebellion, Li Bai saw the perfect opportunity to employ the theories of stratagem. Shortly before the An-Shi Rebellion broke out, Li Bai wrote "Presented to Governor Zhao Yue of Xuancheng," in which he wrote: "If the dark sea does not churn / How will it indulge the great whale and *peng* bird?" When the world is at peace, great geniuses of stratagem like him have no opportunity to put their abilities to use. Only at times of chaotic "sea-change" can a *peng* stretch its wings and fly high. He believed that his opportunity to realize his ambitions had arrived.

Li Bai was the only universally known scholar in Prince Yong's government. Prince Yong welcomed him with great pomp and a banquet. Li Bai followed Prince Yong east: "Poems arising out of drums and pipes / Wine made the sword and song strong." ❶ He is bold and brave, full of ambition.

省著作郎，是永王璘的谋臣之一。永王再三请求，又以平定动乱、安定天下为号召，李白就同意入幕了。他在《赠韦秘书子春》一诗中说："苟无济代心，独善亦何益？……谈天信浩荡，说剑纷纵横。谢公不徒然，起来为苍生。……终与安社稷，功成去五湖。"中国向来有"达则兼济天下，穷则独善其身"的说法，李白认为，如果没有济世之心，只是自己做一个高洁的人又有什么益处呢？李白称赞韦子春渊博而善辩，谈天论道，滔滔不绝，与战国时期号称"谈天衍"的邹衍一样；论兵说剑，侃侃而谈，可与战国纵横家相媲美。诗人何曾不是在说自己呢？"谢公"即东晋谢安。谢安屡与朝廷意旨不合，高卧东山，然胸怀济世之志，最终出来做官，拯济天下苍生。诗借谢安说出了李白自己的理想。

李白入幕，与他早年跟随赵蕤学习纵横术有关。战国征战，正是纵横术大行其道之时。而安史乱起，国家陷入危难，在李白看来，也正是用得着纵横术的时候。安史之乱爆发前不久，李白在《赠宣城赵太守悦》诗中说："溟海不震荡，何由纵鹏鲲？"天下太平之时，像他这样的纵横奇才，自然无法施展才能；只有遇到震荡四海的"海运"，一举千里的大鹏，才能展翅高飞。他认为，实现自己抱负的机会到了。

在永王幕下，李白是唯一举国皆知的大名士。永王隆重欢迎，设宴款待。李白随永王一路东下，"诗因鼓吹发，酒为剑歌雄" ❶，意气风发，踌躇满志。到达金陵后，作《永王东巡

---

❶ 李白《在水军宴韦司马楼船观妓》。

❶ Li Bai, "In the Navy, Feasting Adjutant Wei on a Turreted Junk, Watching Singing Girls."

After arriving at Jinling, he composed eleven poems titled "Songs of Prince Yong Marching East" in which he expresses his ambition and joy. The second song says:

> The Northern bandits in the Three Rivers are tumultuous and unruly;
> The Four Seas rush south, just as in the Yongjia era.
> Yet if Xie Anshi of East Mountain were employed;
> In chatter and laughter, he would settle the Hunnish sands for his lord.

In the region around Luoyang are the Yellow River, the Luo River, and the Yi River, which is why he refers to the "Three Rivers." This region was occupied by the rebel forces, and was in a state of complete disorder. The aristocrats and common people all fled to the south, much like during the chaos of the Yongjia administration at the end of the Western Jin Dynasty. Li Bai compares himself to Xie An, believing that if only he were employed, "In chatter and laughter, he would settle the Hunnish sands for his lord." The eleventh song also says:

> Let me borrow the lord's jade horse whip;
> To direct the nomadic rebels to sit on the jade mat.
> Once the southern winds sweep the Hunnish dust clean;
> We can enter west into Chang'an in the evening dusk.

"Jade horse whip" is a metaphor for military authority. Li Bai is saying that, if he is given responsibility, he could direct military affairs even from a banquet seat. Just like the southern winds, he could have Prince Yong's army sweep clean the rebel forces and smoothly advance westward to retake Chang'an. In the ninth song, Li Bai mentions his battle plans. He recommends that Prince Yong's forces use Jinling as their base of operations, from which they can send naval forces north by sea to capture An Lushan's territory of Youzhou and Yanzhou. This just may be Li Bai's most valued strategy.

Prince Yong commanded four circuit military commissioners of the South from Jiangling, encompassing several thousand miles, including the economically rich southern regions as of yet unaffected by battle. He could almost control the entire southern region from his place in Jinling. This was the route and blueprint designed for Prince Yong by his advisors. Of course, Suzong noticed this. This is why, when Prince Yong began recruiting troops and gathering provisions to form a navy, the situation became very tense.

The more astute people were measuring the abilities of Suzong and Prince Yong. When Xuanzong assigned his various sons to subdue the rebels in different regions, he assigned Li Xian, Governor of Changsha, to be Prince

歌》十一首，抒发他的抱负和欣喜之情。第二首说：

> 三川北虏乱如麻，四海南奔似永嘉。
>
> 但用东山谢安石，为君谈笑静胡沙。

洛阳一带有黄河、洛水、伊水，故称"三川"，当时为叛军所占，一片狼藉。士民惊恐南逃，一如西晋末永嘉之乱时。李白自比谢安，认为只要能用自己，即可"为君谈笑静胡沙"。第十一首亦曰：

> 试借君王玉马鞭，指挥戎虏坐琼筵。
>
> 南风一扫胡尘静，西入长安到日边。

"玉马鞭"比喻军权，李白表示，只要任用他，即可在筵席之间指挥军事，使永王军队像南风一样清扫乱军，顺利西进，收复长安。第九首诗中，李白提出了他的战略计划，主张永王军队以金陵为根据地，派遣舟师从海上行进，直取幽燕安禄山的老巢。这或许就是李白最为看重的长策。

永王在江陵领南方四道节度都使，总握兵权，封疆数千里，加上南方未受战争影响，经济富裕，他似乎可以坐拥金陵，保有江南。这已经是永王的谋臣为他设计好的蓝图以及行动路线。肃宗自然看到了这一点，因此，永王招募兵马，组成水师，形势即刻变得紧张起来。

精明之士都在掂量肃宗与永王两者的份量。玄宗下达分镇诏书的时候，即任命长沙太守李岘为永王的都副大使，但过不

Yong's Chief Commissioner, but before long, Li Xian feigned illness and resigned, then escaped to Suzong's court. When Li Lin led his army east, the litterateur Xiao Yingshi was living in seclusion in Jiangdong. Prince Yong wrote a letter inviting him to join his government, whereupon Xiao Yingshi quickly fled. Shortly thereafter, Xiao Yingshi accepted the invitation of Suzong's Administrator of Guangling Li Chengshi's invitation and became a member of the Guangling military administration. Li Bai's friend Kong Chaofu retired in hiding, not accepting Li Lin's invitation. Li Bai must have known the danger he was in, but all he could think of was how to realize his lofty aspirations. He had no time to worry about the details of reality. Unfortunately, history never makes allowances for the individual's wishes. The details of reality often rewrite people's aspirations and the developments of history. Prince Yong did let Li Bai down.

Prince Yong, Li Lin, was not very well versed in worldly affairs. He had no experience in military or political matters, and he did not have any extraordinary people in his administration. As heir apparent, Li Heng had already established himself as emperor. Under these circumstances, Li Lin's chances of pacifying the rebellion and establishing merit were very small indeed.

Prince Yong's army in Jiangling was a serious threat, and Emperor Suzong was unusually apprehensive, so he immediately ordered Prince Yong to go to Sichuan to see their father, the abdicated emperor. Prince Yong would have nothing of it.

This caused Suzong to be even more uneasy, so he immediately ordered the Military Commissioner of Huainan, Gao Shi, who was also Li Bai and Du Fu's friend, to lead an army to subdue Prince Yong. Facing the rebels, while the empire was on the verge of calamity, Suzong redirected Gao Shi's troops and sent them to attack his own brother to solidify his own power. By early 757, Prince Yong's army arrived in Danyang (or Runzhou, modern Zhenjiang, Jiangsu Province), near Jinling, but morale among the troops was low, and they surrendered without a fight. Prince Yong fled, but he was captured and killed by regional troops. When Prince Yong's army dispersed, Li Bai fled from Danyang southward. On the road, he composed "Fleeing South, Expressing My Heart," in which he wrote:

> The main generals were moved by slander and suspicion;
> The prince's marshals suddenly fled and mutinied.
> I came from the white sands;
> Noise and clamor on the banks of Danyang.

多久，李岘声称自己生病而辞了官，很快投奔到肃宗那里。李璘统兵东下时，文学家萧颖士正在江东避难，永王写信请他出山，他赶紧逃走。可是不久萧颖士却接受了肃宗方面的广陵长史李成式的聘请，成了广陵幕府中的僚属。李白的朋友孔巢父抱着避祸的态度，隐藏起来，没有接受李璘的聘请。李白未必不知道其中的风险，但他一心想着实现自己宏伟的理想，实在无暇顾及许多复杂细微的现实因素。但历史从不迁就人的愿望，各种现实因素都足以从任何地方改写人们的理想方案和历史进程。永王李璘实在让李白大失所望。

永王李璘不谙世事，没有军事、政治经验，而他的臣僚当中也没有什么特异之士，因此，在李亨已经以皇太子的身份自立登基的情况下，他要想平定叛乱，建立功勋，希望实在很渺茫。

但永王起兵江陵，无疑是一个严重的威胁。唐肃宗异常不安，立刻命令永王璘到蜀中看望父亲太上皇，永王根本不听。

肃宗更加着急，立刻令淮南节度使高适，也是李白、杜甫的朋友，率军前往阻挡永王。叛军当前，四海百姓水深火热，可是，肃宗为了坐稳自己的皇位，不惜抽调高适军队对付自己的兄弟。至德二载（757）二月，永王军队抵达金陵附近的丹阳（润州，今江苏镇江），可是军心涣散，不战自溃。永王奔逃，被地方部队擒住杀害。永王军队溃散，李白从丹阳慌忙向南奔逃，途中作有《南奔书怀》，诗曰：

> 主将动谗疑，王师忽离叛。
>
> 自来白沙上，鼓噪丹阳岸。
>
> 宾御如浮云，从风各消散。

> Guests and servants were like floating clouds;
> The wind blew, and they all dispersed.
> In the boat, fingers could be grabbed;
> On the wall, bones were being burned.
> In a rush, leaving the closest gate;
> Running and running, ignorant of a plan.
> Fleeing south, relying on the stars and fires;
> The northern bandits have no shores or banks.
> Seeing as I have no seven-jewel whip;
> I dawdle, playing by the road side.

He calls Prince Yong's troops "the prince's marshals," and Suzong's troops "northern bandits." His support of Prince Yong is evident. Li Bai intended to return to Mount Lu, but after he arrived in Pengze, he was arrested and thrown in prison. Under the circumstances of the times, all remaining members of Prince Yong's party should be put to death. When Du Fu heard that Li Bai had been apprehended, he said in "Cannot See" : "All should be killed / I believe only the talented should be forgiven." Du Fu felt pity for such a genius of poetry as Li Bai.

In the fall of 757, Guo Ziyi first retook Chang'an, and then Luoyang. A month later, Suzong returned to Chang'an. Even though remnants of the rebel army remained, they had lost their momentum, and two years later, the An-Shi Rebellion was completely quelled.

After being imprisoned, Li Bai was very depressed. Appointing Prince Yong to lead pacification troops was Xuanzong's command, and he acted with loyalty to the throne when he joined Prince Yong's camp. The desire to establish merit by suppressing the rebellion should have been good, but in the turn of an eye, he became an imprisoned outlaw. He could not even be sure of his chances of coming out alive. When he thought of this, he could not help feeling indignant anger. He presented a poem to his old friend Gao Shi, who by this time was already Chief Administrator of Yangzhou and Military Commissioner of Huainan, asking to be rescued. He also submitted a petition defending himself, claiming to be innocent, and that all the accusations claiming he was plotting rebellion were lies. In "Petition Presented to District Defender Jia," Li Bai wrote: "(Prince Yong's) letters of invitation came three times. My status was low and the gifts were grand. The deadline was quickly approaching, and I could not easily refuse. I mustered the strength for the trip, and went to watch the progress." He claimed that he joined the camp under duress. At the time, he had no choice. Once he was in prison, some people not only did not defend him, but rubbed salt in his wounds, causing him extra pain.

舟中指可掬，城上骸争爨（cuàn）。

草草出近关，行行昧前算。

南奔剧星火，北寇无涯畔。

顾乏七宝鞭，留连道傍玩。

他称永王的军队为"王师"，称肃宗的军队为"北寇"，于此可见他拥戴永王的态度。李白打算回到庐山，但逃到彭泽后，就被捕入狱了。在当时的情势下，永王余党皆当死罪，杜甫得知李白被捕，在《不见》诗中说："世人皆欲杀，吾意独怜才。"对李白这样的诗歌天才，杜甫感到十分惋惜。

至德二载（757）九月，郭子仪收复长安，继而收复洛阳。十月，肃宗还长安。叛军的余部虽在，但气焰已弱，在随后的两年中，安史之乱终于被彻底平息。

李白入狱之后，心中忧郁。永王分镇领兵是玄宗的旨意，自己出于救国的至诚，参加永王幕府，渴望在平乱中建立奇功，本是好事，可转眼之间，却成为罪人而身陷牢狱，生死未卜。想到这里，不由满怀激愤。他献诗给过去的友人，此时已是扬州大都督长史、淮南节度使的高适，请他解救自己。又上书鸣冤叫屈，为自己辩护，连称自己清白如白璧，诬陷他谋逆的言论都是不实之辞。在《与贾少公书》中，李白说："（永王）辟书三至，人轻礼重。严期迫切，难以固辞。扶力一行，前观进退。"称入永王幕是情势所迫，在当时实属不得已。他身遭囚禁，一些人非但不为之辩解，反而落井下石，尤使诗人倍感痛

"With Extreme Indignance, Submitted to Director Wei" said: "Those that like me pity me, but how can those that do not like me bear to push me over the edge?" Li Bai's wife whose family name was Zong was in Mount Lu when she heard that Li Bai had been imprisoned. "Upon hearing of the disaster, she was moved to cry / Running in tears, she entered the military camp." ❶ She was extremely panicked and distressed. She rushed down the mountain, hoping to rescue her husband as quickly as she could. Li Bai also wrote many poems begging the Chief Concilor Cui Huan and Vice Censor-in-chief Song Ruosi, lamenting to heaven and banging the ground, asserting his regret in hopes that Cui and Song would appeal the injustice against him.

Thanks to Cui Huan and Song Ruosi's rescue, Li Bai was released from prison and spared his life. Song Ruosi looked after Li Bai, and even allowed him to serve in his administration. Li Bai was extremely excited, and once again regained his courage. In his "Self Introduction," he said of himself: "I have the talent to govern, the integrity to resist Chao [Fu] and [Xu] You; my literature can change customs and my learning encompasses the human and natural realms. ... humbly request an appointment in the capital. Please you submit my request to illuminate the court array." Li Bai says he has the same pure character as Chao Fu and Xu You of ancient times, outstanding literary accomplishments, and administrative talents, and so humbly requests that the court allow him to take on the responsibilities of an official position so that he may serve the empire.

Just as Li Bai was about to set off on his new future, ill fortune once again visited. The court re-opened investigations into past events, and Li Bai was exiled to Yelang. At the end of this year, Li Bai had no choice but to set off from Xunyang for Yelang. His wife and her younger brother Zong Jing came to see him off, and Li Bai composed "Fleeing to Yelang, I Part with Zong Jing the Sixteenth at Wu River." Li Bai was quite ashamed facing his family members, and said "I have not yet left my mark on the world / Only my name echoes in the capital / The clouds only just opened / And now I grieve my exile to Yelang." Even though his fame echoes throughout the capital, his fame cannot help him now. He had been exiled to a distant land under criminal charges. Such grief! The poet "Gazes off in the distance, at the straights under the bright moon / Heading west, he bears such longing." It is truly a bleak scene.

Being a famous poet, Li Bai did not encounter any abuse on his way to his place of exile. The local officials and his old friends were happy to receive him. Li Bai composed poems thanking his hosts the whole way. Nonetheless, he was now after all a criminal, and his heart was filled with grief.

苦。《万愤词投魏郎中》云："好我者恤我，不好我者何忍临危而相挤！"李白妻子宗氏时在庐山，听说李白被捕入狱，"闻难知恸哭，行啼入府中" ❶，极为惶恐悲伤，下山竭力奔走，希望早日解救丈夫。李白又多次写诗，求助宰相崔涣和御史中丞宋若思，他呼天抢地，申述自己的痛苦，希望崔、宋能为自己申诉冤屈。

　　幸有崔涣、宋若思等人的营救，李白才释放出狱，免于一死。宋若思对李白很照顾，还让他担任自己的幕僚。李白十分兴奋，重新鼓起勇气。他在《自荐表》中称自己"怀经济之才，抗巢由之节，文可以变风俗，学可以究天人。……特请拜一京官，献可替否，以光朝列"。李白称自己像古代高士巢由一样具有高洁的品行，文章学术成就卓著，具有行政才能，恳请朝廷让自己担任一定的官职，为国效力。

　　就在李白重新展望前程的时候，厄运再次袭来。朝廷重新追究前事，李白被判流放夜郎。这一年的年底，李白只得从浔阳启程，奔赴夜郎。宗夫人与弟宗璟前来送行，李白作《窜夜郎于乌江留别宗十六璟》诗。面对家人，李白十分愧疚，自称"浪迹未出世，空名动京师。适遭云罗解，翻谪夜郎悲"。诗人虽然名动京师，可此时却于事无补，不得不带着罪名，流放远方，真是令人心悲！诗人"遥瞻明月峡，西去益相思"，确是一番凄苦的景象。

　　作为著名诗人，李白在流放路上没有遭到什么虐待。地方官员、各地朋友都还乐意接待他，李白一路赋诗，答谢主人。但毕竟身为罪人，心中满怀悲凉。

---

❶ 李白《在寻阳非所寄内》。

❶ Li Bai, "In Prison in Xunyang, Sent to My Wife."

李白诗意画 "轻舟已过万重山"
Painting according to Li Bai's poem of "The light
boat has already passed infinite mountain ranges"

十　晚境：天夺壮士心

Chapter X　　Late Years: Heaven Robs the Mighty
　　　　　　Man's Heart

Li Bai passed Dongting and followed the Yangtze River upstream. As he was passing Kuizhou in the Three Gorges, he was fortunate to meet with a general amnesty. This was already the second year, i.e. 758. The court did not grant this amnesty exclusively to Li Bai, exonerating him of the injustice. It was a general amnesty, granted to the entire empire. The emperor gave an edict saying: "All convicts now imprisoned, all criminals with death sentences are reduced to exiles, while, all exiles are hereby excused." Having reached Kuizhou, he was almost at Yelang. Nonetheless, upon hearing of the amnesty, he was delighted and immediately turned his boat and floated back downstream. The river surged forward, and the joyous gibbon calls from the forests along the banks sounded on and off. Li Bai was extremely excited, and sang out:

In the morning, departing Baidi among the rosy clouds;
To Jiangling one thousand *li* away, I return in one day.
The cries of gibbons from the banks sound with no end;
The light boat has already passed infinite mountain ranges.

This is Li Bai's famous "Departing Baidicheng in the Morning." The ancient city of Baidi is in Kuizhou. Li Bai departed Baidicheng in the morning, and by evening, he had arrived in Jiangling (modern Jingzhou, Hubei Province). This waterway just happens to be the Three Gorges of the Yangtze River. The rapids of the Three Gorges is swift and the mountains on both banks dense, with steep cliffs blocking the sun. Swift rapids and a small boat, a distance of one thousand *li* can be covered in one day. With the calls of gibbons on the two banks loud and clear, the boat had already passed many mountain ranges. The speed of the boat was a perfect match for the anxious mood of the poet.

After regaining his freedom, Li Bai was well received by the officials along his trip back home. When he arrived at Yuezhou, Li Bai met the poet Jia Zhi. Jia Zhi had once served as Secretariat Drafter, but was exiled at the time to be Adjutant of Yuezhou. The both had experience serving as officials in the capital, and both had met with exiles to the provinces, so when they met this time, they both had empathy as partners in misery. They wrote poetry together, leaving behind many great works. Both of them reminisced about their days in Chang'an. Ever since he was bestowed gold and permitted to retire to the mountains, Li Bai often longed after his life in Chang'an, and felt grief and resentment. He expressed this in "At Jiangxia, Sent to Hanyang Auxilary Office Manager": "I had lofty aspirations to dedicate myself to the state / The dragon's face would not turn my way." He had aspirations to serve his state, but heaven is high and the emperor distant, and he had no way of being entrusted by the court. After being pardoned,

李白过洞庭，沿着长江而上，行经三峡夔（kuí）州时，幸运地遇到了大赦。这已经是第二年，即乾元元年（758）了。这并不是朝廷知道了诗人的冤屈，专门为他昭雪，而是全国性的大赦。皇帝诏书说："天下现禁囚犯，死罪从流，流罪以下，一切赦免。"到了夔州，就已经快到夜郎了。但不论怎样，李白听到赦令，还是满怀喜悦之情，立即掉转船头，顺流而下。江水奔腾，岸边树林里传来猿猴的阵阵嬉闹声，此起彼伏。李白万分激动，吟诵道：

> 朝辞白帝彩云间，千里江陵一日还。
>
> 两岸猿声啼不住，轻舟已过万重山。

这是李白的名篇《早发白帝城》。白帝古城在夔州，李白早晨从白帝城出发，晚上就到了江陵（今湖北荆州）。这段水路正好是长江的三峡，三峡水流湍急，两岸群山连绵，重岩叠嶂，遮天蔽日。急流轻舟，千里之遥，朝发夕至。两岸猿声犹在耳边，轻舟早已越过重重山峦。行舟之快正切合诗人兴奋激动的心情。

李白恢复了自由，回家的途中，受到沿途官员的热情招待。李白到达岳州时，遇到诗人贾至。贾至曾任中书舍人，此时被贬为岳州司马。两人都有京城做官的经历，又都有贬谪放逐的遭遇，此时相遇，颇有同病相怜的感受，唱和酬答，留下了不少佳作。二人都对长安的岁月极为留恋。自赐金还山后，李白一直怀念长安的生活，心中充满着失落与幽怨。正如他在《江夏寄汉阳辅录事》中所说："报国有壮心，龙颜不回眷。"报国有心，然而天高皇帝远，无由得到朝廷重用。不过，被赦放回，

though, his mood was much happier. He was optimistic about his future.

As he passed through Jiangxia, he met his old friend Wei Liangzai. Wei Liangzai's term as Governor of Jiangxia was about to come to an end, and he was about to return to the capital to take up his new position. Li Bai enjoined: "As you ascend the Phoenix Pool / Forget not the talent of Scholar Jia." Li Bai was already sixty years old by this time, yet he still had lofty aspirations, and hoped that he could employ his talents, which he compared as equal to those of Jia Yi of the Han Dynasty. He still believed that his literary talent could attract the attention of the new emperor. He said in "Returning from Hanyang with a Hangover, Sent to District Magistrate Wang" :

> Last year, I was exiled to Yelang Circuit;
> The glazed tile ink has long been dry.
> This year, I was pardoned on the north slope of Mount Wu;
> The writing brush of the dragon gives off brilliant light.
> The sagely ruler even listens to "Rhapsody on Sir Vacuous" ;
> Xiangru however wishes to discuss essays.

Being exiled to distant Yelang, Li Bai was unable to give full play to his literary talent, but now that he was returning, he could again use his dragon-brush to write brilliant masterpieces. In the past, the sagely ruler Wudi of the Han Dynasty liked only the great rhapsody on "Sir Vacuous," yet Sima Xiangru had ambitions to govern the world. Li Bai compared himself to Sima Xiangru, hoping to have a new chance in Suzong's administration.

After a circuitous route, Li Bai finally returned home in 760. After being exiled to Yelang, suffering the difficulties and strains of the road, Li Bai was in a delicate state of mind, and his health was not what it used to be. At this time, rebel forces were still active in the southeastern region of Zhejiang, and the people were attacking the government and rebelling. The court sent the Defender-in-chief Li Guangbi to put down the upheaval. When Li Bai heard the news, he immediately went to join Li Guangbi's forces, but on the way, he fell very ill and was not able to continue. He had no choice but to return to Jinling. He also composed a poem saying farewell to the government officials of Jinling entitled "Hearing that Defender-in-chief Li Recruited a Large Army of Millions and Set off to the Southeast, I Cowardly Ask for an Appointment, Requesting that I Could Be of Some Use; Half Way There, I Returned with an Ailment, and Now Compose Rhymes to Say Farewell to Attendant Censor Cui the Nineteenth of Jinling," in which he wrote: "(The great army) plans to behead the giant turtle / Much less mince the long whale / I regret I do not have the strategies of

李白这时的心情，总是开朗了很多，对前途充满着希望。

经过江夏时，遇到了旧友韦良宰。韦良宰江夏太守的任期将满，即将回到京城任职，李白嘱咐："君登凤池去，勿弃贾生才。"李白此时已是六十岁的人了，但他仍怀着壮志雄心，希望自己如汉代贾谊一样的才能，能够得到发挥。他仍然相信自己的文学天才可以得到新皇帝的欣赏。《自汉阳病酒归寄王明府》曰：

去岁左迁夜郎道，琉璃砚水长枯槁。

今年敕放巫山阳，蛟龙笔翰生辉光。

圣主还听《子虚赋》，相如却欲论文章。

长流夜郎，李白无法施展文学才能，而今回来，又可以让自己蛟龙之笔写出辉煌巨作。当年圣主汉武帝只喜欢《子虚》大赋，而司马相如却怀有济世之心。李白自比司马相如，期望着在肃宗时代能有新的机会。

经过一番曲折，李白终于在上元元年（760）回到家中。长流夜郎，旅途劳顿，李白心力交瘁，健康大不如前。此时，东南浙江一带仍有叛军残部活动，又有平民攻占官府，聚众暴动。朝廷派遣太尉李光弼前往，平定动乱。李白闻讯，立刻前往投奔李光弼军队，可是走到途中，大病一场，无法成行，只好回到金陵，并作诗与金陵群官告别，诗题曰：《闻李太尉大举秦兵百万，出征东南，懦（nuò）夫请缨，冀申一割之用，半道病还，留别金陵崔侍御十韵》，其中说："（大军）意在斩巨鳌，何论鲙长鲸！恨无左车略，多愧鲁连生。……半道谢

Zuoju / I am embarrassed by Lu Lian / ... Half way, I return due to illness / I have no fate to march southeast." Li Bai regrets not having the strategies of Li Zuoju, a general during the transition from the Qin to the Han Dynasty. Neither does he have the skill to repel the Qin forces among chatter and laughter, as did Lu Zhonglian. Although he still had the ambition, he could not help that "heaven robbed me of my heart of the brave warrior / With a long cry, I part from the Wu capital (Jinling)." Li Bai expended his last strength in the name of his dream, but in the end, it could not be fulfilled.

Due to illness, after leaving Jinling, he had no choice but to settle in Dangtu and rely upon the District Magistrate Li Yangbing. Li Yangbing was skilled at composition, and especially skilled at writing the small seal script, for which he was known throughout the empire. If people were successful in requesting Yan Zhenqing to write a stele inscription, they would then ask Li Yangbing to write the header in seal script. A stele with both would then receive the appellation of "combined gem." Li Bai was seriously ill. Lying in bed, he gathered his manuscripts which he had collected over many years and gave them to Li Yangbing. He asked Li Yangbing to edit them into a collection and write a preface for him. Li Yangbing accepted the invitation.

Li Bai was truly old. Looking at himself in the mirror, he said: "I laugh at the man in the mirror / White hair like frosted grass / Grasping my bosom, I give an empty sigh / And ask my image how I became so withered." ❶ When he was feeling slightly better, Li Bai traveled to the Xie Mountain Pavilion. He sighed: "Reduced by old age, I lay by the river and sea / Again enjoying the blueness of the sky / Idle in illness, I have long been lonesome / Years and matter are but fragrant blossoms / I borrow your Western Pond to roam / Just to entertain myself." During this trip, it was a local farmer that joined him and treated him to wine and entertainment: "The farm family has fine wine / I tip a cup with him in the dusk / Once drunk, I enjoy the moon on the way back / From afar, I am pleased that my youngest son welcomes me." ❷

He was very sick. At times, he was distracted, and at times clear minded. At times, he would laugh out loud, and at times, he would cry. So many dreams now dispersed like smoke and mist; so many yearnings now already gone with the tide; so many desires now forgotten by all; and so many obsessions now dispersed and dissipated. Looking back on the past, he felt infinite lament; tasting life, he could only sigh to no end. At the end of the day and the end of the road, Li Bai sang "Song for Taking the Road" :

The great *peng*, how it shakes the eight directions;

病还，无因东南征。"李白自恨没有秦汉之际李左车的计谋，又无鲁仲连谈笑退却秦军的本领，但壮志仍在，无奈"天夺壮士心，长吁别吴京（金陵）"。李白为了自己的梦想，做出了最后的努力，可惜未能如愿。

他离开金陵，因病无奈，只得来到当涂，投靠县令李阳冰。李阳冰善词章，尤工小篆，篆书妙天下。当时人如果请到颜真卿书写碑文，那么一定要请李阳冰用篆书题其额，这样就可以得到"连璧"的美称。李白病得很厉害，躺在床上，他拿出自己积存多年的诗稿，交给李阳冰，请他编集并写序言。李阳冰答应了。

诗人真的老了。他临镜自照："自笑镜中人，白发如霜草。扪心空叹息，问影何枯槁？"❶ 病稍好一点，李白就到附近的谢氏山亭游赏。他叹息道："沦老卧江海，再欢天地清。病闲久寂寞，岁物徒芬荣。借君西池游，聊以散我情。"此时与之交往的、请他唱酒的是附近的农夫："田家有美酒，落日与之倾。醉罢弄归月，遥欣稚子迎。"❷

诗人真的病倒了。他时而恍惚，时而清醒。时而大笑，时而哭泣。多少梦想，如今已经烟消云散，多少眷恋，如今已是付诸东流，多少渴望，如今已是无人记起，多少沉醉，如今也已是月白风清。回首往事，他感慨万千；咀嚼人生，他叹息不已。日暮途穷，李白吟唱《临路歌》：

　　大鹏飞兮振八裔，中天摧兮力不济。

❶ 李白《览镜书怀》。
❷ 李白《游谢氏山亭》。

❶ Li Bai, "Looking in a Mirror, I Express My Emotions."
❷ Li Bai, "Traveling to Xie's Mountain Pavilion."

Ravaged in the middle of the sky, how its strength is inadequate.

The wake of its wings, how it stirs the infinite generations;

Roaming about the hibiscus, how I hook my stone cuff.

Later generations hear of this and pass it on;

When Confucius died, how no one shed a tear for him?

Ancient Chinese believed that if a sage were to be born, auspicious signs such as the "River Picture" or the "Document of the Luo" would appear. When the ruler of Lu was hunting, he captured a mythical chimera. At the time, only Confucius could tell that it was an ominous sign, and sighed: "My way has come to an end!" The great *peng* bird in the first chapter of *Zhuangzi*, "Free and Easy Roaming," ascended into the sky, "beating its wings and ascending ninety thousand *li*." All his life, Li Bai loved this myth. Even now, he still compares himself to the great *peng*. He imagines that he is the *peng* bird, spreading its wings and flying high in the sky, except that the chance is not right, and the great *peng* falls from the sky. It no longer has the strength to fly to where it aspires. Despite this, the *peng* flies high in the sky, and when it struggles in the sky, the "wake of its wings, how it stirs the infinite generations," generating deep influences on later generations. Ancient Chinese mythology says that the sun emerged from the "Hot Spring Valley" and bathed in the "Salty Pond." As it brushed past the divine *Fusang* (hibiscus), it rose. Li Bai imagined himself to be like the great *peng*, which passing by the *Fusang*, hooked its sleeve on a branch. Why is it a sleeve? The Western Han writer Yan Ji composed a rhapsody "Command of Sad Times," in which he lamented that his times were not as good as ancient times. He was born in the wrong age, so he could not fulfill his aspirations. In it, he says: "Cap so lofty that it cuts the clouds, ahh / Sword so long and uninhibited / Robes wrap leaves to keep, ahh / My left cuff (sleeve) hookes on the *Fusang* / My right lapel rubs on Buzhou, ahh / Creation is not sufficient to roam." Yan Ji says his aspirations are grand. He wishes to roam throughout the realm, but as he goes east, he hooks his great sleeve on the eastern most hibiscuss tree; as he goes west, he hangs his lapel on the western most Mountain Buzhou. Li Bai uses this to express that the universe is not large enough to allow him to roam freely, so he is not able to realize his own ambitions. Li Bai says that when he, like the great *peng* bird, passes by the hibiscus, he will hook his sleeve on the tree. Years later, it will petrify, which is why he says "stone cuff." Later generations will pass it from generation to generation, but, as of the death of Confucius, who will shed tears when looking at this "stone cuff"? Who can comprehend the regret of unfulfilled grand ambitions encompassed by this "stone cuff"?

余风激兮万世，游扶桑兮挂石袂。

后人得之传此，仲尼亡兮谁为出涕？

中国古人认为圣人在世，一定会出现"河图"、"雒书"这样的征兆。鲁国君主狩猎，捕获神兽"麟"，当时只有孔子看出它是不祥的征兆，悲叹："吾道穷矣！"《庄子·逍遥游》中的大鹏，横空出世，"抟扶摇而上者九万里"，李白一生都很喜爱这个传说，至此仍自比大鹏。他想象着自己是展翅高飞的鹏鸟，可是时运不济，大鹏中天陨落，气力不济，再也无法飞到自己的目的地。然而，鹏鸟飞行高远，中天摧折也可以"余风激兮万世"，对后世产生深远的影响。中国古代神话说，太阳从"汤谷"出来，在"咸池"沐浴，拂过神木"扶桑"之后，就升起来了。诗人想象自己像大鹏一样经过"扶桑"时，将袖子挂断在了树上。为什么是袖子？西汉文学家严忌写过一首辞赋《哀时命》，主要哀叹自己的时命不及古人，生不逢时，不能实现心中的志愿。其中说："冠崔嵬而切云兮，剑淋离而从横。衣摄叶以储与兮，左袪（袖子）挂于榑（扶）桑。右衽拂于不周兮，六合不足以肆行。"严忌说自己理想远大，渴望纵横天地之间，可是，向东走，自己宽大的袖子就要挂在天地最东面的扶桑树上；向西行，自己的衣襟就要扯到最西边的不周山上了。诗人借此表达天地六合仍不足以让他肆意行游，无法实现自己的理想的意思。李白说，我像鹏鸟一样经过扶桑树时，将袖子挂断在了树上。经过若干年后，化而为石，即所谓"石袂"。后人得之，代代相传，可是，自孔子去世以后，有谁看到这个"石袂"还会涕泣呢？有谁还能理解这个"石袂"所包含的壮志未酬的遗憾呢？

The poet died.

Even though the poet died, we are still reading his poems. Generations will continue to read his poems into the infinite future.

Li Bai died in Dangtu in 762 at the age of sixty-two. He was buried at the foot of local Dragon Mountain. Shortly thereafter, seeking overlooked talents, the court appointed Li Bai as Assistant Advisor, but this appointment came too late, as he had already passed on.

There are different stories about Li Bai's death. In "Passing by Li Bai's Grave," the Tang poet Xiang Si wrote: "Retuning from Yelang, he was not yet old / He died from wine by this river." *Jiu Tang Shu* (*Old Book of Tang*) also said that Li Bai died from drinking too much wine. It is evident that, already in the Tang times, there was the saying that Li Bai died from drinking too much. In *Tang Zhiyan* (*Selected Topics of the Tang*), Wang Dingbao of the Five Dynasties period said that, while drinking on the Caishi River, he drowned to death when he jumped into the water to capture the moon. Although these stories have no basis, they certainly do reflect the later generations' views of Li Bai. Li Bai was an uninhibited drinker all his life. For the poet, what death could fulfill his wishes better than dying from drinking too much? Li Bai loved the moon, and composed many poems describing the brilliant moon. The moon represented Li Bai's quest for pure character. What action could better represent the poet's quest for pure ideals than to jump into the water to capture the moon?

When Li Bai and his wife whose family name was Zong went south to avoid the chaos of the An-Shi Rebellion, their children remained in Shandong. Li Bai was extremely concerned by this. He once sent his pupil Wu E to fetch them, but he seems to have failed. When Li Bai was in exile, his children were still not by his side. It was most likely when Li Bai was seriously ill that Boqin came to Dangtu to care for him. Boqin never did hold an official position, and passed away in 792. Shortly after his daughter Pingyang married, she too passed away. His other son, Poli, never appeared in the records.

The son of a friend of Li Bai, Fan Chuanzheng, was later appointed to an official position. He traveled to Xuanzhou to seek descendants of Li Bai. He found the two daughters of Boqin. They both married local peasants. They said they also had a brother, but he left twelve years ago, and they did not know of his whereabouts. They told Fan Chuanzheng that Li Bai used to love Xie Tiao, and that he often climbed the "Xie family knoll" (*Qingshan*). Now that Li Bai's grave site was in disarray, they wished that they could move it to here. On February 12, 817, Fan Chuanzheng moved Li Bai's grave to the northern slope of Qingshan and composed "Tang Assistant Advisor Hanlin Academician Sir

诗人死了。

诗人死了，我们仍在读他的诗，千百年后人们仍会不断地阅读他的诗。

代宗宝应元年（762）十一月，李白在当涂病逝，时年六十二岁。人们将他葬在当地龙山的山脚下。不久，朝廷搜求遗逸，拜李白为左拾遗，但这个官职的任命来得太晚，诗人已经去世。

关于李白之死，后世有不同的传说。唐诗人项斯《经李白墓》说："夜郎归未老，醉死此江边。"《旧唐书》也说李白饮酒过度而卒。可见唐代就已经有诗人醉酒而亡的说法了。五代王定保《唐摭言》说，诗人醉游采石江，入水捉月而死。这些传说虽然没有什么根据，但颇能反映后人对李白的看法。李白一生豪饮，对于诗人而言，还有什么样的死法比醉死更符合他的愿望呢？李白喜爱月亮，描写明月的诗作很多，月亮是李白追求高尚品格的象征，还有什么能比入水捉月的举动更能形象地传达出诗人对高洁理想的追求呢？

当年李白与宗氏避安史之乱而南下时，儿女仍滞留东鲁，李白为此极为担忧，曾托门人武谔前往接取，看来未能如愿。李白流放的时候，子女仍不在身边。大约李白病重，儿子伯禽来到当涂照料父亲。伯禽从未做官，后于贞元八年（792）去世。女儿平阳嫁人之后不久去世。另一儿子颇黎，则始终未见相关的记载。

李白一个朋友的儿子范传正，后来做了官，到宣州来寻访李白的后代。他找到伯禽的两个女儿。她们都嫁给了当地的农民，她们说，还有一个哥哥，但出外十二年，不知下落。她们告诉范传正，李白生前很喜爱谢朓经常登临的"谢家青山"，如今李白的坟墓日益崩坏，希望能够迁葬在那里。元和十二年（817）正月二十三日，范传正将李白之墓迁到青山之阳，并写

Li's New Grave Inscription," in which he wrote: "Xie Family Knoll, ahh, is Sir Li's grave / The flow of poetry of different ages will still follow this path." This was fifty-five years after Li Bai's death. All his life, Li Bai admired Xie Tiao, so moving his grave to Qingshan was a form of comfort for the poet's spirit in heaven.

Li Yangbing collated Li Bai's works into the ten-chapter *Caotang Ji* (*Collected Works from the Grass Hut*), for which he composed a preface. In it, he wrote: "Of [Li Bai's] works, nine tenths have been lost, and those that remain came from others." It is evident that most of Li Bai's compositions have been lost, and only an extremely small part of them remain extant. Fan Chuanzheng collected additional manuscripts of Li Bai's works, and edited them into a twenty-chapter collection. Both of the collections have been lost, though. During the Song Dynasty, many people continued to collect and organize Li Bai's works, of which, Song Minqiu's thirty-chapter collection of poems and prose was more complete. It is still extant today. Refering to all other collections, Wang Qi of the Qing Dynasty edited *Li Taibai Shiji* (*Collected Poems of Li Taibai*), to which he also added annotations and appendices. This collection is very detailed and complete.

了一篇《唐左拾遗翰林学士李公新墓碑》，铭文中说：“谢家山兮李公墓，异代诗流同此路。”此时距李白逝世已过了五十五年。李白一生钦慕谢朓，改葬青山，对诗人的在天之灵也是些许慰藉。

李阳冰将李白的作品汇编成集，编成《草堂集》十卷，并写了一篇序文。序中说：“（李白）当时著述，十丧其九，今所存者，皆得之他人焉。”可见，李白的作品当时散失极多，留存下来的只是极少的一部分。范传正重新搜集李白的遗稿，编为文集二十卷。但这两种集子后来都散失了。宋人不断收集、整理李白的作品，其中宋敏求所编的诗文集三十卷比较完备，流传至今。清代王琦参考各本，重新编定《李太白诗集》，并作注、增加附录等，颇为详备。

李白墓

Tomb of Li Bai

结语： 蓬莱文章建安骨

Conclusion: Words of the Penglai, Bones of the Jian'an

Even in his own time, Li Bai was known for his poetry. He Zhizhang called Li Bai an exiled immortal. Du Fu said: "Bai's poems are beyond comparison / Soaring ideas have no peers / Fresh and novel, like Commander Yu / Elegant and remote, like Adjutant Bao." Yin Fan of the Tang Dynasty collated a selection of poems, *Heyue Yingling Ji*, in which he included works from twenty-four poets of the Kaiyuan (713-741) and Tianbao (742-756) administrations of Emperor Xuanzong. He included Li Bai's poems in this anthology. In it, he said that most of Li Bai's poems are decadent and indulgent. Of such works as "The Road to Shu Is Difficult," he said: "One could say they are the more extraordinary of the extraordinary." One can be sure that he was famous for his poetry, but he was still not installed in an esteemed position in the kingdom of poetry.

This is most likely because these people were still too close in time and location to Li Bai, and were not able to see him accurately. This is why, even though Li Yangbing said in "Preface to *Collected Works from the Grass Hut*" : "Since the beginning of history and after the *Songs of the South*, driving Qu [Yuan] and Song [Yu], whipping Yang [Xiong] and Ma [Sima Xiangru], the only one to go it alone in these thousand years has been Sir [Li Bai]" ; however, he most likely did not comprehend the historical significance of "going it alone in these thousand years." By the Middle Tang period, the creative magnificence of the High Tang was already beginning to receive recognition. Han Yu was a great poet of the Middle Tang period. He was obviously more aware of Li Bai's significance when he said "Where ever Li and Du's compositions are / Brilliance extends ten thousand yards." ❶ Han Yu's evaluation of Li Bai and Du Fu established their exalted positions in the history of classical Chinese poetry.

From this point, the admiration and notoriety of Li Bai was almost unbroken. This focused mostly on two aspects. The first is the recognition of Li Bai's extraordinary poetic talent. Pi Rixiu of the Late Tang period said of Li Bai: "Oh, pity! In one thousand, no ten thousand years / This talent cannot be had." ❷ Du Xunhe also said: "On Qingshan, an evening with a bright moon / Throughout history, there is but one poet." ❸ In *Nanbu Xinshu* (*New Book of the South*), Qian Yi said: "Li Bai was the ultimate heavenly talent, Bai Juyi was the ultimate human talent, and Li He was the ultimate ghostly talent." Zhu Xi of the Song Dynasty praised Li Bai as "sagely in poetry." The poetry critic Yan Yu also believed that the compositions of Li Bai and Du Fu reached the level of "enthrallment," the level of "ultimate superiority." There was no

　　李白生前就享有很高的诗名。贺知章称李白是谪仙人。杜甫说："白也诗无敌，飘然思不群。清新庾开府，俊逸鲍参军。"唐人殷璠（fán）选编过一部诗歌选集《河岳英灵集》，选录开元、天宝年间二十四位诗人，其中就有李白。他说李白写诗，大多"纵逸"，《蜀道难》等作品"可谓奇之又奇"。李白诗名天下知，这一点在当时是肯定的，但他还没有被安排到诗国最崇高的位置上。

　　这多半是因为当时人在时空上与李白靠得太近，不容易看得十分真切，所以，尽管李阳冰《草堂集序》中说："自三代已来，风骚之后，驰驱屈（原）、宋（玉），鞭挞扬（雄）、马（司马相如），千载独步，惟公（李白）一人。"但恐怕他还不能完全体会到"千载独步"的历史份量。到了中唐时代，人们已经领略到了盛唐诗歌所创造的辉煌。韩愈是中唐时期的大诗人，当他说"李杜文章在，光焰万丈长"时❶，则显然更清楚李白的意义。韩愈的评价奠定了李杜在中国古典诗歌史上崇高的地位。

　　此后，人们对于李白的推崇与称赞几乎从没有间断。主要集中在两个方面，一是充分肯定李白超凡的诗才。晚唐皮日休评李白："惜哉千万年，此俊不可得。"❷　杜荀鹤也说："青山明月夜，千古一诗人！"❸　钱易《南部新书》曰："李白为天才绝，白居易为人才绝，李贺为鬼才绝。"宋代朱熹称李白是"圣于诗者也"。诗论家严羽也认为李白、杜甫的创作达到了"入神"的境界，达到了"至矣、尽矣"、无以复加的地步。李

---

❶ 韩愈《调张籍》。
❷ 皮日休《七爱诗》。
❸ 杜荀鹤《经谢公青山吊李翰林》。

❶ Han Yu, "Inciting Zhang Ji."
❷ Pi Rixiu, "Poem on Seven Loves."
❸ Du Xunhe, "Passing Sir Xie's Qingshan, Mourning Hanlin Academician Li."

further to go. The most outstanding aspect of Li Bai's poetic talent was "extraordinariness." Pi Rixiu said it well when he said Li Bai's poems could "speak of that beyond heaven and earth, and think beyond the surface of the ghostly and divine." ❶ He already transcended the imagination of the average person. Hu Yinglin also said Li Bai's poems "Came from the ghostly and went to the divine, dispersed and unpredictable." Such lines as "The great road is like the blue sky / Only I have no way out" ; ❷ "I don't know the spring breeze / Why does it enter my gauze curtain?" ❸ "The fresh breeze and brilliant moon do not cost anything / Mountains of jade fall on their own, and are not pushed by anyone" ; ❹ and "When young, I did not know of the moon / But suddenly wrote of the white jade platter / I also suspected the jade table mirror / Flew to the peaks of the dark clouds" ; ❺ such lines of poetry are plain as spoken words, yet fantastic beyond compare. They make people wonder how they could possibly have formed in the poet's mind. Many of his poems are luminous, rich in imagination, as if fallen from the heavens. Each poem is unexpected. Poets and critics throughout the ages are fairly consistent in their belief that Li Bai's poetic talent was "heaven sent," and not attained through "human effort," and so he was truly a "divine person," "heavenly genius." Simply put, Li Bai's poems are incomprehensible. They cannot be imitated. The artistic level that his poetry reached was of course partly due to long periods of tireless effort, but it was even more due to the inborn talent of the poet.

The second aspect of his acclaim was the extreme admiration of Li Bai's bold and uninhibited nature. Li Bai was arrogant and independent, wild and unrestrained. Not only did Li Bai admit this, but all who knew him agreed. Li Bai was bold, with a strong sense of justice, and acted upon impulse: "I play with the lords as with peers / View comrades as reeds." He treated aristocracy as equals, unmoved by their authority. This unconstrained personality was not only displayed in his legendary life, but was truthfully expressed in his poetry. One thousand years later, when reading his poetry, no one can help feeling this deeply.

Li Bai was a great poet, but he was also a controversial person. This was even truer in a time when Confucian ideology held a prominence. There were several points of major criticism against him.

白诗才最突出的表现就是"奇"。皮日休说得好，李白诗能够"言出天地外，思出鬼神表" ❶，完全超越了一般人的想象。胡应麟也说李白诗"出鬼入神，惝恍莫测"。诸如"大道如青天，我独不得出" ❷；"春风不相识，何事入罗帏" ❸；"清风朗月不用一钱买，玉山自倒非人推" ❹；"小时不识月，呼作白玉盘。又疑瑶台镜，飞在青云端" ❺之类的诗句，明白如话，却又奇妙无比，不禁使人想问，它们究竟是怎样从诗人的脑海中酝酿而成。他的许多诗歌色泽明丽，意象丰富，想落天外，每每出人意料。历代诗人、诗论家相当一致地认为，李白的创作才能得之于"天授"，而非"人力"所能到达，即真正所谓"天人"、"天才"、天生之才。简单地说，李白诗歌无迹可寻，是学不来的。他所达到的诗歌艺术水平，当然得益于长期不懈的努力，但更多地依赖于诗人的天赋。

二是极力赞赏李白的豪气、狂放。李白傲世独立，狂放不羁，这一点不仅李白自称如此，也是所有了解李白的人所公认的。李白为人豪爽仗义，任侠使气，"戏万乘如僚友，视俦列如草芥"，平交王侯，面对权贵，不为所动，这种独立的人格，不仅体现在他充满传奇的一生中，也真实地表现在他的诗歌当中。千载之下，朗读他的诗歌，无不能够深切地感受到这一点。

李白是一位伟大的诗人，也是备受争议的人物。这在传统儒家思想占主导地位的时代更是如此。对他的指责主要有几点：

---

❶ 皮日休《刘枣强碑文》。
❷ 李白《行路难》三首之二。
❸ 皮日休《刘枣强碑文》。
❹ 李白《襄阳歌》。
❺ 李白《古朗月行》。

❶ Pi Rixiu, "Grave Inscription for Liu Zaoqiang."
❷ Li Bai, "The Road Is Hard," the second of three poems.
❸ Pi Rixiu, "Grave Inscription for Liu Zaoqiang."
❹ Li Bai, "Song of Xiangyang."
❺ Li Bai, "Ballad of the Ancient Brilliant Moon."

One was his support of Prince Yong, Li Lin. In the context of extreme authoritarianism, this was seen as a complete failure of morality. The Song Dynasty philosopher Zhu Xi criticized him, saying: "His mindlessness brought this on." From today's perspective, though, we no longer have a reason to blame Li Bai.

Another criticism was some of Li Bai's extreme beliefs. We have already discussed that, due to unusual life experiences and exposure to multifarious cultural influences, Li Bai had many beliefs that, from an orthodox perspective, appeared to be extreme. Li Bai was genuine, and never hid these beliefs. He even frequently expressed them in his poetry. These extremes were often difficult for the orthodox scholars of the Song Dynasty to accept. This is why the Song scholars both appreciated Li Bai's talent, but were also dissatisfied with his unusual beliefs. They criticized Li Bai as being "unreasonable" and "oblivious to reason." In fact, some of Li Bai's ideas were not within the realm of these Song scholars' "reason."

Some even believed that Li Bai was "shallow." This is to say, they believed Li Bai had no taste. He had no ideas. In his *Tiaoxi Yuyin Conghua* (*Collected Sayings of the Secluded Fisherman of Tiao Stream*), the Song writer Hu Zi recorded Wang Anshi as saying: "Bai's poems are almost vulgar. This is why they easily please. Bai has polluted and lowly knowledge. In his poetry, nine out of ten poems speak of women and wine." Hui Hong's *Lengzhai Yehua* (*Evening Stories from Cold Studio*) also recorded Wang Anshi as saying: "Taibai was quick with his lines, and did not filter them, but his knowledge was lowly. Nine out of ten lines speak only of women and wine." This did not come from Wang Anshi's firsthand material, so it is worth investigating whether it was said by Wang Anshi. Nine out of ten poems and nine out of ten lines are obviously an exaggeration. This is not difficult for anyone who has read Li Bai's collected poetry to see. Actually, other than his support of Li Lin, the main reason Song scholars were not happy with Li Bai's "knowledge" was that he did not have the ambition to save the world that Du Fu had. Su Shi's "Record of Li Taibai's Tombstone" says: "Li Taibai ...how was he a talent for saving the world?" Zhao Cigong said: "Li and Du are called the greatest of poets, yet Bai's poems are more about the breeze and the moon among the grass and trees, about empty words, gods and immortals. What good does this do for culturing the people? Only Wild Man Du Ling (Du Fu) had the talent to serve the ruler and the desire to serve the state." In *Helin Yulu* (*Jade Dew in Crane Forest*), Luo Dajing wrote: "When the empire was in crisis and the state was in chaos, Li Taibai composed poems, boldly bragging, wildly drunk

　　一是他追随永王李璘。这在过分尊崇君权的意识形态氛围中，完全被看做是失节的行为，宋代朱熹批评他"没头脑至于如此"。但现在看来，我们已经没有理由苛责李白了。

　　二是李白的某些异端思想。我们已经说明，由于特殊的人生经历以及接受多元文化的影响，李白具有许多在正统观念看起来完全属于异端的思想。李白率真，从不掩饰自己的这些思想，而且经常表现在诗歌当中。这些异端，往往为恪守正统观念的宋人所无法接受。所以，宋人一方面欣赏李白的才气，另一方面又很不满意他怪异的想法。他们批评李白"不达理"、"不知义理之所在"，其实李白的一些想法本来就不在宋人的"义理"范围内。

　　还有一些人认为李白"识度甚浅"，就是说李白没有什么眼光，没有什么思想。宋人胡仔《苕溪渔隐丛话》载王安石说："白诗近俗人，易悦故也。白识见污下，十首九说妇人与酒。"惠洪《冷斋夜话》亦记王安石的话："太白词语迅快，无疏脱处，然其识污下，诗词十句九句言妇人酒耳。"这话并非出于王安石的第一手材料的记载，是否王安石所说，有待细考。十首九首、十句九句之说明显夸张过分，任何读过李白诗集的人都不难看出这一点。其实，宋人不满李白"识见"、"识度"，除了从璘一事之外，差不多都集中在李白没有杜甫那样的济世之心上。苏轼《李太白碑阴记》说："李太白……岂济世之人哉！"赵次公说："李杜号诗人之雄，而白之诗多在于风月草木之间、神仙虚无之说，亦何补于教化哉！惟杜陵野老（杜甫），负王佐之才，有意当世。"罗大经《鹤林玉露》中也说："李太白当王室多难，海宇横溃之日，作为歌诗，不过豪侠使气，狂

among the flowers and the moon. He never had his mind on the people of the state. When considering the concern for state and people of Du Shaoling (Du Fu), how can they be mentioned in the same breath?" We now understand that Li Bai's ambitions were not one bit less than Du Fu's. If one recites Li Bai's poetry seriously, one cannot help but feel his strong enthusiasm for serving the state.

Even though he has been long misunderstood, there are still innumerable lovers of Li Bai. Many aspiring writers and poets have studied Li Bai. Not only are they moved by his haughty personality, but also encouraged by his enthusiastic and unrestrained poetry. It is worth noting that advocates of Li Bai are rarely successful officials. They are usually inconspicuous people who have had rich experiences and live in seclusion. It is Li Bai's unbridled personality, insolent attitude toward authority, and optimistic spirit despite his difficult life that attract them.

Li Bai's poetry reached Japan very early. The compositions of the cultural circles revolving around the Zen monks of Kyoto and Kamakura, the Gosan Bunraku Ha, were greatly influenced by Li Bai's poetry. There are many Sinologist who have studies Li Bai. Their criticisms, translations, and studies are considerable. Japanese middle school textbooks still include Li Bai's poetry. Even today, many Japanese are able to recite Li Bai's poems from memory.

Li Bai was not only a great poet, but also an extraordinarily charismatic person. He was a unique genius in Chinese poetry. Those magnificent poems that he left behind are gorgeous rarities. They will bloom forever in the literary garden of China, and the world.

醉于花月之间耳。社稷苍生，曾不系其心膂（lǚ）。其视杜少陵（杜甫）之忧国忧民，岂可同年语哉！"现在我们知道，李白的济世之心丝毫不减杜甫。只要认真通读李白的诗歌，不会不感受到其中强烈的为国效力的热情。

尽管李白长期以来受到不少误解，但热爱李白的人仍不胜枚举，许多仁人志士、作家诗人都曾学习李白，不仅为他一生傲岸的人格所打动，也为他热情豪放的诗篇所鼓舞。值得注意的是，推崇李白的人很少有显赫的官员，他们大都名位不显，经历曲折，身处逆境，正是李白豪放不羁的个性、笑傲王侯的态度、漂泊潦倒一生却又自信乐观的精神吸引了他们。

李白的诗歌很早就传到日本。京都、镰仓的以禅宗僧侣为中心的文学团体即五山文学派的创作就受到李白诗歌的巨大影响。在日本，研究李白的汉学家有很多，注释、翻译、研究李白诗的成果十分可观。日本中学教科书仍选录李白的诗歌，直到今天仍有很多日本人能够流利地背诵李白诗。

李白不仅是伟大诗人，也是具有强烈人格魅力的杰出人物。他是中国诗坛上独一无二的千古奇才，他留给我们的那些惊天动地的诗文，犹如绚丽的奇葩，将在中国乃至世界文苑中永远绽放。

Translator's Notes

Li Bai (李白) has often been transliterated as "Li Bo" (*in hanyu pinyin*) or "Li Po" (in Wade-Giles Romanization). "Bó" is the literary pronunciation of 白, and "bái" is the modern vernacular pronunciation. In modern mandarin, when referring to the great Tang poet, the modern pronunciation is commonly used. As most Chinese will pronounce the great Tang poet's name "Lǐ Bái," this translation uses "Li Bai."

All official titles and office titles have been translated in accordance to Charles O. Hucker's *A Dictionary of Official Titles in Imperial China* (Stanford: Stanford University Press, 1985).

All references to years by their reign dates (i.e. the year of a specific administration of an emperor) in the original have been converted to the corresponding year of the Common Era. For example, the third year of the Tianbao Administration of the Tang Emperor Xuanzong, the year in which Li Bai first met Du Fu, is converted to 744. In the rare reference to a precise date, the Academia Sinica calendar conversion tool (http://db1x.sinica.edu.tw/sinocal/) was used to present the date in the Western calendar.

A frequent topic in this volume is immortal (*xiān* 仙). *Xiān* can be translated as "fairy," but is usually translated as "immortal." It usually refers to celestial beings in heaven or perfected beings on earth that do not age or die. They do not eat food or drink wine, but survive on dew and universal energy. As immortals are transcendent beings, they do not usually appear in the common mortal realm. Celestial immortals live in the heavens and travel on clouds or float on the wind, and earthly immortals live in remote high mountains, often in caves, or heavenly grottoes. A practitioner of Daoist alchemy, if successful in working and ingesting the elixir of immortality, can also become an immortal, and may even ascend to the heavens on a cloud or on the back of a crane. As such, a Daoist practitioner can also be respectfully referred to as a *xiān*. *Xiān* is also used in a metaphorical manner, as it often is in this volume. It can represent a certain transcendent and aloof attitude, or even to the lifestyle of a mountain hermit. Although I suspect "hermit" may better represent the authors' intension when they use *xiān* in some discussions of Li Bai's poems, this translation uses the word "immortal" for consistency, and because it better retains the rich imagery of Li Bai's original poems.

Curtis Dean Smith

图书在版编目(CIP)数据

李白:汉英对照/周勋初,童强著:史国兴译. —南京:
南京大学出版社，2010.3
（中国思想家评传简明读本）
ISBN 978-7-305-06609-2

Ⅰ.李… Ⅱ.①周…②童…③史… Ⅲ.李白(701～762)—
评传一汉、英 Ⅳ.K825.6

中国版本图书馆CIP数据核字(2009)第239818号

出 版 者 南京大学出版社
社　　　址 南京汉口路22号　邮　编 210093
网　　　址 http://www.NjupCo.com
出 版 人 左 健

丛 书 名 《中国思想家评传》简明读本(中英文版)
书　　　名 李 白
著　　　者 周勋初 童 强
译　　　者 Curtis D. Smith
审　　　读 张 静
责任编辑 赵 丽　　　编辑热线 025-83597520

照　　　排 江苏凤凰制版印务中心
印　　　刷 江苏凤凰盐城印刷有限公司
开　　　本 787×1092 1/16 印张 15.75 字数 306千
版　　　次 2010年3月第1版 2010年3月第1次印刷
ISBN 978-7-305-06609-2
定　　　价 37.80元

发行热线 025-83594756
电子邮箱 Press@NjupCo.com
　　　　　Sales@NjupCo.com (市场部)